THE SELECTED LETTERS OF

GUSTAVE FLAUBERT

THE

SELECTED LETTERS OF

GUSTAVE FLAUBERT

TRANSLATED AND EDITED
WITH AN INTRODUCTION BY
FRANCIS STEEGMULLER

Biography Index Reprint Series

BOOKS FOR LIBRARIES PRESS
FREEPORT, NEW YORK

Reprinted 1971 by arrangement with
Farrar, Straus & Giroux, Inc.

INTERNATIONAL STANDARD BOOK NUMBER:
0-8369-8082-4

LIBRARY OF CONGRESS CATALOG CARD NUMBER:
78-160919

PRINTED IN THE UNITED STATES OF AMERICA

This presentation of a portion of
Flaubert's correspondence is dedicated
to
GERDA STEIN

NOTE

In French, the best-known printed letters of Gustave Flaubert occupy, together with their index, nine volumes of the Conard edition of his collected works. There are also two or three small additional, separate volumes of letters. Still other letters, which have been printed in magazines only, together with many others which have never been printed anywhere, have recently been copied and edited by a group of French scholars, and their publication is planned for the near future: they will make another nine volumes or so. My selection for translation has been made from the letters already in print; dates and text have been corrected when necessary and possible.

The 275 surviving letters to Louise Colet (the largest group of letters to any one correspondent) were sold by her daughter and are now in the possession of a Paris publisher. Most of these have been printed in the Conard edition, but with many excisions; only some of the indicated omissions in my English text have been made by me. The French text of the letters to Louise included in my second section contains long discussions of Louise's poetry, which are of little interest to the modern reader. The portions I have translated form a discourse by Flaubert, chiefly on problems of art and on the progress of his novel.

F. S.

CONTENTS

INTRODUCTION

THOSE who uphold the affirmative in the debate sometimes engaged in by critics and others interested in literature—Resolved: that the study of a writer's life and letters is useful for the understanding of his works—can scarcely be provided with any more effective ammunition for their cause than the correspondence of Gustave Flaubert. Apart from the facts that he hated the bourgeois, sought the *mot juste,* and wrote *Madame Bovary,* what is best known about Flaubert is perhaps a portion of his artistic credo that declares: "No lyricism, no comments, the author's personality absent!"—to quote but one of the many forms in which he expressed it. Due to the meager supply of translations, it is somewhat less well known in the English-speaking world that he wrote several thousand letters—when fully published in France they will fill about twice as many volumes as his novels—in which he may be said to have taken what the French call his "revenge."

In the evening, or often in the early morning, when the day's work was done, the determinedly objective novelist who had spent hours seeking a phrase, or a week revising a page, was capable of letting himself go in lengthy, almost unblotted letters to friends; and here, in free-flowing prose—often careless, abounding in the tautologies, assonances, and chain-like relative clauses that he relentlessly banished from his works—he analyzes himself, discusses the social forces that shaped his period, and expounds his ideas on art and the creative process. The reading of a portion of this correspondence, in serving to acquaint one to a considerable extent with its writer's psychology, may serve also to test the validity of certain deductions and conclusions concerning Flaubert and his art commonly offered in more or less good faith by his admirers and detractors.

Of Flaubert's personality, the conventional idea (so far as one exists at all) is perforce vague and fragmentary, due to the rigid objectivity of his novels; but in general it seems to be that the man was a chilly recluse with an exclusive passion for the *mot juste*. This conception the correspondence corrects. The writer of the letters is often, at first sight, highly contradictory; and yet in each case the letters supply also the solution to the apparent contradiction. "There is little use in living," he constantly laments, at the same time recording his pleasure in aspects of life as diverse as the goodness of George Sand and the unfurling of the new leaves outside his study window; and as one reads on one realizes that it was precisely his very great artistic sensibility that made him suffer—often to such a point that he wondered whether he could bear to go on.

He claims that everyone bores him, that he meets no one with whom he can discuss art, which is the only thing worth discussing; and yet the list of his correspondents, with whom he energetically exchanges ideas, is actually quite long. The boredom, we come to realize, is a habit of mind resulting from the disappointments of early longings to communicate with those about him—his early bourgeois surroundings were unresponsive; we know that his father scoffed at his literary ambitions and fell asleep while listening to him read his own work aloud —and this habit of mind was furthered by a quite amazingly high incidence of defection and death among his confidants. "Oh no!" he writes to Louise Colet. "I do not *seek* to free myself of every bond, to separate myself from all affection; those things quit me of their own accord, like knots that loosen and untie themselves without being touched. How much love and enthusiasm, how many deep friendships and lively sympathies I have enjoyed, only to see them melt away like snow! I clutch at the little that remains to me." He devoted his life to art, but he managed to do so without mutilating himself as a human being; he remained affectionate and generous—generous with sympathy, with money, and with literary services; it is difficult to imagine anyone surpassing him in friendship. The letters confirm what Henry James said of him: "My main remembrance is of a conception of courtesy in him, an accessibility to the human relation, that only wanted to be sure of the way taken or to take."

The intricate structure of the novels, so obviously impossible of accomplishment without the scrupulous taking of pains, is in itself a convincing indication that the author was an "honest" man in the fullest possible sense of that complex term; and in the correspondence we see to what an extent he was honest not only in his art, but with himself and others—most especially Maxime Du Camp and Louise Colet. As an artist, Flaubert had the utmost respect for words, and not only in his novels but in daily life as well he insisted on using them only when he meant them, and on giving them their true meaning. This was an inevitable source of misunderstanding with persons addicted to the much more widespread habit of using words for effect—pragmatically, as it were. Neither Du Camp nor Louise Colet was capable of believing that Flaubert meant what he said. Du Camp could not believe his friend when he said openly that he had chosen the cloistered way of art; Louise could not believe her lover when he declared frankly that he had no expectation of loving her "always." In dealing with the clashes that ensued, modern biographers tend to react by denigrating Du Camp and pitying Louise. Du Camp is usually ridiculed because of his opportunism, and Flaubert's attitude toward him is praised as evidence of artistic purity. On the other hand, Flaubert's treatment of Louise is condemned on moral grounds as heartless, while psychoanalytical critics see in it proof of a persistent infantile incestuous fixation. In reality, it is Flaubert's uncompromising, utterly unconventional, almost naïve attitude toward language and communication, as similarly revealed in both conflicts, which is most relevant if the letters are to be studied as an aid to greater understanding of the novels.

Concerning Flaubert and Louise, moralists will decide who wronged whom, and there is ample opportunity for disagreement as to which was the more neurotic of the two. Whatever the conclusions, it cannot be denied that with Louise as with Du Camp, Flaubert's cards were on the table from the beginning.

Flaubert's best-known aspect is undoubtedly his hatred of the bourgeois, which in his artistic work found its culminating expression in the ferocious concept of *Bouvard et Pécuchet.* This hatred has been accounted for in various ways: as a heritage from romanticism, which identified the bourgeois with anti-art; as a reaction against his own immediate milieu (once again we recall the scene, described by Maxime Du Camp in his *Souvenirs littéraires,* of Dr. Flaubert falling asleep while his son read aloud from the first *Education sentimentale*) ; as an expression of anti-authoritarianism, the French middle class being in Flaubert's formative years at the height of its power. The correspondence, in its intimacy, expresses the hatred directly, and even more violently than do the novels; and yet the letters also suggest that behind this negative attitude there is to be found a positive, though frustrated, aspiration. They suggest that just as Flaubert loves individuals while saying "everybody bores me," so he has a vague but driving vision of a good society. The hatred, the letters hint, contains more love than is commonly realized.

His specific references to the bourgeois often give one the

impression that his condemnation of their ways is associated with his realization that the path of modern society leads away from communication between men; that personal relationships are being supplanted by the dominance of the machine, money, and the state. Speaking of Alfred de Vigny's *Servitude et grandeur militaires,* he writes to Louise Colet in 1846: "The book . . . shocked me a little at first, because I saw in it a systematic depreciation of blind devotion (the cult of the Emperor, for example), of the fanaticism of man for man, in favor of the abstract, dry concept of duty—a concept that I have never been able to grasp and that seems to me not inherent in the human heart. What was fine in the Empire was the adoration of the Emperor, a love that was exclusive, absurd, sublime, really human; . . . I have little understanding of what the concept of Fatherland can mean to us today." And five years later he writes to his mother: "Why did France want Louis XVIII after Napoleon? . . . As a result of old sympathies, we had faith in a community of feeling that exists no longer. . . . Between a man and another man, between a woman and another woman, between a heart and another heart—what abysses exist! The distance between one continent and another is nothing in comparison."

In so far as people accept this deplorable, anti-human development, in so far as they further it and profit from it, they are bourgeois and worthy of hatred, whether they are shopkeepers or workmen, aristocrats or proletarians, writers of popular literature or pompous academicians, monarchists or republicans, conservatives or socialists. (It was always the fundamental social forces that interested Flaubert—much more than their political expression, concerning which his statements are often as extreme as the expression itself. And whether we agree or disagree with his specific political statements it is not difficult for us today to sympathize with his fears about "progress.") Whatever their class or profession, all these people think meanly, and that is precisely one of Flaubert's definitions of the bourgeois: *"J'appelle bourgeois tous ceux qui pensent bassement"*—those people who, as André Gide says, hate everything they "cannot put to use"; people who have become cogs in a machine, who cannot communicate with their fellow-men except in slogans, and who have no awareness of anything "beyond."

When Flaubert writes to Turgenev that he feels "an invincible flood of barbarism rising out of the depths," he is referring to this process of dehumanization characteristic of his era—not to speak of our own; and in order to understand his conception of art it is important to bear in mind this despair with which he confronts the modern world. The correspondence provides important clues as to how he arrived at his idea of art as the only remaining haven of human values.

In letters written to Louise Colet during the composition of *Madame Bovary* he defines the subject matter of his art as "ordinary life," "humdrum details"; but he makes clear that he has exalted standards of presentation: "A good prose sentence should be like a good line of poetry—*unchangeable* . . . no one has ever conceived a more perfect type of prose than I." And he keenly realizes the originality, the daring, of this attempt to depict the commonplaces of existence in the most precious colors: "It is perhaps absurd to want to give prose the rhythm of verse (keeping it distinctly prose, however) and to write of ordinary life as one writes history or epic (but without falsifying the subject). I often wonder about this. But on the other hand it is perhaps a great experiment, and very original, too."

There is indeed a seeming "absurdity" in Flaubert's choosing to depict precisely the world which he despises, but there was necessity in the choice. For he was perhaps the first to realize the real absurdity of the romantic attempt to ignore this ever-more-ugly world. At twenty-five he wrote warning Maxime Du Camp against daydreaming, that "vicious monster . . . siren of the soul," which had already "destroyed much of [his] substance"; and in passages of the letters in which he discusses romantic writing it is clear that he sees the unmanliness, the ostrich-like behavior, the surrender of lucidity, inherent in the romantic form of escape. Worst of all, such escape represents the complete surrender of one's will to the detestable pressure of the world: the unrealistic dream is ultimately the acceptance of this pressure.

While as an artist he withdraws from any practical intervention in the concerns of this society which he detests, and despises all political attempts to reform it because the reformists are as blind to the things he loves as everyone else—Flaubert's withdrawal is not a capitulation. It is a form of resistance: in his works he continues to face reality. And by facing it, by transfiguring it, he is enabled not only to endure it, but to gain over it the only kind of revenge within his power. "It is small consolation, I know," he writes to Mademoiselle de Chantepie, "to realize that all this [the evil of the world] has always existed. But the conviction that rain makes you wet, that rattlesnakes are dangerous, should help you endure them." And to George Sand: "What form should one use to express one's opinion on the things of this world without running the risk of being taken later for a fool? It is an arduous problem. It seems to me that the best thing is quite simply to depict those things that exasperate you."

Flaubert's famous realism, his dogged determination to render the slightest detail correctly, is thus seen to be not an aim in itself, but rather one of his weapons: by nailing down reality in words that will resist the ravages of time he is enabled to "rub the noses of the bourgeois in their own turpitudes."

From all this it is clear that Flaubert is utterly consistent in seeking, for the presentation of his subject matter, a perfect stylistic medium. The *mot juste* is not merely the "right word" in the grammatical or dictionary sense; it is also the word that strikes the hardest, that espouses most tightly the reality it denotes, that obtrudes the least upon the vision of the reality on exhibit and sets it off most strikingly—the word that is, in short, the most perfect vehicle of communication. Flaubert's phobia concerning repetitions, his almost neurotic concern with smooth transitions and with the musicality of his phrase: these are weapons in his arsenal; every word transfixes an element of reality and is at the same time a plate in his armor against it. Flaubert's preoccupation with form is anything but formalistic. It is as though all those human virtues which no longer find any scope in society discover their outlet in his art: untrammeled communication; universal sympathy, as displayed in his supreme ability to give life to his many characters, to experience their sufferings in his own flesh; a sense of the continuity of history in an era that glories in destroying tradition; a sense of order; and above all absolute honesty and authenticity.

But to be this kind of an artist in that kind of an age, Flaubert had to pay a price. Self-abnegation was necessary. Not only of a material kind—the giving up of worldly pleasures for work was the least of it; a more subtle payment had to be made. The nature of this payment is clarified when we become aware that Flaubert's creative process had in it something of the very character of his age which he so detested. His pitiless, self-imposed discipline and his constant compulsive sense of *having* to be busy at his task are highly symptomatic: the price he had to pay was—spontaneity.

Of this, the letters show us that he was quite conscious. Time and again he laments that the art he produces is not the art he admires most. His great heroes among the artists are in their method, or their lack of it, his very opposite. ". . . how easily the great men achieve their effects by means extraneous to Art. What is more badly put together than much of Rabelais, Cervantes, Molière, and Hugo? But such quick punches! Such power in a single word! We have to pile up a lot of little pebbles to build our pyramids; theirs, a hundred times greater, are made with a single block." In the long list of his charges against his age, that is surely not the least weighty, nor can it have been the least anguished. For in this respect he sees that he is caught. He has to accept this limitation imposed on him by his age because only on this condition can he resist the age with his art. His lucidity in this acceptance, in this defeat that leads to the only possible victory, is not the least of our reasons for admiring him. And the fact that in his letters he actually did achieve the spontaneity that was elsewhere denied him—the "quick punches," the effects produced "by means extraneous to Art" that he was unable to put into his books—is not the least of our reasons for treasuring the correspondence.

Today there is a tremendous and open pressure on the writer to comply with various social demands: to take part in hot or cold wars, to suit his work to the ever-tightening strait-jacket of the magazines, to spend his time treating subjects preferred by publishers and foundations rather than by himself, and treating them in ways which publishers and foundations think best. Although in Flaubert's age this kind of pressure had not yet become as overt as it is today, he realized its nature and the challenge it constituted to the integrity of the artist. He met this challenge magnificently. His correspondence is probably the most complete statement in existence of the artist's duty to maintain his independence—a statement even more valid today than when Flaubert made it. The words applied to it by the French critic Albert Thibaudet can scarcely be bettered: *"Elle doit être tenue pour un bréviaire de l'honneur littéraire."*

Francis Steegmuller

FLAUBERT'S FAMILY AND OTHER CORRESPONDENTS

ANNE-JUSTINE-CAROLINE FLAUBERT (1794-1872), *née* Fleuriot, Flaubert's mother, born in the Norman town of Pont-l'Evêque, lost her mother at her birth and her father, a doctor, at the age of nine. A few years later she was sent to live with the family of a Dr. Laumonier, who was head of the Hôtel-Dieu, the municipal hospital of Rouen, capital of the province of Normandy. There she became acquainted with one of the doctors on the staff, ACHILLE-CLEOPHAS FLAUBERT (1784-1846), brought up at Nogent-sur-Seine in Champagne, and married him in 1812. Seven years later he succeeded to the position of Dr. Laumonier, and from then until his death the family lived in a wing of the hospital.

Their older son, ACHILLE (1813-82), with whom Gustave had little in common, succeeded his father as head of the hospital in 1846.

Their daughter, CAROLINE (1824-46), Gustave's only sister, married on March 3, 1845, EMILE HAMARD, an uninteresting, unstable young Rouennais of whom Gustave disapproved. She died five weeks after her father, four weeks after giving birth to a daughter (1846-1931), who was also christened CAROLINE and who—her father being too alcoholic and incompetent to act as a parent—was brought up by Flaubert and his mother at Croisset.

At the age of eighteen this Caroline married ERNEST COMMANVILLE (born 1834), a young Rouennais lumber merchant. When Commanville's business failed Flaubert sacrificed his patrimony to save the "good name" of his niece and nephew; Caroline exploited her uncle's affection ruthlessly. As his literary executor she similarly exploited his writings, publishing a mutilated version of his correspondence and in general impeding the activities of scholars.

PAUL ALEXIS (1847-91) was one of the naturalists, a fervent disciple of Zola.

PIERRE-CHARLES BAUDELAIRE (1821-67) and Flaubert met at the home of Théophile Gautier, to whom Baudelaire later dedicated his *Fleurs du mal,* calling him *"poète impeccable . . . parfait magicien ès lettres françaises."* For Gautier's magazine, *L'Artiste,* Baudelaire wrote the only review of *Madame Bovary* which Flaubert felt "entered into the secrets of the book." The publication of *Les Fleurs du mal* cost Baudelaire a fine of 300 francs for "outrage of public morals and religion" and the suppression of six of the poems in its first edition.

FREDERIC BAUDRY (1818-85), author of a Sanskrit grammar, was a philologist and the son-in-law of MARIE-ANTOINE-JULES SÉNARD (1800-85), Flaubert's lawyer at the time of the attempted suppression of *Madame Bovary* in 1857. After Sénard's successful defense, Flaubert dedicated the novel to him, but this did not prevent Sénard, twenty-two years later, when he was a member of the Chamber of Deputies, from intriguing to secure for his son-in-law a post which Flaubert was also seeking (see page 261).

AUGUSTE-EMILE BERGERAT (1845-1923) was a great writer of literary articles for French newspapers. He married a daughter of Théophile Gautier and became a member of the Académie des Goncourt.

LOUIS BONENFANT was the husband of Flaubert's cousin Olympe Parain, of Nogent-sur-Seine.

LOUIS BOUILHET (1822-69) was a native of the village of Cany, near Le Havre. He and Flaubert (who grew to look strikingly alike) had known each other vaguely at the Rouen lycée, where he was a scholarship student, and later he had been among Dr. Flaubert's medical students. But their friendship came to flower only about the time of Alfred Le Poittevin's marriage in 1846, and by then Bouilhet had abandoned medicine and was devoting himself to poetry, earning his living in a tutoring school. With Maxime Du Camp he urged Flaubert to put aside the first version of

La Tentation de Saint Antoine, and after his return from Egypt and the Near East encouraged him to undertake a less exotic subject. Flaubert consulted him about every page, every phrase, of *Madame Bovary, Salammbô,* and *L'Education sentimentale.* "In losing my poor Bouilhet," Flaubert wrote in 1869, "I have lost my *accoucheur,* the man who saw more deeply into my thought than I did myself."

Bouilhet is a poet who can be read with pleasure, though he is not universally recognized as the poetic genius his friend thought him. Flaubert spent much time and labor arranging for the publication of his posthumous poems, the production of a posthumous play, *Mademoiselle Aïssé,* and the erection of a memorial in Rouen.

Bouilhet was always a poor man, and in 1867 was glad to accept the post of chief librarian at the Rouen municipal library. He never married, but maintained for many years a happy liaison with a woman named Léonie Leparfait. Also a member of the ménage was Léonie's son, Philippe Leparfait, by a previous liaison with the Marquis Charles-Philippe de Chennevières-Pointel, Inspector of Provincial Museums and Director of the Department of Fine Arts.

MADAME JEAN-BAPTISTE BRAINNE (1836-1883), *née* Marie-Louise Léonie Rivière, was the daughter of the editor of the *Nouvelliste de Rouen,* one of the city's leading newspapers. After the death of her husband, a literary man, she devoted herself to journalism. Her sister, Marie-Valérie, married Charles Lapierre, who succeeded his father-in-law as editor of the *Nouvelliste.* Flaubert called the sisters *"mes anges,"* and they were among the few Rouennaises whom he cared to visit.

MADEMOISELLE MARIE-SOPHIE LEROYER DE CHANTEPIE (1800-89) was a provincial lady, a spinster of Angers who spent her time writing novels and wrestling with religious doubts. Moved by *Madame Bovary* (whose heroine she felt she resembled), she wrote to its author, and there ensued a long correspondence which has done more than her novels to make her name remembered.

GEORGES CHARPENTIER (born 1849), the publisher, inherited

a business founded by his father, who had published Victor Hugo, Alfred de Musset, Gérard de Nerval, and Théodore de Banville. Young Charpentier added to his list the Goncourts, Alphonse Daudet, Zola—and Flaubert, who enjoyed his relations with him after the unpleasantness of his earlier publisher, Lévy. Charpentier was a charming man, and his wife, painted by Renoir, presided over an enjoyable, informal *salon.*

ERNEST CHEVALIER (1820-87) was one of Flaubert's schoolmates at the Rouen lycée. He studied law, became a judge, and rose to be attorney general. He resigned in 1870, and was later a conservative member of the Chamber of Deputies. In his maturity he was thus an arch-bourgeois, and as their paths diverged he and Flaubert had less and less to say to each other; but they continued to correspond occasionally, paying rather constrained tribute to their youthful friendship.

LOUISE COLET (1810-76), *née* Revoil at Aix-en-Provence, was a beautiful blonde of thirty-six and a well-known poet when the twenty-four-year-old Flaubert met her on July 29, 1846 in the Paris studio of the sculptor JAMES PRADIER. (In the letters Pradier is sometimes called "Phidias" and Louise "the Muse." MADAME PRADIER, whose husband in 1845 obtained a legal separation on grounds of adultery, was—like Louise herself—one of Flaubert's models for Emma Bovary.) Louise knew everyone, and everyone had long known her: Achille Flaubert, seeing her portrait in his brother's room in 1846, remembered having danced with her at Pradier's ten years before and offended Gustave by his cold way of speaking of her. Her mediocre husband, Hippolyte Colet, was professor of harmony and counterpoint at the Conservatoire, having achieved that rank thanks to the favor of his wife's long-term lover, the philosopher VICTOR COUSIN (sometimes called "Plato" or "the Philosopher" in the letters). Louise was also at various times close to other literary men, among them Alfred de Musset and the critic Abel-François Villemain. She was a great *intrigante* and winner of Academy prizes, and once out of revenge for unfavorable mention in a gossip column she had attacked the journalist Alphonse Karr with a knife.

Her relationship with Flaubert was divided into two separate periods. The first lasted until August, 1848—two years, during which in voluminous correspondence she kept reproaching Flaubert with his indifference to her and to physical passion, and during which she succeeded in seeing him only six times; and the second extended from Flaubert's return from his oriental journey in 1851 to their final rupture, which seems to have occurred in 1854. The fullest account of the affair in English is in Francis Steegmuller's *Flaubert and Madame Bovary*.[1]

When Louise read *Madame Bovary* she was made indignant by the realization that she had unwittingly supplied material for it, and she published in a fashion magazine a poem declaring that the novel gave the impression of having been written by a traveling salesman. She castigated Flaubert in two novels of her own, sent him anonymous letters, and made the most of other opportunities to insult and offend him. But in 1876 he wrote a friend: "I have just learned by chance of the death of poor Madame Colet. This news fills me with many emotions. Surely you understand." And he always felt an upsurge of emotion when his train for Paris or Rouen passed through Mantes, where he and Louise had had some of their earliest meetings at the Hôtel du Grand Cerf.

LOUIS DE CORMENIN (François-Louis-Justin-Eugène de La Haye, Baron de Cormenin) (1821-66) was the son of a prominent liberal politician. He studied law and showed signs of journalistic promise, but he lacked energy and his dynamic father was a stifling influence. Some of his articles were collected and published with a preface by his childhood friend Maxime Du Camp, in 1868, under the title *Reliquiae*.

MADAME HORTENSE CORNU (1809-75), *née* Hortense-Albine Lacroix, was a literary lady, a childhood friend of Napoleon III.

MAXIME DU CAMP (1822-94) was, like Flaubert, a doctor's son. He had ample private means, traveled extensively, practised the new art of photography, wrote large amounts of journalism, and in 1880, the year of Flaubert's death, was elected to the French Academy. He and Flaubert met in Paris while Flaubert was at law school. There was an immediate sympathy, and Flaubert read him some of his early writings. After he and Louis Bouilhet persuaded

[1] Farrar, Straus & Young, New York.

Flaubert to put aside the first version of *La Tentation de Saint Antoine* in 1849, he and Flaubert traveled in Egypt, the Near East, Greece and Italy. He bought a part-interest in the *Revue de Paris,* and in this magazine *Madame Bovary* was first published, with cuts.

He tried unsuccessfully to inculcate Flaubert with his own increasing worldliness, love of activity, and desire for honors, and the friendship cooled. It was occasionally revived at moments of emotion, as on the death of Bouilhet and in 1870.

Du Camp is known today chiefly as an early photographer (the figure of Flaubert can be dimly detected against an Egyptian background in his sumptuously published album) and for his *Souvenirs littéraires,* in which he makes unpleasantly clear his inability to forgive Flaubert his genius.

ERNEST-AIME FEYDEAU (1821-73), a Parisian gentleman connected with the stock exchange and the author of an archaeological treatise, published in 1858 a novel, *Fanny,* which Sainte-Beuve considered superior to *Madame Bovary* and which enjoyed considerable success.

MADAME CHARLES ROGER DES GENETTES (1818-91), *née* Mlle. Letellier-Valazé, maintained a literary and artistic *salon,* frequented by Cousin, Hugo, Sainte-Beuve, Lacordaire, Père Didon, and many others. A volume of letters addressed to her by famous men was published after her death.

EDMOND (1822-96) and JULES (1830-70) DE GONCOURT, brother novelists and social historians, were, in 1862, with Sainte-Beuve, Gavarni, and others, the founders of the "Magny dinners" —a bimonthly reunion of literary men at the Magny restaurant in Paris. These dinners, attended by Turgenev, Taine, Flaubert, Renan, Gautier, and others, were in a sense the precursor of the Académie des Goncourt, still functioning in Paris today, still awarding an annual literary prize, under terms laid down by Edmond in his will. The Goncourts' famous *Journal* contains frequent references to Flaubert, many of them uncharitably stressing the "ridiculous aspects" of which he himself had earlier written to Louise Colet that "There are plenty of them."

HENRI-HONORE GOURGAUD-DUGAZON had been one of

Flaubert's teachers at the Rouen lycée and had also given him private lessons. In 1842 he was teaching at Versailles.

VICTOR-MARIE HUGO (1802-85), whose life-span encompassed Flaubert's, was the latter's lifelong admiration and the great god of French romanticism. Flaubert was too young to attend the riotous first performance of Hugo's *Hernani* in 1830, at which Théophile Gautier in a scarlet waistcoat led his fellow youthful romantics in their booing of the classicists who tried in vain to impede this triumph of romanticism; but he pored over Hugo's *Feuilles d'automne* with Alfred Le Poittevin and his sister, and he and Maxime Du Camp were unwilling to be separated from those poems and from *Les Orientales* even when traveling. "There has been only one poet in this century," Flaubert wrote Louise Colet in 1852, *"c'est le père Hugo."* After the *coup d'état* of Napoleon III in December, 1852, Hugo spent eighteen years in exile, first at Brussels and then on the islands of Jersey and Guernsey.

LEON LAURENT-PICHAT (1823-86) was co-director, with Maxime Du Camp and Louis Ulbach, of the *Revue de Paris,* in which *Madame Bovary* first appeared, serially, in 1856. Later he became a deputy and senator.

ALFRED LE POITTEVIN (1816-48), the brilliant and romantic son of a prosperous Rouen cotton manufacturer, although devoted to literature and philosophy cynically obeyed his father and studied law. But his sensitivity took its revenge, his spirit and his body sickened, and he ended his days in a kind of despair. Even before his early death, however, he had already once been lost to his adoring, jealous friend Flaubert, five years younger than himself: by his marriage, in 1846, to Louise de Maupassant. Flaubert never forgot the rapture of his friendship with Alfred. "I am now acquainted with what are commonly called 'the most intelligent men of the day,'" he wrote to Alfred's sister Laure in 1862, "and I compare them with him and find them mediocre. Not one of them has ever dazzled me the way he used to. What excursions into the empyrean he used to take me on, and how I loved him! I think I have never loved anyone, man or woman, as much." And in 1874 he dedicated to Alfred's memory the final version of *La Tentation de Saint Antoine,* whose first version, composed in the late 1840's, had been heavily influenced by Alfred's romanticism. Alfred's own writings were published in 1924, under the title *Une Promenade de Bélial et œuvres inédites.*

MADAME GUSTAVE DE MAUPASSANT (1821-1903), *née* Laure Le Poittevin, was the sister of Alfred Le Poittevin. She secured a separation from her husband (the brother of Alfred's wife) after a few years of marriage. Her son GUY DE MAUPASSANT (1850-93) found Flaubert's affection open to him as a young man because of the Le Poittevin relationship. During the 1870's, while working as a civil servant, he showed most of his early writings to Flaubert, who coached him and called him "my disciple." He had the first of his many great successes with *Boule de suif* in 1880, shortly after Flaubert's death.

GEORGE SAND (1803-76), *née* Amandine-Aurore-Lucie Dupin, was the only woman in France sufficiently respected as an artist to be invited to the Magny dinners. It was at one of these, in 1863, that Flaubert was presented to her by Sainte-Beuve and the younger Dumas. From his earliest youth he had loved her novels; in 1848 he hated her republican activities; later, after their meeting, he continued to deplore her humanitarianism but fell in love with her humanity. By this time her celebrated series of love affairs was over, and Flaubert's relation with her—literary, largely epistolary, almost filial—was more warmly satisfying than with any other woman. She visited him at Croisset, and he her at Nohant, where she lived with children and grandchildren. "She is the best and best-natured of women, not at all a blue-stocking," he wrote Madame Roger des Genettes in 1866. "She is a little over-benevolent, a little too overflowing with kind words, but full of acute perceptions and excellent sense—as long as she stays off her socialist hobbyhorse."

In 1875, when it seemed that Flaubert's niece was about to sell the house at Croisset for the benefit of herself and her husband, leaving her uncle homeless, George Sand wrote him: "If the price were not beyond my means, I should buy it, and you would live there the rest of your life. I have no ready money, but I would try to invest a little of my capital in it. Answer me seriously, please; if I can do it, it will be done." Flaubert wrote his niece of this offer, and the house was not sold.

MAURICE SCHLESINGER (1797-1871) and MADAME MAURICE SCHLESINGER (1810-88), *née* Elisa Foucault at Vernon in Normandy, were the models for Monsieur and Madame Arnoux in *L'Education sentimentale*. Elisa Schlesinger, the object of Flaubert's lifelong affection, remains a remote and colorless figure despite the efforts of countless scholarly investigators. She was twenty-six, and the mother of an infant, when the fourteen-year-old Flaubert met her and fell in love with her at Trouville in the summer of 1836. The Flaubert family had come there from Rouen for a long seaside holiday (Madame Flaubert owned property at nearby Deauville that needed occasional visiting) and they found at their hotel Schlesinger, a German-Jewish music publisher in Paris, and his "wife" and child. (Actually the Schlesingers were not married until 1840, due to the existence of a previous husband of Elisa's of whose existence Flaubert probably never had any inkling.) Flaubert did not lose his adolescent infatuation, and while he was in Paris studying law in 1843 he saw much of the Schlesinger household. It was probably Elisa's gratitude to Schlesinger for marrying her and regularizing her situation that made her refuse Flaubert's plea that she become his mistress; for the jovial Schlesinger was an unfaithful husband, and Elisa undoubtedly returned the passion of the handsome younger man. As an unattainable feminine ideal she helped shape Flaubert's course along with the other factors: his childhood in a hospital, the romanticism into which he was born, the break-down which prevented his leading an active life, and the rest.

Later the Schlesingers lived chiefly in Baden. In 1872 Elisa, whom Flaubert addressed in a letter of that year as *"Ma vieille Amie, ma vieille Tendresse"* visited him at Croisset—their last meeting. In his memoirs Maxime Du Camp claims to have seen her, insane, in Baden in 1881. Her tremendous importance in Flaubert's life goes far beyond the meager number of biographical facts available, and far beyond the meager number and mediocre quality of those of Flaubert's letters to her which have survived. For her the more vivid Louise Colet was but a poor substitute, emotionally speaking; and yet it is to the substitute, not the ideal, that we owe the finest letters.

HIPPOLYTE-ADOLPHE TAINE (1828-93) wrote a number of books dealing with the philosophy and psychology of art and the history of literature; he emphasized especially the role of environmental factors in shaping the creative process.

IVAN TURGENEV (1818-83) spent much of his time in France beginning in 1854; he lived chiefly at Bougival, a suburb of Paris, with the singer Pauline Viardot and her husband, and many of his books were written there. He and Flaubert first met at one of the Magny dinners, on February 23, 1863; but it was Flaubert's loneliness after the deaths of Louis Bouilhet and George Sand that caused their friendship to flower. Turgenev translated Flaubert's *Légende de Saint Julien l'Hospitalier* and *Hérodias* into Russian. He also saw to it that a Russian translation was made of *La Tentation de Saint Antoine,* but the censor in St. Petersburg forbade its publication.

EMILE ZOLA (1840-1902) was greatly admired by Flaubert for the strength of his novels, but Flaubert was somewhat uneasy about Zola's admiration for him. For the seeker after the *mot juste* found Zola's style careless and slipshod; and although he was proud of his own meticulous documentation he deplored what he considered the tendency of Zola and the other naturalists to make factual accuracy an end in itself. And Zola's publicity-seeking—his manifestoes, his brandishing of the word "naturalism," his flamboyant essays in so-called literary criticism—Flaubert found lamentable: "His aplomb as a critic is explained by his unimaginable ignorance," he wrote his niece in 1877.

THE SELECTED LETTERS OF

GUSTAVE FLAUBERT

I

CHILDHOOD AND YOUTH

1821-1851

GUSTAVE Flaubert was born (December 12, 1821) and lived until the age of twenty-five in a wing of the Hôtel-Dieu, or Municipal Hospital, of Rouen, of which his father was resident head. "The dissecting-room of the hospital gave on our garden," he wrote to Louise Colet when he was thirty-two. "How many times my sister and I used to climb the trellis, hang onto the vines, and peer curiously at the cadavers on their slabs! The sun shone on them, and the same flies who were flitting about us and about the flowers would light on them and fly buzzing back to us. . . . I can still see my father raising his head from his task of dissection, and telling us to go away." He was a handsome boy, blond, blue-eyed and Norman-looking, and was given to daydreaming and scribbling. His great joy was in presenting and acting in plays, some of them written by himself, in his family's billiard room, using the billiard table as a stage. When he was eleven he was sent as a boarder to the Rouen lycée, and there he quickly allied himself with those of his co-evals who were enraptured by Byron and Hugo, slept with daggers under their pillows, dreamed of romantic adventure, and lamented the flatness and dreariness of life in bourgeois France.

In school, or, in his later adolescence, at home (for at seventeen he ceased to be a boarder at the lycée) he wrote numerous romantic prose effusions: *Agonies, Mémoires d'un fou, La Danse des morts, Smarh,* the first two dedicated to his friend Alfred Le Poittevin, the last a kind of precursor of *La Tentation de Saint Antoine.* In the summer of 1836, when he was fourteen, he conceived a passion for the twenty-six-year-old Madame Schlesinger at Trouville—a passion of great personal and literary importance, though of it few epistolary traces remain. As a graduation present in 1840 he was given a trip to the Pyrenees, to Marseilles (where he had a brief erotic interlude with a lady named Madame Foucaud, picked for him as a suitable wild-oat by a doctor friend of Dr. Flaubert, in whose charge he was), and to Corsica. The sensuality of Marseilles and the romantic air of Corsica combined to increase his reluctance to study the law—his father's choice of career for him. He spent 1841 at home, and just before and just after matriculating at the law school in 1842 he wrote two romantic novels—*Novembre* and *L'Education sentimentale.*

Restless, unhappy, bored, hating the subject he was studying, and studying it with absurd and defeatist incompetence, he remained at the law school until the Christmas and New Year holidays of 1843-44; and during that period, which he spent with his family, he suffered a dramatic break-down—a seemingly epileptic seizure, followed by others, which left him quivering, nervous, and wretched, unable to pursue the hated studies. "One good thing has come out of my illness," he wrote a friend from his sickbed, "and that is that I am allowed to spend my time as I please—no small item in life. I can think of nothing in the world I enjoy more than a nice room, well heated, with the right books and plenty of leisure."

His father bought an estate at Croisset, on the banks of the Seine outside Rouen, and there during the summer Flaubert slowly recovered his strength. By the spring of 1845 he was well enough to accompany his parents and his newly married sister on her wedding journey to Italy, where, at Genoa, he fell in love with Breughel's picture of *The Temptation of Saint Anthony*—a subject which he had previously seen acted out by puppets at a Rouen fair. Another year of idleness followed, and then, early in 1846, his father and his sister died one after the other. With his mother and his baby niece Flaubert at once left the quarters in the hospital and moved to Croisset, which now became his principal residence; and here, in the grief-laden atmosphere, he suffered another loss in the engagement and the marriage on July 6 of his beloved Alfred Le Poittevin.

On July 29, 1846 he went to Paris, taking with him his sister's death-mask. To commission a bust of her he visited the studio of the sculptor Pradier, whom he had previously known during his period of law study and who had recently advised him to end the celibacy in which he had been living for the past two years. There in the studio, standing near a bust which Pradier had done of her, wearing a blue dress, blond curls falling to her shoulders, was the poet Louise Colet. Pradier introduced them with some words about Madame Colet's possible usefulness to this young man who wanted to make a name for himself in literature, and a day or two later they were lovers. On August 4, despite Louise's protests, Flaubert returned to Croisset; and there, despite her increasingly shrill and incredulous protests, he remained most of the two years during which this phase of the liaison lasted. Tied to his mother, to his habits, to his books, to his ideas of what love should be, he consented during that period to meet the more fleshly Louise only six times—in Paris or in Mantes, which is on the railroad from Paris to Rouen. His letters were long, frequent, and, in their way, undeniably passionate; but she, fading, carnally aroused, and aggressive, made no attempt to hide her dissatisfaction that the affair should be so largely epistolary; and before its end it had degenerated into an intolerable quarrel.

During the strange liaison Flaubert saw much of Maxime Du Camp and Louis Bouilhet at Croisset; Louise raged bitterly at his willingness to spend time with them and not with her, and she was particularly jealous of a trip he made with Max to Brittany in the spring of 1847. On their return the two friends composed alternate chapters of an account of their journey, entitled *Par les champs et par les grèves,* published only posthumously.

At the same time Flaubert was doing wide reading for his drama about the temptation of Saint Anthony; and the actual beginning of this was precipitated by Alfred Le Poittevin. Since his engagement and marriage Flaubert had seen little of him; but when he felt that he was dying he called his old friend to him and the last few months of his life were a period of intensely emotional reconciliation. Alfred died on April 3. On "Wednesday, the 24th of May 1848, at quarter-past three in the afternoon," Flaubert set down the first words of *La Tentation de Saint Antoine*—destined to be published in book form, during his lifetime, only in its third version, in 1874, dedicated to Alfred Le Poittevin.

The crumbling liaison with Louise did not long survive this immersion in Alfred and Saint Anthony, and its first phase came to an end in August.

Except for brief references in letters written later, the correspondence is silent about the composition of the first version of *La Tentation de Saint Antoine* in 1848-49 and about Flaubert's dramatic reading of the piece to its judges, his friends Du Camp and Bouilhet, in September, 1849. The account contained in Du Camp's memoirs is probably roughly correct: about how Flaubert summoned his two friends to Croisset, read them the 541 pages of his manuscript aloud, and was at first infuriated, then crushed by their verdict that it was unoriginal bombast, "an imitation of imitations of *Faust*," and that it should not be published, but put away. Saddened and not entirely convinced, he followed their advice.

Meanwhile the apprehensive and possessive Madame Flaubert had reluctantly given her son permission to accompany Du Camp on a long tour of Egypt and the Near East, and they left Marseilles for Port Said on November 4, 1849. Flaubert recorded his travels not only in many letters to his mother and to Bouilhet, but also in voluminous *Notes de voyages,* which have been published in his collected works. In the spring of 1851 he and his mother were reunited in Venice and returned together to Croisset.

To ERNEST CHEVALIER

[*Rouen, December 31, 1830*]

Dear Friend

You are right in saying that New Year's Day is stupid. My friend, they have just dismissed the greatest of them all, the white-haired Lafayette, freedom's champion in the old world and the new.[1] Friend, I'll send you my political and constitutional liberal speeches. You are right in saying that you will give me pleasure in coming to Rouen—you will give me a great deal. I wish you a happy 1831—embrace your good family for me. The friend you sent me seemed like a nice fellow even though I only saw him once. I'll also send you some of my comedies. If you'd like us to work together at writing, I'll write comedies and you can write your dreams. And since there's a lady who comes to see papa and always says stupid things, I'll write them too. I'm not writing this letter well because I'm expecting a box of candy from Nogent. Adieu, answer me as soon as possible.

Adieu; good health; your friend for life.

Answer as quickly as possible, please.

To ERNEST CHEVALIER

February 4, 1831

Dear Friend

I'm answering you by return of mail. I told you I'd write some plays, but no—I'll write some novels that I have in my mind; they are the beautiful Andalusian, the masked ball, Cardenio, Dorothy, The Moorish Woman, the impertinent eavesdropper, the prudent husband. I have arranged the billiard table and the scenery. In my dramatic proverbs there are several plays that we can put on. Your father is still the same. See—I was right in saying that my marvelous explanation of constipation and my eulogy of Corneille would go down to posterity—that is, down to the posterior. Nor do I forget the dauntless Mayeux. Try to answer me as precisely as I do you. But for you

[1] The nine-year-old Flaubert refers to Lafayette's dismissal as commander-in-chief of the National Guard, following disagreements with King Louis Philippe. More precisely, Lafayette's office had been abolished by the Chamber of Deputies, in compliance with the king's wishes, on December 24.

that's scarcely possible, since you're now pope, priest, devil, scholar, author, and the three patriarchs Abraham, Isaac, and Jacob rolled into one. Rather a jacobin than Jacob. So long, Happy New Year, come to Rouen.

Your dauntless friend till death.

Answer.

To ERNEST CHEVALIER

Rouen, this fifteenth of January,
year of Our Lord Jesus Christ 1832

Dear Friend

Your father is a little better, the medicine papa gave him helped him and we hope that he'll soon be well. I am making notes on *Don Quixote* and Monsieur Mignot says they're very good. Somebody has had my eulogy of Corneille printed—I think your Uncle Amédée—and I am sending you a copy. The billiard table is deserted—I'm not putting on any plays since you're not here. The Sunday you left seemed to me ten times as long as the others. I forgot to tell you that I am going to begin a play which will be called The Stingy Lover—it will be about a stingy lover who refuses to give presents to his mistress, so his friend gets her away from him. All my greetings to your family; I will tell you the end of my play in another letter. Make your parents promise to come here with you for Carnival, work at your geography. I'm going to start also a History of Henry IV, Louis XIII and Louis XIV; I must get to work. Don't forget Mahieu[1a] or The Stingy Cuckold. Adieu, my best friend till death, by God.

Good-night. Your old friend.

Answer.

[1a] The name of a character in contemporary caricature, representing the petit-bourgeois. Misspelled "Mayeux" in the preceding letter.

To ERNEST CHEVALIER

[*March 31, 1832*]

Dauntless One:

You know I told you in one of my letters that we were not having any more theatre, but just the last few days we've been busy on the billiard table again, I have about 30 plays and there are many which Caroline and I act together. But if you come at Easter you'll be a good boy and stay at least a week. You'll hear me recite my catechism. You'd start out from your house on Sunday at six o'clock after vespers, you'd be at Rouen by eleven, and you'd leave us with great regret the next Saturday afternoon. Your father is better. I am writing a poem called A Mother which is as good as The Death of Louis XVI. I am also doing several plays, among others one called The Ignorant Antiquary which makes fun of stupid antiquaries and another which is called Preparations to Receive the King, a farce.

You know there is a pupil in old Langlois's class named Alexis, called by everybody Jesus. The other day he almost fell into the trench. At the moment he was placing his façade on the hole the boards broke and if someone hadn't caught hold of him he'd have fallen into old Langlois's excrement. Adieu.

Answer quickly at the first opportunity.

Rouen, this 31 of March 1832.

To ERNEST CHEVALIER

[*April 3, 1832?*]

Victory, Victory

Victory, Victory, Victory, you'll be coming some day soon, my friend; the theatre, the posters, everything is ready. When you come, Amédée, Edmond, Madame Chevalier, mama, two servants, and perhaps some of the medical students will come to see us act, we'll give 4 plays that you don't know but you'll learn the lines quickly. The tickets for the first, second, and third are done; there will be regular seats; there are also real roofs and decorations. The curtain is ready, perhaps there will be 10 or twelve people. So you must be brave and fear nothing, we'll have a doorman (young Lerond), and his sister will be an extra. I don't know whether you have seen *Poursognac,*[2] we'll give it along with a play by Berquin, one by Scribe and a dramatic proverb by Carmontelle, no reason for me to tell you their titles I don't think you know them. When they told me you weren't coming I was in a frightful rage. If by any chance you didn't come I'd go to Les Andelys to get you on all fours like the dogs of King Louis *Fils-Lippe* (see the newspaper *Caricature*), and I think that you would do the same for me, for you and I are bound by a love that can be called fraternal. Yes, I, who have deep feeling, yes, I would walk a thousand leagues if necessary to be reunited with the best of my friends, for nothing is so sweet as friendship oh sweet friendship how much has been done in the name of that sentiment, without attachments how would we live. We see this sentiment even in the smallest animals, without friendship how would the weak live, how would women and children subsist?

Permit me, my dear friend, these tender reflections but I swear to you they were not prepared in advance and I've not been trying to indulge in rhetoric but am speaking to you with the truthfulness of the true friend. The cholera morbus has almost disappeared here. Your father is the same. Come to Rouen; adieu.

2 Molière's *Monsieur de Pourceaugnac.* For a description of a scene from this comedy adapted by the children, see page 158.

To ERNEST CHEVALIER

Rouen, this Friday August 14, 1835

Dear Ernest

It is with much pleasure that I can now tell you with certainty that we'll soon be coming to see you—I have papa's word. Then you will owe us a return visit, and I hope you will adopt the good habit of coming to spend a week with us. It's about two weeks since I finished my *Frédégonde,* I've even recopied an act and a half. I have another drama in mind. Gourgaud is assigning me narrative compositions.

Since you saw me I've read *Catherine Howard* and *La Tour de Nesle.* I've also read the works of Beaumarchais: that's the place to find new ideas. Now I am entirely absorbed in the plays of old Shakespeare, I am reading *Othello,* and then I am going to take with me for my trip the *History of Scotland* in three volumes by W. Scott, then I'll read Voltaire. I am working like a demon, getting up at half past three in the morning.

I see with indignation that dramatic censorship is going to be re-established and freedom of the press abolished! Yes, this law will pass, for the representatives of the people are nothing but a filthy heap of sold-out wretches. They see only their own interests, their natural bent is toward baseness, their honor is a stupid pride, their soul a heap of mud; but some day, a day which will come before long, the people will unloose the third revolution: heads will fall, blood will run in rivers. Now they are depriving the man of letters of his conscience, his artist's conscience. Yes, our century is rich in bloody peripeties. Adieu, au revoir—let us devote ourselves always to Art which greater than peoples, crowns, and kings is always there, enthroned on high in our inspiration, wearing its divine diadem.

To ERNEST CHEVALIER

Rouen, Thursday, September 13, 1838

Your remarks on Victor Hugo contain as much truth as they do lack of originality. Modern criticism now generally accepts that antithesis of body and soul so profoundly expounded in all the works of the great author of *Notre-Dame*. This man has been much attacked because he is great and arouses envy. People were at first astonished, and then they blushed, to see before them a genius as immense as any of those whom they'd been admiring for centuries; for human pride doesn't enjoy paying its respects to laurels that are still green. Is not V. Hugo as great a man as Racine, Calderon, Lope de Vega, and many another long admired?

I am still reading Rabelais, and have also taken up Montaigne. I even propose to make a special philosophical and literary study of these two later. Together they mark the taking-off point, as I see it, of French literature and the French spirit.

Really I profoundly value only two men, Rabelais and Byron, the only two who have written in a spirit of malice toward the human race and with the intention of laughing in its face. What a tremendous position a man occupies who places himself in such relation to the world!

No, the view of the sea is not conducive to gaiety or the making of quips, though I have smoked considerably and eaten pantagruelistically of fish stew, brill, lettuce, sausages, onions, bunions, radishes, turnips, beets, sheep, pigs, lambs, and larks.

By now I have come to look on the world as a spectacle, and to laugh at it. What is the world to me? I shall ask little of it, I'll let myself float on the current of my heart and my imagination, and if anyone shouts too loudly perhaps I shall turn like Phocion, and say "What is that cawing of crows?"

To ERNEST CHEVALIER

Rouen, November 30, 1838

You see that I'm answering you quite promptly—a pleasure for me, even more than a duty owed to friendship. Your letter, like all letters from those we love, gave me great pleasure. For a long time I have been thinking of you and imagining how you look walking in Paris, cigar in mouth, etc.; so I greatly enjoyed getting details about your daily life; I assure you there weren't too many of them.

You do well to see much of Alfred; the more time you spend with him, the greater treasures you'll discover in him. He is an inexhaustible mine of good feelings, generosities, and grandeur. And he entirely reciprocates the friendship you feel for him. Why am I not with you, dear friends! What a fine trinity we should make! How I look forward to joining you! We'll have some good times, the three of us, philosophizing and pantagruelizing.

You tell me that you have come to a definitive belief in a creative force (God, fatality, etc.) and that having done so you expect to spend some agreeable moments. To tell you the truth, I cannot imagine what will be agreeable about them. When you have seen the dagger that's to pierce your heart, the rope that's to strangle you, when you're ill and learn the name of your illness—I cannot imagine what consolation you have achieved. Try to attain belief in a universal design, in morality, in the duties of man, in the future life; try to believe in the integrity of statesmen, in the chastity of whores, in the goodness of man, in the happiness of life, in the truth of all possible lies. Then you'll be happy, and able to call yourself a believer and three-quarters a fool; but in the meantime continue to be intelligent, a skeptic and a drinker.

You have read Rousseau, you say? What a man! I recommend especially his *Confessions*. It's in them that he bares his soul.

Poor Rousseau, so calumnied because thy heart was nobler than that of other men, thy pages dissolve me in delectations and amorous reveries!

Continue your style of life, dear Ernest, it could not be better. And I, what am I doing? I am still the same, facetious rather than gay, distended rather than great. I am writing speeches for old Magnier, historical studies for Chéruel, and smoking pipes for my own pleasure. As far as living arrangements are concerned, I have never been so well off as this year: I no longer suffer any of the annoyance of the college, I am quiet and peaceful.

As for writing, I am doing none of it or almost none; I content myself with drawing up outlines, creating scenes, dreaming of disjointed, imaginary situations in which I picture myself and live intensely. It's a strange world, my mind!

I have read *Ruy Blas;* all in all it is a fine work, apart from a few blemishes and the fourth act which, though comic and amusing, lacks high and true comedy; not that I want to attack the grotesque element in drama. There are two or three scenes, and the last act, which are sublime; have you seen Frédérick in this play? What's your opinion of him?

Tell Alfred to hurry and write me, and that I'll answer him immediately.

Farewell, dear Ernest, keep well. My best to Pagnerre and Alfred. . . .

The last three or four days I have been debating, in old Magnier's class, with one of the Abbé Eudes' pupils. There were two debates, especially, in which I was magnificent. All the pupils in my row were impressed by the uproar I made. I began by saying that I was well known as a priest-hater, and every day there's a new round. I invent the most absurd rubbish about the Abbé Eudes and about Julien; the poor church mouse looks stricken; the other day he was sweating.

To ERNEST CHEVALIER

[*Rouen, March 18, 1839*]

To begin with I am dazzled by the fires of your genius, all admiration for your description of Palmyra! It really deserves the honor of being printed and entered in the academic competition: nay, more! the entire collection of the *Colibri*[3] would pale before it, and Orlowski[4] with his twelve cups of coffee would prostrate himself in the dust in oriental style.

As to your horror for *those ladies*—who are, I might say in passing, very worthy people without prejudices—I leave to Alfred the task of changing it logically into a philosophical love conformant to the rest of your moral opinions. Yes a thousand times I prefer a whore to a grisette, for of all the types of human beings the grisette is what I abominate the most. Such, I believe, is the name given to that wriggly, twisty, proper, coquettish, simpery, perky, stupid something that's always getting on your nerves and wanting to play scenes of passion with you the way she's seen them played in the vaudeville dramas. No, I much prefer the frankly ignoble. This is a pose like any other, a fact which I realize better than anyone else.

With all my heart I could love a woman who was beautiful, ardent, with the soul of a whore. Such is the point I have reached. Such pure and innocent tastes! Long live idyllic pleasures!

You tell me that you have an admiration for G. Sand; I share it keenly and with the same reticence. I have read few things as fine as *Jacques*. Speak to Alfred about it.

At present I am reading scarcely at all. I have resumed a work long since abandoned, a mystery play, a ragout—I think I've

3 Three hundred and one numbers of this magazine had already appeared, beginning in 1836; and it was to continue to appear every Thursday and Sunday through 1844.

4 Caroline Flaubert's piano teacher, popular with the children. He was a Polish friend of Chopin's, living in exile in Rouen.

told you about it already. Here, in two words, is what it is: Satan leads a man (Smar)[5] into the infinite; they both rise immense distances into the air. In thus discovering so many things, Smar is filled with pride. He believes that all the mysteries of creation and the infinite are revealed to him, but Satan leads him still higher. Then he is afraid, he trembles, all this abyss seems to engulf him, he feels weak amid the emptiness. They return to earth. There he is on his own ground; there he should live, he says; everything in nature is subject to him. Then a storm arises, the sea is about to swallow him. Again he confesses his weakness and nothingness. Satan proceeds to lead him among men; first, the savage sings of his happiness, his nomadic life; but suddenly a desire to move toward the city seizes him, he cannot resist it; he departs. (These are the barbaric races becoming civilized.) Second, they enter the city, visit the king stricken with sorrows and prey to the seven deadly sins, visit the poor, the married, the church, which is deserted. All parts of the edifice give voice to complaints; from the nave to the tombstones, everything speaks and curses God. Then the church, become impious, crumbles. Throughout all this there is a character who takes part in all the events and caricatures them. This is Yuk, god of the grotesque. Thus in the first scene, while Satan is debauching Smar through pride, Yuk is persuading a married woman to give herself to every man who happens by, without distinction. (This is laughter side by side with tears and suffering, mud side by side with blood.) So: Smar is thus disgusted with the world; he would like everything to be ended at that point, but Satan on the contrary makes him experience all the passions and all the miseries he has seen. He takes him on winged horses to the shores of the Ganges. There, monstrous and fantastic orgies, sensual pleasure such as I am able to conceive it; but sensuality wearies him. And so he

5 Flaubert later decided to spell his hero's name "Smarh." This "ragout" has been published among his juvenilia.

again becomes ambitious. He becomes a poet; after his lost illusions, his despair is immense, the cause of heaven is being lost. Smar has not yet experienced love. A woman appears . . . a woman . . . he loves her. He regains his earlier beauty, but Satan also falls in love with her. So, each one proceeds to seduce her. Who will be the victor? Satan, as you are thinking? No: Yuk, the grotesque. The woman is Truth; and the whole thing ends with a monstrous copulation. Marvelous plot: full of pitfalls. Show it to Alfred along with my last letter . . . that way I won't have to write the same thing twice.

I write works which will never receive the Montyon prize,[6] and which are *not recommended for young girls.* I'll be sure to put that last fine phrase on the title page.

Adieu.

Always yours

To ERNEST CHEVALIER

Monday afternoon, [*Rouen, April*] *15,* [*1839*]

Class on the theory of eclipses—Prof. Amyot, whose own mind is severely eclipsed.

You pity me, dear Ernest, and yet am I to be pitied, have I any reason for cursing God? On the contrary, when I look about me at the past, at the present, at my family, at my friends, my attachments, I find little lacking to make me bless Him. The circumstances surrounding me are favorable rather than otherwise. And with all that I am not content; we give vent to endless jeremiads, we create imaginary troubles for ourselves (alas! that's the worst kind) ; and we build up illusions which collapse; we sow our own path with brambles, and then the days pass, real troubles come, and we die without having had a single ray of

[6] Awarded annually by the French Academy for the most virtuous action performed in France during the year.

pure sunlight in our souls, a single day of calm, a single cloudless sky. No, I am happy. And why not? Who is there to distress me? The future will be black, perhaps? Let us drink before the storm; too bad if the tempest shatters us, but the sea is calm now.

And you, too! I thought you had more good sense than I, dear friend. You too are bawling and sobbing! Good Lord, why? Do you realize that the young student generation is wildly stupid? It used to be more intelligent; it spent its time on women, duels, orgies; now it patterns itself on Byron, dreams of despair and for no reason at all puts its heart under padlock. Each vies with the other as to who shall look the palest and most convincingly say "I am blasé." Blasé! What a sorry thing! Blasé at eighteen! Is there no longer such a thing as love, or glory, or work? Is everything finished? Does nature no longer exist for youth, nor flowers? Let's have no more of all this. Let's go in for sadness in Art, since that is the aspect of things we feel the best, but let's have gaiety in our lives: I'm for the popping cork, the stuffed pipe, the naked whore! If we have the spleen some evening, at twilight, during an hour of fog and snow, let it come, but not often: from time to time we must scrape the scale from our hearts with a little suffering. That is what I advise you to do, what I try to put into practice.

Another bit of advice: write me often, ill-bred, ill-mannered oaf. Tell me what you are doing with yourself morally, physically. Yesterday I finished a mystery play that takes three hours to read. Only the subject is respectable. It won't be forbidden to young girls.

Achille is in Paris. He is passing his thesis and buying furniture. He's going to settle down, like a polyp on a rock.

To GOURGAUD-DUGAZON

Rouen, January 22, 1842

Mon cher Maître:

I begin by saying that I'd like an answer. I count on seeing you in April, and since your letters usually take whole trimesters and semesters to arrive, you might easily leave me without news until then. So—surprise me, be punctual: it's a scholastic virtue which you should make a point of possessing, since you have all the others. I was in Paris at the beginning of this month; I stayed two days, but was deep in business and errands and had no time to come and embrace you. In the spring I'll come find you some Sunday morning, and willy-nilly you'll have to make me a present of your entire day. Hours pass quickly when we are together; I have so many things to tell you, and you listen so well!

Now more than ever I need to talk to you, need your wisdom, your friendship. My moral position is critical: you saw that when we were last together. From you I hide nothing, and I speak to you not as though you were my former teacher, but as though you were only twenty and were here, opposite me, beside my fireplace.

I am, as you know, studying law; that is, I have bought my lawbooks and matriculated. I'll start studying in a little while, and expect to pass my entrance examination in July. I continue to busy myself with Greek and Latin, and shall perhaps busy myself with them always. I love the flavor of those beautiful languages; Tacitus is for me like bronze bas-reliefs, and Homer is beautiful as the Mediterranean: the same pure blue waters, the same sun and the same horizon. But what keeps coming back to me every minute, what makes me drop my pen as I take notes, and obliterates my textbooks as I read, is my old love, the same fixed idea: writing! That is why I am not accomplishing much, even though I rise very early and go out less than ever.

I have arrived at a decisive moment: I must go forwards or backwards. It is a question of life and death. When I decide, nothing will stop me, even though I be booed and jeered at by everyone. You are sufficiently acquainted with my stubbornness and stoicism to believe me. I will pass my bar examination, but I scarcely think I shall ever plead in court about a party-wall or on behalf of some poor father of a family cheated by a wealthy climber. When people speak to me of the bar, saying "This young fellow will make a fine trial lawyer, he's such a fine figure of a man, his voice is so booming," I confess that my stomach turns and I don't feel myself made for such a completely material, trivial life. On the contrary, every day I admire the poets more and more, I discover in them a thousand things that formerly I never saw. I grasp relationships and antitheses whose precision astonishes me, etc. This, then, is what I have resolved: I have in mind three novels, three tales, each of them different, each requiring a particular way of writing. This is enough to prove to myself whether I have talent or not.

Into them I'll put everything I have—all the style, all the passion, all the intelligence—and then we'll see.

In April I expect to have something to show you: that sentimental and amatory hodgepodge of which I spoke to you. There is no action. I wouldn't know how to give you an analysis of it, since it consists of nothing but psychological analyses and dissections. It is perhaps very fine; but I fear it may be very false, and not a little pretentious and stilted.

Adieu; I leave you, for you've perhaps had enough of this letter in which I've done nothing but speak of myself and my wretched passions. But I have nothing else to talk to you about: I don't go to dances, and don't read the newspapers.

Again adieu; all my affection.

P.S. Answer me soon. I should dearly love to correspond with you more often, for after a letter is finished I find myself only at the beginning of what I want to tell you.

To ERNEST CHEVALIER

[*Paris, July 22, 1842*]

What a charming science law is! How beautiful! Above all, how literary! Messieurs Oudot and Ducoudray: they have such fine styles! Monsieur Duranton: his face—the face of a true artist! His appearance: pure Greek! To think that for a month I haven't read a line of poetry, listened to a note of music, dreamed quietly for three hours, lived a single minute! I am so harassed by it all that the other night I dreamed of the law! I felt ashamed at having so dishonored dreaming. I sweat blood and tears, but if I can't find somebody's notes on Oudot it's the end —I'll be rejected for next year. Yesterday I went to watch some other students taking their examinations; I have nothing better to do than that. Soon I too will have to wear that filthy harness. I care nothing for the law, as long as they don't pass one against my smoking my pipe and watching the clouds, lying on my back and half-closing my eyes. That is all I wish for. Do you think I have any desire to be important, a great man, a man known in an arrondissement, in a department, in three provinces, a lean man, a man with indigestion? Do you think I have ambition, like the bootblacks who aspire to be boot-makers, coachmen who long to be grooms, valets who yearn to be the masters—the ambition to be a deputy or a minister, to receive a decoration, to become municipal counselor? All that seems very dreary to me and makes my mouth water as little as a 40-sou dinner or a humanitarian speech. But it's everybody's mania. And even if only to achieve distinction and not to follow one's taste, even if only for the sake of good form and not out of inclination, it is well nowadays to keep to oneself and leave all that sort of thing to the rabble, who are always pushing themselves forward and crowding the public places. As for us, let us stay at home; from our balcony let us watch the public go by, and if at times we're too bored, then let's spit on their heads, and continue to talk quietly and watch the sun sink below the horizon.

Good-night to you.

To his sister CAROLINE

Paris, July 26, 1842

Your letter of this morning, sweet Carolo, gave me much more pleasure even than the others, because Monsieur T., whom I saw yesterday, had told me that you were tired out from doing some over-long errands. Thank God, that was mere passing fatigue. Take care of yourself, dear child, always think of those who love you and of the suffering your slightest discomfort causes us.

I dined yesterday at Monsieur T.'s, with Monsieur and Madame D. Distinguished in dress and manner, like Murat, I conducted myself very well through dinner. But later, the company took it into their heads to speak of Louis Philippe and I took it into mine to rail against him because of the museum of Versailles. Think of that pig deciding that a picture by Gros wasn't big enough to fill a wall panel, and conceiving the idea of tearing off a side of the frame and adding two or three feet of canvas painted by some mediocre artist. I'd enjoy meeting that artist, just to see what he looks like. Naturally Monsieur and Madame D., who are frantic *philippistes,* who attend court, and who therefore, like Madame de Sévigné after dancing with Louis XIV, cry "What a great king!"—were very shocked by the way I spoke of him. But as you know, the more indignant I make the bourgeois, the happier I am. So, I was very satisfied with my evening. They doubtless took me for legitimist, because I made just as much fun of the men of the opposition.

To his sister CAROLINE [*1842*]

The study of law is souring my character in the extreme; I'm constantly grumbling, growling, grousing; I mutter even against myself, and when I'm alone. The day before yesterday I'd have given a hundred francs (which I didn't have) to have been able to give somebody—anybody—a good thrashing.

To his sister CAROLINE

[*Paris, December, 1842*]

My nerves are so on edge that I have to let myself go a little in a letter to you. I am leaving definitely next Friday. I want to finish up as soon as possible because things can't go on like this any longer. I'd end up in a state of idiocy or fury. This evening, for example, I'm enjoying both these feelings simultaneously. I am so furious, so impatient to pass my examination, that I could weep. I think I should even be happy if I failed, so heavy a weight do I find this life I've been leading for six weeks. Some days are worse than others. Yesterday, for example, the weather was mild as May: all morning I had a terrible longing to take a cart and drive out into the country. I kept thinking that if I were in Déville I'd be under the cart shed with Neo watching the rain and quietly smoking my pipe. One mustn't pay attention to all the good, delightful things that come into one's mind when preparing for an examination; I reproach myself for wasting time whenever I open my window to look at the stars (there's a beautiful moon just now) and take my mind off things a little. To think that since leaving you I haven't read a line of French, not six lines of poetry, not a single decent sentence. The Institutes are written in Latin and the Civil Code in something even less resembling French. The gentlemen who edited it didn't offer up much of a sacrifice to the Graces. They made of it something as dry, as hard, as stinking, as dully bourgeois as the wooden benches of the Law School, where you go to harden your buttocks and hear it explained. Those who aren't very sensitive about intellectual comfort may find themselves not too badly off there; but for aristocrats like me, who are accustomed to enthroning their imaginations in seats that are more ornate, richer, and above all more softly luxurious, it's damned disagreeable and humiliating. . . .

To his sister CAROLINE

[*Paris, end of January, 1843?*]

Good-morning, mouse. I gather your precious health is satisfactory, and that you are beginning to acquire a good constitution. Keep on taking care of yourself, so that when I come to Rouen next month I'll find you more vigorous and flourishing than ever. If you continue well, what a time we'll have at Trouville this summer! You know my vacation begins in June. May God make it as good as I hope to make it long. . . .

You are waiting for details about Victor Hugo. What can I tell you? He is a man like any other, with a rather ugly face and a rather common appearance. He has magnificent teeth, a superb forehead, no eyelashes or eyebrows. He talks little, gives the impression of being on his guard and not wanting to give himself away; he is very polite and a little stiff. I greatly like the sound of his voice. I took pleasure in watching him from nearby; I stared at him with astonishment, as I would stare at a casket full of gold and diamonds; I kept thinking of everything that has come out of him—that man who was sitting just next to me on a little chair and staring at his own right hand, that hand that has written so many fine things. *That* was the man who all my life has done more than any other to make my heart throb; the man whom I have loved best, perhaps, of all those whom I do not know. We spoke of torture, revenge, thieves, etc. The great man and I did most of the talking, and I no longer remember whether what I said was good or stupid, but I said rather a good deal. As you see, I go rather often to the Pradiers'. It's a house that I greatly like; one doesn't feel at all constrained there; it's my kind of place.

To ERNEST CHEVALIER

[*Rouen, late January or early February, 1844*]

Dear Ernest

You didn't know it, but you almost went into mourning for the man who is writing you these lines. Yes, my worthy sir; yes, young man; I came close to paying my respects to Pluto, Rhadamanthus, and Minos. I am still in bed, with a seton in my neck—a collar even stiffer than the kind worn by an officer of the National Guard—taking countless pills and tisanes, and above all plagued by that specter, a thousand times worse than all the illnesses in the world, called a diet. Know then, dear friend, that I have had a cerebral congestion, a kind of attack of apoplexy in miniature, accompanied by nervous symptoms which I retain because it's good form to do so. I very nearly passed out in the midst of my family (with whom I had come to spend two or three days to recover from the terrible scenes I had witnessed at H's).[7] They bled me in three places simultaneously and I finally opened my eyes. My father wants to keep me here a long time and to watch me carefully; my morale is good, however, because I don't know what it is to be worried. I'm in a rotten state; at the slightest excitement, all my nerves quiver like violin strings, my knees, my shoulders, and my stomach tremble like leaves. Well, *c'est la vie, sic est vita,* such is life. It is probable that I shall not soon be returning to Paris, except perhaps for two or three days toward April, to give my landlord notice and attend to a few small matters. I'll be sent to the seashore early this year and will

[7] Probably Emile Hamard.

be made to take a good deal of exercise and above all kept very quiet. No doubt I'm boring you frightfully with this tale of my woes, but what can I do? If I'm already suffering from old men's illnesses, I must be allowed to drivel the way they do.

And you? What has become of you? How is everything? What are you doing with yourself in the new Athens? Write me. When you get to Les Andelys, don't forget to come to Rouen. Adieu, a thousand greetings to all friends.

Adieu.

To ERNEST CHEVALIER

[*Rouen, February 9, 1844*]

Our two letters crossed. You sent me a merry one that made me laugh and unwrinkled my forehead; by now you have received one from me that must have surprised and distressed you. Your uncle Motte has been here to get news of me, and he has probably passed it on to you. Yes, I am wearing a seton that keeps running and itching, holding my neck stiff and driving me crazy. They purge me, bleed me, cover me with leeches, keep me away from good food and from wine: I'm a dead man.

I go on binges with orange-flower water, on sprees with pills; I have myself socratized with a syringe, and wear a stiff collar under my skin. What a voluptuous existence! Double damn it all.

I have suffered horribly, dear Ernest, since you saw me, and I have had occasion to consider to what extent human life is flower-sprinkled and festooned with delights. I'll spend all summer in the country, at Trouville. I'd like to be there now, and keep sighing for the sun.

You will marvel that I am alive when I tell you to what depths of sorrow I have descended, when I tell you that my pipe, yes, my pipe, yes, you read correctly, my pipe, my old pipe:

To ERNEST CHEVALIER [*1844*]

MY PIPE IS FORBIDDEN ME!!!

Forbidden *me,* who loved it so, who loved it alone, with cold grog in summer and coffee in winter!

I'll probably go to Paris within six weeks or two months, to put my affairs in order, and then I'll return here. I am like a melon. Fortunately this melon isn't runny: that would be the last straw. . . .

To ERNEST CHEVALIER

June 7, [*1844*]

Well, poor wreck—so you keep being badgered by bad health, infuriated by illness, maddened by ailments! You're continuing your system of falling ill at examination time, thus retarding your prodigious successes, your university ovations. As to your faithful servant, he is better without being precisely well. Not a day passes that I don't see, from time to time, what looks like bundles of hair or Bengal lights passing in front of my eyes. That lasts varying lengths of time. Still, my last severe attack was lighter than the others. I still have my seton, a pleasure I hope you may never have to experience, and I am still deprived of my pipe—a horrible torture never inflicted on the early Christians. And they say the emperors were cruel!!! You see how history is written, dear sir! *Sic scribitur historia.* I am not ready to enjoy the freedom of navigating alone, so that it will still be some time before I can stand with you on the Roche-à-l'Hermite and roll in the grass in the Bois de Cléry. Ah! Those wonderful days when I climbed into Jean's carriage, my pockets well stuffed with tobacco and cigars, and drove off to Les Andelys! Who will ever tell of our pranks, our mouth-waterings!

My father has bought a house outside Rouen, at Croisset. We are going there to live next week. Everything is upset by this move; we'll be rather uncomfortable there this summer in the midst of workmen, but next summer I think it will be superb. I go boating with Achille.

Tell me how you are and what you are doing. Do you sometimes see Oudot in your dreams? Is Duranton an incubus on your chest in your nightmares? What a marvelous idea it was of somebody's to invent the Law School for the express purpose of boring the shit out of us! It's without doubt the most poisonous invention in all creation.

Adieu, good health, my best to your parents.

To LOUIS DE CORMENIN

June 7, [*1844*]

How guilty I must seem to you, my dear Louis! But what can you do with a man who is ill half the time and so bored the other half that he has neither the strength nor the intelligence to write even the friendly, easy words that I should like to send you? Do you know what boredom is? Not that common, banal boredom that comes from idleness or illness, but that modern boredom that eats the very entrails of a man and turns an intelligent being into a walking shade, a thinking ghost. Ah! I pity you if you're acquainted with that leprosy. Sometimes you think yourself cured; but one fine day you wake up in greater pain than ever. You know those stained-glass windows you sometimes see in ugly little bourgeois houses? Seen through them the countryside is red, blue, yellow. It's the same with boredom. The most beautiful things, seen through it, take on its color and reflect its sadness. In my case it's a childhood disease that comes back on my bad days, like today. It can't be said of me as of Pantagruel: "And then he would spend a half hour in study, but his mind was always in the kitchen." My mind is on worse things: on the leeches they put on me yesterday and which are scratching my ears, on the pill that I just swallowed and that is still navigating in my stomach, on the water that followed it.

To LOUIS DE CORMENIN [*1844*]

We have little reason to be gay—Maxime is gone, his absence must weigh on you; and I have my nerves, which give me little rest. When shall we all meet again in Paris, in good health and good humor? What a fine thing to be one of a group of good fellows, all artists, living together and meeting two or three times a week to eat a good roast washed down by good wine, all the while relishing some succulent poet! I've often had that dream; it is less ambitious than many another, but perhaps no more realizable. I have just seen the sea and returned to my stupid city; that is why I am in worse humor than usual. The contemplation of beautiful things always makes one sad for a certain length of time. We would seem to be made to endure only a certain dose of beauty; a little more fatigues us. That is why mediocre natures prefer the view of a river to that of the ocean, and why so many proclaim Béranger the greatest of French poets. And let us not confuse the yawning of the bourgeois as he listens to Homer, with the profound meditation, the intense, almost painful reverie that enters the heart of the poet when he measures himself beside the colossi and utters an anguished *"O altitudo"*! So I admire Nero: he is one of the climactic men of the antique world! Woe to him who does not tremble as he reads Suetonius! I recently read the life of Heliogabalus in Plutarch. This man has a different beauty from Nero's. More Asiatic, more fevered, more romantic, more unbridled: it is the close of the day, delirium by torchlight. But Nero is quieter, more beautiful, more antique, more sober: in sum, superior. The masses have lost their poetry since Christianity. Do not speak to me of modern times as far as the grandiose is concerned. There is nothing to satisfy the imagination of even a tenth-rate hack-writer.

I am flattered to see that you join me in hating Sainte-Beuve and his like. I love above all the phrase that is nervous, substantial, clear, well-muscled, swarthy-skinned; I like male phrases, not female phrases like those of Lamartine, very often, and, on a lower level, those of Villemain. The writers I constantly read, my bedside books, are Montaigne, Rabelais, Régnier, La Bruyère, and Le Sage. I confess that I adore the prose of Voltaire and find in his tales an exquisite savor. I have read *Candide* twenty times; I once translated it into English, and have since reread it from time to time. Now I am re-reading Tacitus. In a little while, when I am better, I shall take up my Homer and Shakespeare. Homer and Shakespeare: everything is in them! The other poets, even the greatest, seem small beside them.

One of these days a small boat will arrive for me from Le Havre. I'll float on the Seine, sailing and rowing. The heat is beginning; soon I'll strip and go swimming. Those are my only pleasures. . . .

To ALFRED LE POITTEVIN

Nogent-sur-Seine, April 2, 1845

It would truly be wrong for us to part, to be false to our vocation and our sympathy. Each time we have tried to do it we have found ourselves the worse for it. Once again, at our last separation, I had painful feelings; I felt less dazed than on previous occasions, but still grieved. For three months we were together, alone, alone in ourselves and sufficient unto ourselves. There is nothing in the world to equal those strange conversations we had in that dirty chimney-corner where you have just now sat down—isn't it so, dear poet? Plumb the depths of your life and you will admit, as I do, that we have no better memories: that is, no memories of things more intimate, more profound and even more tender, because they were all so lofty. I enjoyed seeing Paris again; I looked at the boulevards, the rue de Rivoli, the sidewalks, as though I had returned after being away a hundred years, and I don't know why, but I felt happy in the midst of all that noise and all that human flood. But I have no one with me, alas! The moment you and I part, we set foot on some strange land where no one speaks our language and where we cannot make ourselves understood. No sooner was I arrived in Paris than I put on my city shoes . . . and began my visits. The stairs at the Mint left me out of breath, because there are a hundred of them and also because I remembered the time, gone never to return, when I used to climb them on my way to dinner. I greeted Madame and Mademoiselle Darcet,[8] who were in mourning; I sat down, talked for half an hour, and then decamped. Everywhere I went I was walking in my own past, pushing through it as though striding against the current of a river. I went twice to the Champs-Elysées, to see the two women[9] with whom I used to spend entire afternoons. The invalid was still half-lying in an armchair. She greeted me with the same smile and the same voice. The furniture was still the same, and the rug no more worn. In exquisite affinity with former days, one of those harmonious correspondences that can be felt only by the artist, a street-organ began to play under the windows, just as when I used to read them *Hernani* or *René*. Then I made my way to the home of a great man.[10] Alas! He was away. "Monsieur Maurice left just this afternoon for London." You may imagine that I was sorry, that I'd like to have seen someone for whom I feel such unconquerable affection. Maurice's clerk found me taller; am I, do you think?

Having secured from Panofka the address of Madame Pradier, I hurried to the rue Lafitte and asked the concierge for the apartment of that lost lady. Ah! How I observed *that* situation!

8 The mother and sister of the adulterous Madame Pradier.

9 Henrietta and Gertrude Collier, daughters of the British naval attaché in France. Flaubert had met them one summer holiday at Trouville in 1835 and seen much of them in Paris during his period of law study. Gertrude Collier is the girl mentioned on page 80.

10 Maurice Schlesinger.

You should have seen how I behaved! I acted the role of the gallant, the blackguard. I approved her conduct, declared myself the champion of adultery, and perhaps even surprised her by my indulgence. She was certainly extremely flattered by my visit and invited me to lunch on my return. All that wants to be written, detailed, painted, chiseled. I would do it for a man like you if it weren't that I hurt my finger the other day, and it forces me to write slowly and hampers me at every word.

I pitied the baseness of all those people at the throat of that poor woman. They have taken away her children, taken away everything. She lives on six thousand francs a year in a furnished flat, no maid—wretchedness. When I saw her the time before the last she was in her glory—two salons, purple silk chairs, gilded ceilings. When I came in she had been weeping, having learned that morning that the police had been following her for two weeks. The father of the young man with whom she had her affair is afraid that she'll get her hands on him, and is doing everything he can to break up this illicit union. Can't you just see the father, terrified of the gold-digger? And the son, nervous and uneasy? And the girl, pitilessly prosecuted?

We leave tomorrow from Nogent, and proceed immediately to Arles and Marseilles. We'll visit the Midi at leisure on our way back from Genoa. At Marseilles I shall call on Madame Foucaud; that will be singularly bitter and funny, especially if I find her grown ugly, as I expect. A bourgeois would say that I'll be greatly disillusioned. But I have rarely experienced disillusions, having had few illusions. What a stupid platitude it is, always to praise lies and to say that poetry lives on illusions! As if disillusion weren't a hundred times more poetic in itself! Both words are immensely inept, really.

Today my boredom was terrible. How beautiful the provinces and the chic of the comfortably-off who inhabit them! Their talk is of *The Wandering Jew* and the polka, of taxes and road improvements; and their neighbors are very important!

To ALFRED LE POITTEVIN

Milan, May 13, [*1845*]

Once again I have left my beloved Mediterranean. I bade it farewell with a strange sinking of the heart. The morning we were to leave Genoa I left the hotel at six o'clock as though to take a stroll, but instead I hired a boat and went out as far as the entrance of the harbor, to see one last time the blue waters I so love. The sea was running high; I let myself be rocked with the boat, thinking of you and missing you. And then, when I began to feel that any minute I might be seasick, I went back to shore and we set out. I was so depressed for the next three days that more than once I literally thought I should die. No matter how great an effort I made, I could not utter a word. I begin to disbelieve that people die of grief, since I am alive.

I saw the battlefields of Marengo, Novi, and Vercelli, but I was in such pitiable state of mind that it all left me unmoved. I kept thinking of those ceilings in the Genoa palaces, beneath which one would love so proudly. I carry the love of antiquity with me in my very entrails. I am moved to the depths of my being when I think of the Roman keels that once cut the changeless, eternally undulant waves of this ever-young sea. The ocean is perhaps more beautiful, but here the absence of the tides which divide time into regular periods seems to make you forget that the past is far distant and that centuries separate you from Cleopatra. Ah! When shall you and I stretch out on our stomachs on the sands of Alexandria, or sleep in the shade of the plane trees of the Hellespont?

You are wasting away with boredom, you are bursting with rage, you are dying of sadness, you are stifling . . . have patience, oh lion of the desert! I too stifled for long; the walls of my room in the rue de l'Est still record the frightful curses, the foot-stampings, the cries of distress that I gave vent to when I was alone: how I roared and how I yawned, one after the other! Train your lungs to use little air: they will expand with all the more pleasure when you're on the high peaks and have to breathe hurricanes. Think, work, write, roll up your sleeves and cut your marble, like the good workman who doesn't turn his head and sweats and laughs over his task. It is in the second period of the life of an artist that travel is good; but in the first it is better to express everything that is truly intimate, original, individual within you. Think what a long wandering in the Orient will mean to you a few years from now! Give your muse free rein, ignoring human concerns, and each day you'll feel your mind expanding in a way that will astonish you. The only way not to be unhappy is to shut yourself up in Art and to count all the rest as nothing; pride takes the place of everything else when it rests on a broad foundation. As for me, I've really been fairly well since resigning myself to be perpetually ill. You're aware, aren't you, that I miss many things, that I had it in me to be as lavish as the richest man in the world, as tender as lovers, as sensual as the most unbridled? However, I do not miss riches, or love, or the flesh, and everyone is astonished to see me behave so well. I have said an irrevocable farewell to the practical life. From now until a day that's far distant I ask for no more than five or six quiet hours in my room, a big fire in the winter, and a pair of candles to light me at night.

You distress me, my dear sweet friend, you distress me when you speak of your death. Think of what would become of me. A soul wandering like a bird over the flooded earth, I wouldn't have the tiniest rock, a single square inch of ground, where I could rest my weariness. Why are you going to spend a month in Paris? You'll be even more bored than in Rouen. You'll return even more exhausted. Besides, are you sure that steam baths will do any good to your Moechus-like head?

I long to see what you have written since I left. In four or five weeks we shall read it over together alone, by ourselves and sufficient unto ourselves, far from the world and from the bourgeois, secluded as bears in winter, growling under our layers of fur. I still think about my oriental tale, which I shall write next winter, and for the past few days I have had an idea for a rather good play about an episode of the Corsican war which I read in a history of Genoa. I have seen a picture by Breughel, *The Temptation of Saint Anthony,* which made me think of arranging the subject for the theatre, but that would need a different sort of person from me. I would certainly give the entire collection of the *Moniteur*—if I had it—and a hundred thousand francs besides, for that picture, which most people who see it undoubtedly think bad.

To ALFRED LE POITTEVIN

Geneva, May 26, [*1845*]

Two days ago I saw Byron's name written on one of the pillars of the dungeon where the prisoner of Chillon was confined. This sight afforded me exquisite joy. I thought more about Byron than about the prisoner, and no ideas came to me about tyranny and slavery. All the time I thought of the pale man who one day came there, walked up and down, wrote his name on the stone, and left. One would have to be very daring or very stupid to write one's name in such a place after that.

Byron's name is scratched on one side and it is already black, as though ink had been rubbed into it to make it show; indeed it does stand out on the gray column, and one sees it the minute one enters. Below the name the stone is a little eaten away, as though the giant's hand which rested on it had worn it with its weight. I was sunk in contemplation before those five letters. This evening, just now, I lit my cigar and walked to a little island attached to the shore of the lake opposite our hotel, called the Ile Jean-Jacques because of Pradier's statue which stands there. This island is a favorite walking-place, where they have music in the evening. When I arrived at the foot of the statue, the brasses were sounding softly; it was so dark that one could scarcely see; people were sitting on benches, facing the lake, at the foot of tall trees whose tops, almost motionless, were nonetheless swaying slightly. Rousseau stood on his pedestal and listened to it all. I shivered; the sound of the trombones and flutes went to my very entrails. After the andante came something merry, full of fanfares. I thought of the theatre, the orchestra, boxes full of powdered women, of all the thrills of glory, and of this paragraph of the *Confessions: "J.-J. tu doutais, toi qui quinze ans plus tard, haletant, éperdu . . ."* The music continued a long time. From symphony to symphony I put off returning to my room; finally I left. At the two ends of Lake Geneva there are two geniuses whose shades loom higher than that of the mountains: Byron and Rousseau, a pair of powerful, shrewd fellows who would have made "very good lawyers."

You tell me that you are more and more in love with nature. My own passion for it is becoming uncontrollable. At times I look on animals and even trees with a tenderness that amounts to a feeling of affinity; I derive almost voluptuous sensations from the mere act of seeing—when I see clearly. A few days ago I met three poor idiot women who asked me for alms. They were terrible, disgusting in their ugliness and cretinism; they could not speak, they could scarcely walk. When they saw me they began to make signs to tell me that they loved me; they smiled at me, lifted their hands to their faces and sent me kisses. At Pont-l'Evêque my father owns a pasture where the shepherdess is an imbecile girl; the first times she saw me she too evidenced a strange attachment to me. I attract madmen and animals. Is it because they sense that I understand them, because they feel that I enter into their world?

We crossed the Simplon last Thursday. Up until now, it is the most beautiful thing in nature that I have seen. You know that beautiful things cannot stand description. I missed you badly; I'd have liked you to be with me, or else I'd have liked to be in the soul of those tall pines which stood, all hanging and snow-covered, at the rim of the abysses. I kept measuring myself against that immensity. At Domodossola I visited a Capuchin monastery (I had already seen one in Genoa, and another, Carthusian, near Milan). The Capuchin who showed us about offered us a glass of wine; I gave him two cigars, and as we parted we shook hands warmly. He seemed like an excellent fellow. One brushes against many friendships when traveling; I don't speak of love affairs.

It's a singular thing, the way I have withdrawn from women. I am satiated, as those must be who have loved too much. The marvelous fluids of love have seethed in me too furiously ever to escape, and this has made me impotent. In the presence of no woman do I experience that passionate curiosity that impels you to strip the veil from the unknown and to seek something new.

Stay in Rouen, so that I'll find you when I come, toward the fifteenth of June. Try to stay there at least until August, so that we may have time to tell each other what we have to tell. I am sick of being alone. Are you aware that there is great logic in our union? It is inevitable that sound should rise, and that the stars should follow their parabolas. It is the same with us. Unique in our natures, isolated in immensity, Providence makes us think and feel in harmony.

To MAXIME DU CAMP

Rouen, March [*20*], *1846*

Hamard has just left my room, where he has been standing sobbing beside the fire. My mother is a weeping statue. Caroline speaks to us, smiles, caresses us, says gentle and affectionate things to all of us, but her memory is going and her ideas are confused: she didn't know whether it was I or Achille who had gone to Paris. What a grace there is about the sick, what strange movements they make! The baby sucks and cries. Achille says nothing, not knowing what to say. What a house! What a hell! My own eyes are dry; it is strange how sorrows in fiction flood me with facile emotion, while actual sorrows remain hard and bitter in my heart, crystallizing there as they come. Calamity is in this house, intending, it seems, to remain until it shall have glutted itself on us. Once again[11] I shall see funeral cloths and hear the ignoble sound of the undertakers' hobnail boots descending the stairs. I prefer to have no hope, to plunge, rather, in thought, into the grief that is coming. Dr. Marjolin is arriving tonight. What can he do? I had a premonition yesterday that when I next saw you I should not be gay.

To MAXIME DU CAMP

Croisset, March [*23 or 24*], *1846*

I didn't want you to come here: I was afraid of your affection. It was enough for me to see Hamard, without seeing you. Perhaps you would have been even less calm than we were. In a few days I shall send for you; I count on you. It was yesterday at eleven o'clock that we buried the poor girl. They dressed her in her wedding-dress, with bouquets of roses, immortelles, and violets. I watched beside her all night. She lay there on her bed, in that room where you have heard her play. She seemed much

11 Flaubert's father had died January 15.

taller and much more beautiful than when she was alive, with the long white veil coming down to her feet.[12] In the morning, when everything was done, I gave her a last kiss in her coffin. I bent over her, and as I lowered my head I felt the lead buckle under my hands. It was I who attended to the casts. I saw the big hands of those rustics touching her and covering her with plaster. I shall have her hand and her face. I shall ask Pradier to make me her bust and shall put it in my room. I have her big colored shawl, a lock of her hair, her table and writing-desk. That is all—all that remains of those we love! Hamard insisted on coming with us. There, in the cemetery—around whose walls I used to walk with my class—he knelt on the edge of the grave, blew kisses to her, and wept. The grave was too narrow, the coffin wouldn't fit. They shook it, pulled it, turned it every which way; they took a pick and some crowbars, and finally a gravedigger stamped on it—just over Caroline's head—to force it down. I was standing to one side, holding my hat in my hand; I threw it down with a cry. I'll tell you the rest when we're together, for I'd write it all too badly. I was dry-eyed as a tombstone, but horribly tense. I wanted to tell you all this, thinking it would give you pleasure. You are sufficiently intelligent, and love me enough, to understand that word "pleasure," which would make the bourgeois laugh.

We have been back in Croisset since Sunday. What a journey! Alone with my mother, and the baby crying all the way. The last time that I left Croisset, it was with you: you remember. Of the four who lived here, two remain. The trees are still leafless,

12 Recalling this scene in a later letter to Louise Colet, Flaubert adds the following details:

"I was reading Montaigne; my eyes kept turning from my book to the corpse; her husband and the priest were snoring; and I kept telling myself, as I saw all this, that forms disappear, that the idea alone remains; and I kept feeling thrills at turns of phrase in the Montaigne, and reflected that he, too, would be forgotten. It was freezing; the window was open because of the odor, and from time to time I got up to look at the stars, calm, shining, radiant, eternal."

the wind is blowing, the river is high; the rooms are cold and bare. My mother is better than one would think she could be. She busies herself with her daughter's child, puts her to bed in her room, rocks her, does everything she can. She is trying to make herself into a mother again: will she succeed? The reaction has not yet set in, and I dread its coming. I am crushed, numb; I must resume my quiet life, for grief and wretchedness are stifling me. When can I begin to lead it again, my poor life of tranquil art and long meditation? I laugh with pity at the vanity of the human will, when I think that for the past six years I have wanted to get back my Greek, and that circumstances are such that I haven't yet got as far as the verbs.

To MAXIME DU CAMP

[*Croisset*], *April 7, 1846*

I've chosen a large sheet of paper with the intention of writing you a long letter; perhaps I shall send you only three lines; we'll see how it goes. The sky is grey, the Seine yellow, the grass green; the trees are just beginning to bud; it is spring, the season of joy and love. "But there is no more spring in my heart than there is on the highroad, where the wind wearies the eyes and the dust rises in whirling clouds." Do you remember where that comes from? From *Novembre*. I was nineteen when I wrote it, almost six years ago. It is strange, how I was born with little faith in happiness. While still very young I had a complete presentiment of life. It was like a nauseating kitchen smell that pours through a ventilator: you don't have to eat the food cooked in such a place to know that it would make you vomit. This is not a complaint, however; my recent bereavements have saddened me but not surprised me. Without feeling them any the less acutely, I have analyzed them as an artist. This task has revived my grief. Had I expected better things of life I should have cursed it; but that is just what I have not done. You would perhaps look upon me as heartless were I to tell you that I do not consider this the worst period of my life. At a time when I had nothing to complain of, I felt much sorrier for myself. This, after all, may be only a question of practice. The soul expands in suffering, and in the process its capacity greatly increases; what formerly filled it to the point of bursting now seems a mere drop. At least I have one great consolation, one pillar that sustains me; it is this: nothing worse is likely to happen to me. There is my mother's death, which I think of as more or less imminent; but were I a little less selfish I should wish it for her. Is it an act of humanity to succor those in despair? Have you ever realized how completely we are made for misfortune? Sensual pleasure can make us swoon; anguish, never. Tears are for the heart what water is for fish. I am resigned to everything, ready for everything; I have furled my sails and await the squall, my back to the wind and my head bowed. Religious people are said to stand the evils of this world better than the rest of us. But a man who is conscious of the harmony of the universe, who believes that his body will return to nothingness whereas his soul will sleep in the bosom of the great All until it goes to inhabit the body of a panther, perhaps, or to shine in the stars—he too is unafraid. Too much has been made of mystic bliss. Cleopatra died as serenely as St. Francis. I believe that the dogma of a future life was inspired by the fear of death or by the wish to salvage something from death.

Yesterday my niece was baptized. The infant, the guests, I, and even the curé, who had just had his dinner and was still red in the face—nobody had any understanding of what was taking place. As I observed all those symbols, so meaningless for us, I felt as though I were witnessing a ceremony from some remote religion, exhumed from the dust. It was very simple and very familiar, and yet it struck me as infinitely strange. The priest rattled off a jumble of Latin that he himself did not understand;

the rest of us did not listen; water was poured over the baby's bald little head; the candle burned and the beadle answered Amen. More intelligent than any of us, certainly, were the stones, which had understood it all long ago and perhaps still retained something of its meaning.

I am going to get to work, at last, at last. I crave and hope to work hard and long. Is this because I have had tangible proof of the vanity of ourselves, of our plans, of our happiness, of beauty, of goodness, of everything? But I have the impression of being limited and very mediocre. I am developing an artistic squeamishness that distresses me; I shall end by never writing another line. I think that I could do good things, but I keep asking myself why I should. This is all the more strange since I do not feel discouraged; on the contrary, I am plunging ever deeper in the pure Idea, into the infinite. I aspire to it, it attracts me; I am becoming a brahmin, or rather I am becoming a little mad. It is very doubtful that I shall write anything this summer. If I do, it will be a play. My oriental story is postponed until next year, perhaps until the year after, perhaps forever. If my mother dies, my plans are made: I will sell everything and go live in Rome, in Syracuse, in Naples. Will you follow me? But heaven grant me a little calm! A little calm, great God! A little rest, nothing more—I do not ask for happiness. You seem happy; that is sad. Happiness is a red cloak with a tattered lining; when you try to cover yourself with it, the wind blows it to pieces, and you find yourself floundering in the chilly rags of something you had thought would give you warmth.

To MAXIME DU CAMP

April, 1846

Boredom—*taedium vitae*—has no cause; to try to be logical about it, to fight it by rational arguments, is to show lack of understanding. There was a time when I had everything that makes for happiness and yet was truly pitied; the greatest sorrows are not those for which one wears mourning. I know what emptiness is. Who can tell, though—perhaps it contains the seeds of future greatness. But be on your guard against day-dreaming; it is a vicious monster, very seductive, that has already devoured much of my substance. It is the siren of the soul; it sings and beckons; once you answer its call you never return.

I have a great desire, or rather a great need, to see you. I have a thousand things to tell you, sad things. It seems to me that the stage I have now reached will be permanent. This is probably an illusion, but if it is, it is the only one I have left. When I think of everything that may happen I do not see what could change me; I mean change me essentially, my life, my daily routine; and then I am beginning to acquire a habit of work, for which heaven be thanked. I read or write regularly from eight to ten hours a day; and if I am disturbed it makes me ill. Many a day passes without my going as far as the end of the terrace; my boat hasn't even been taken out of winter quarters. I thirst after long studies and arduous tasks. The life of the mind, which I have always dreamed of, is finally beginning to awaken. In all this, poetry will perhaps be the loser; I mean inspiration, passion, spontaneity. I am afraid of being desiccated by knowledge; and yet I am so ignorant that I blush for myself. It is strange, how since the deaths of my father and my sister I have lost all love of fame. Only at exceptional moments do I think of my future successes as an artist. I often doubt whether I shall ever publish a line. . . . An artist who is truly an artist, who works for himself alone, unconcerned with all else—that would be a wonderful thing; such an artist would perhaps know immense joy. Probably the pleasure of walking in a virgin forest or of hunting tigers is spoiled by the thoughts of having to write a well-composed description that will please as many bourgeois as possible. I live alone, very alone, more and more alone. My father and sister are dead; my friends leave me or change. "He who has understood that sorrow comes from attachment," says Sakiya-Muni, "retires into his solitude like a rhinoceros." Yes, as you say, the countryside is beautiful, the trees are green, the lilacs are in bloom; but this, like everything else, I enjoy only from my window. You would not believe how much I love you; the attachment I feel for you increases constantly. I clutch at what is left to me, like Claude Frollo hanging over the void.[13] You speak of an outline; send me what you want to show me. Alfred Le Poittevin, that strange creature, is busy at something entirely different. I have reread Michelet's *Roman History;* antiquity makes me dizzy. Certainly I lived in Rome at the time of Caesar or Nero. Have you sometimes thought what it must have been like, the night of a triumph—the legions returning, the perfumes burning around the chariot of the conqueror, and the captive kings marching behind? And the circus! That is when we should have lived: then it was possible to breathe, and breathe a true poetic air, whole lungfuls of it, as on a mountaintop, until the heart pounded! Ah, some day I will get drunk on Sicily and Greece! In the meantime I have boils on my legs and keep to my bed.

To ERNEST CHEVALIER

[*Croisset,*] *June 4,* [*1846*]

Poor fellow! I well know that three hundred leagues from me[14] there are eyes that fill with tears when mine are weeping, a heart that fills with anguish when mine is torn. I understand, I pity you for your isolation, the desert of the affections in

13 At the end of Victor Hugo's *Notre-Dame de Paris.*

14 At Calvi, Corsica, where Chevalier had been appointed deputy public prosecutor.

which you live; I wish, like you and for you, that you might return to France. Let us hope that before long they will grant you that favor, or rather that right, for you really begin to deserve promotion considering the trouble your duties give you. Is it not true that one must have lived abroad to love one's country? and lost one's family to know the value of one? I await the vacation with impatience, so that we may spend a few good hours together. My poor mother will be happy to see you again; she will welcome you with joy—you are associated with too many tender things from the time of her happiness not to be dear to her. Do we not love to rediscover in people, and even in furniture and clothes, traces of those who have been near them, loved them, used them?

I'll give you some news of what is happening here. Achille has succeeded my father as resident head of the Rouen Hospital: so there he is established, in the finest medical position in Normandy. The rest of us are living at Croisset, which I never leave and where I work as much as I can, which is not very much, but a step toward something more. In the winter, we spend four months in Rouen. We have taken an apartment there at the corner of the rue Buffon. Our move is almost finished, thank God! That too is a sad task. I have quite a nice room, with a little balcony where I can smoke my morning pipe.

Would you care to hear the announcement of something that will make you utter an "Oh" followed by several exclamation points? It is the marriage—of whom? Of a young man of your acquaintance—not I, rest assured; but of one called Le Poittevin, to Mademoiselle de Maupassant. At this point you will give yourself up to astonishment and reverie. The "holy nuptials" will be celebrated in a fortnight, I believe. The contract was to have been signed last Tuesday. After the wedding they will make a trip to Italy and next winter will live in Paris. There is another lost to me, and doubly so—first because he is marrying and second because he will live elsewhere. How everything comes to an end! How everything comes to an end! On the trees, the leaves are growing again; but for us, where is the May that will restore the beautiful vanished flowers, the virile flavor of our youth? I don't know whether you feel the same, but I have the sensation of being inordinately aged, older than an obelisk. I have lived enormously, and it is probable that when I am sixty I shall feel very young; that's what's so bitterly absurd about it all.

My poor mother is still disconsolate. You have no conception of such grief. If there is a God, you must admit that he is not always in a kind mood. Madame Mignot wrote me this morning to tell me that she will soon come to spend a few days here; I am immensely grateful to her. My courage is not always equal to the task of carrying alone the burden of this great despair that nothing can lighten. Adieu, dear old friend; I embrace you with all my heart.

To LOUISE COLET

Tuesday midnight [*Croisset, August 4, 1846*]

Twelve hours ago we were still together, and at this very moment yesterday I was holding you in my arms! Do you remember? How long ago it seems! Now the night is soft and warm; I can hear the great tulip tree under my window rustling in the wind, and when I lift my eyes I see the reflection of the moon in the river. Your little slippers are in front of me as I write; I keep looking at them. Here, locked away by myself, I have just put away everything you gave me; your two letters are in the little embroidered bag, and I am going to reread them as soon as I have sealed mine. I am not writing to you on my ordinary writing-paper—that is edged with black and I want nothing sad to pass from me to you. I want to cause you nothing but joy, and to surround you with a calm, endless bliss—to repay you a little for the overflowing generosity of the love you have given me. I am afraid of being cold, arid, selfish—and yet, God can see what is going on within me at this moment. What memories! And what desires! Ah! Our two rides in the Bois; how beautiful they were, particularly the second, with the lightning flashes above us. I find myself remembering the color of the trees lit by the streetlights, and the swaying motion of the springs; we were alone, happy: I kept staring at you, and even in the darkness your whole face seemed lighted by your eyes. I feel that I am writing badly; you will read this without emotion; I am not saying anything that I want to say. My sentences run together like sighs; to understand them you will have to supply what should go between; you will do that, won't you? Every letter, every turn of my handwriting will set you dreaming? When I see your little brown slippers I dream of the movements of your feet when they were in them, when the slippers were warm with them. . . .

My mother was waiting for me at the station. She wept at seeing me return. You wept at seeing me leave. In other words, such is our woe that we cannot move a league without causing tears on two sides at once! This is indeed grotesque and sad. Here the grass is still green, the trees as full, the river as placid as when I left; my books are open at the same pages; nothing is changed. External nature shames us, her serenity is a rebuke to our pride. No matter—let us think of nothing, neither of the future nor of ourselves, for to think is to suffer. Let the tempest in our hearts blow us where it will, and as for the reefs—if they are there we shall run onto them, that's all. We shall see.

. . . On the train I read almost the whole of one of your books. More than one passage moved me, but of that I will talk with you more fully later. As you can well see, I am unable to concentrate, and my critical faculties are not with me tonight.

To LOUISE COLET [*1846*]

I wanted only to send you another kiss before sleeping, to tell you that I love you. No sooner had I left you—and the more as I was borne further and further away—than my thoughts flew back toward you, more swiftly even than the smoke I saw flying back from the train. (My simile implies the idea of fire: forgive the reference.) Here: a kiss, quickly—you know the kind—the kind Ariosto speaks of—and another, and another! Still another, and finally one more, just under your chin on the spot I love, where your skin is so soft, and another on your breast, where I lay my heart. Adieu, adieu. All the love you will accept.

To LOUISE COLET

Thursday night, 11 o'clock, [*Croisset, August 6, 1846*]

Your letter of this morning is sad, full of sorrow and resignation. You offer to forget me if that is what I want. You are sublime! I knew you were good, but I did not know you were as noble as that. I repeat: I feel *humble* at the contrast I see between us. Do you know that the things you write me are cruel? And the worst is that it was I who provoked them. You are returning blow for blow—a reprisal. You ask me what it is that I want of you. I cannot tell you that, but I can tell you that what I want of myself is to love you, to love you a thousand times more, even, than I do. Oh! If you could read my heart you would see the place I have given you in it! I can see that you have been suffering more than you admit, your letter is a little strained. You had been weeping, probably? It sounds crushed; I feel in it the weariness of grief, the weakened echo of a sobbing voice. Admit it; admit that you had had a bad day, that it was because my letter had not come that you wrote as you did. Be frank, not proud; do not do as I have done too often. Do not restrain your tears; they fall back into the heart, you know, and leave deep wounds.

To LOUISE COLET [*1846*]

Something occurs to me which I must say. I am sure you think me selfish. The thought grieves you and you are convinced it is true. Is it because I seem so? Well, on this score everyone is mistaken. I am selfish like everyone else—less so than many, perhaps, and perhaps more than others. Who knows? Besides, "selfish" is a word that everyone applies to his neighbor without really knowing what he means by it. Who is not selfish, to a greater or lesser degree? From the moron who wouldn't give a sou to redeem the human race, to him who dives beneath the ice to rescue an unknown, do we not all search, according to our individual instincts, to satisfy our natures? Saint Vincent de Paul obeyed an appetite for charity, Caligula an appetite for cruelty. Everyone takes his enjoyment in his own way and for himself alone. Some direct all activity toward themselves, making themselves the cause, the center, the end of everything; others invite the whole world to the banquet of their souls. That is the difference between prodigals and misers: the first take their pleasure in giving, the second in keeping. As for ordinary selfishness (what we usually mean by the word), although the thought of it is extremely repugnant to me I admit that if it could be bought I should give everything to have it. To be stupid and selfish and to have good health are the three requirements for happiness, though if stupidity is lacking, the others are useless. But there is also another kind of happiness, yes, there *is* another, for I have seen it, you have made me feel it; you have shown me, in the air, its shining light; before my eyes I have seen the glistening of its garment. I hold out my hands to grasp it . . . and then you yourself begin to shake your head, and to suspect it is but a phantom. (What a stupid mania I have for speaking in metaphors that say nothing!) I am beginning to feel that you too have sadness in your heart, that deep sadness which comes of nothing, and which, rooted in the very substance of being, increases as being itself is stirred. I warned you: my misery is contagious. I am infected! Woe to him who touches me!

Oh, what you wrote me this morning is lamentable and painful: I picture your poor face, sad at the thought of me, sad because of me. Yesterday I was so happy, confident, serene, joyful as the summer sun between two showers. Your mitten is here. It smells good, I imagine myself still breathing the perfume of your shoulder and the sweet warmth of your bare arm. Come! Here are thoughts of voluptuousness, thoughts of caresses, overcoming me again; my heart leaps up at the thought of you. I covet all your being, I invoke my memory of you to shake this need that is crying within me; why are you not here! But—Monday, yes? I await the letter from Phidias. If he writes me, everything will be as we agreed.

Do you know what I am thinking of? Of your little boudoir, where you work, where . . . (no word here; the three dots say more than all the eloquence in the world) . I keep seeing your pale, intense face as you lay on the floor, your head in my lap . . . and the lamp! Oh! Never break it; keep it, light it every night, or rather at certain solemn moments of your inner life, when you are beginning or finishing some great work. An idea! I have some water from the Mississippi. It was brought to my father by a sea captain, who gave it to him as a great present. I want you, when you have written something that you think fine, to wash your hands with it; or else I will pour it on your breast, as a sign of my lover's baptism. I am wandering, I think; I don't know what I was speaking of before I thought of that bottle. The lamp, wasn't it? Yes, I love it, I love your house, your furniture; everything, except that frightful caricature in oil hanging in your bedroom. I think also of that worthy Catherine who served us at dinner, of Phidias' jokes, of everything, of a thousand details that amuse me. But do you know how I keep seeing you? As you were when you were standing in the studio, posing, the light falling on you from the side, when I looked at you and you looked at me; and also as you were in the evening, at the hotel—I see you lying on my bed, your hair streaming over my pillow, your eyes raised, your face pale, your hands joined, flooding me with wild words. When you were dressed, you were as fresh as a bouquet. In my arms you're like a warm sweetness that melts and intoxicates. And I? Tell me how I seem to you; what sort of picture of me comes to your mind? . . . What a wretched lover I am! Will you believe me when I tell you that what happened to me with you never happened to me before? (I had been exhausted for three days, and taut as a cello-string.) If I were a man of great self-esteem I'd have been bitterly chagrined. I was, for you. I feared that you might suppose things that you would consider odious; other women would perhaps have found me insulting. They would have thought me cold, or disgusted, or used up. I was grateful to you for your spontaneous intelligence, which kept you from being surprised, whereas I myself was surprised by it as by some unheard-of monstrousness. I must indeed have loved you, and deeply, since with you my first feelings were the opposite of what they have always been with any other women.

You would like to make me into a pagan, O my muse! you who have Roman blood in your veins. But try as I might, any effort in that direction would be useless, for at the very bottom of my soul are the mists of the North that I breathed at my birth. I carry within me the melancholy of the barbarians, with their instinct for migration and their innate disgust for life—which made them leave their own country as though by so doing they could take leave of themselves. They loved the sun, all those barbarians who went to Italy to die; they had a frenzied longing for light, for the blue sky, for a warm, vibrant existence. They dreamed of joyful days, of love drenching their hearts like the juice of ripe grapes squeezed in the hand. I have always had a tender sympathy for them, as one might have for one's ancestors. Haven't I discovered in their boisterous history the entire peaceful, unknown history of myself? Alaric's cries of joy on entering Rome have found their parallel, fourteen centuries later, in the secret ravings of a poor child's heart. Alas! No, I am no man of antiquity; men of antiquity did not have sick nerves like me! Nor you: you are neither Greek nor Latin; you are beyond that, romanticism has touched you, too. The coming of Christianity—defend ourselves against it as we may—has ennobled all that, but has spoiled it, too, by adding the element of suffering. The human heart can expand only by being cut and torn. You tell me ironically, apropos of the article in the *Constitutionnel,* that I have little regard for patriotism, generosity, and courage. Oh no! I love the conquered, but also I love their conquerors. That is perhaps difficult to understand, but it is true. As to the idea of a fatherland—that is, a certain portion of the earth's surface drawn on a map and separated from others by a red or blue line—no! My fatherland is for me the country I love, that is, the one I dream of, the one in which I feel at home. I am as Chinese as I am French, and I rejoice not at all in our victories over the Arabs, because I am saddened by their defeats. I love that fierce, enduring, hardy people, the last type of primitive society; I enjoy thinking of them, as they pause for rest at noon, lying in the shade under the bellies of their camels, smoking their chibouks and jeering at our fine civilization; and I enjoy thinking of how their jeering enrages us. Where am I? Whither do I roam—as a tragic poet of the school of Delille would put it. In the Orient, God help me! Farewell, sultana! . . . To think that I haven't even a silver-gilt perfume-burner, to light when you come to sleep in my couch! Forgive me! But I will offer you all the perfumes of my heart. Farewell, one long, very long kiss, and others besides.

To LOUISE COLET

[*Croisset, Saturday, August 8, 1846*]

I am shattered, numb, as though after a long orgy; I am dying of longing. My heart contains a vast emptiness. I, formerly so calm, so proud of my serenity, working keenly and steadily from morning to night, I cannot read, or think, or write; your love has made me wretched. I can see that you are suffering, and I foresee that I will make you suffer still more. Both for your sake and for my own I wish we had never met, and yet the thought of you is never absent from my mind. In it I find an exquisite sweetness. Ah! How much better it would have been to stop short after our first ride together! I had forebodings that things would turn out as they have! The next day, when I didn't come to Phidias', it was because I already felt myself falling into the abyss. I wanted to stop: what pushed me? So much the worse! So much the better! God did not give me a merry constitution; no one senses more keenly than I the misery of life. I believe in nothing, not even in myself, which is rare. I devote myself to Art because it gives me pleasure to do so, but I have no faith whatever in beauty, any more than in anything else. So the part of your letter in which you speak of patriotism, poor darling, would have made me laugh if I had been in a gayer mood. You will think that I am hard. I wish I were. All those who cross my path would benefit from my being so, and so would I, with my heart that's been eaten down—like meadow grass in autumn by passing sheep. You would not believe me when I told you I was old. Alas, yes, for every sensation that enters my soul turns there to bitterness, like wine poured into jars which have been used too often. If you knew all the inner forces that have consumed me, all the mad desires that have passed through my head, everything I have tried and experimented with in the way of sensations and passions, you would see that I am not so young! It is you who are a child, you who are fresh and new, you whose candor makes me blush. The grandeur of your love fills me with humility; you deserved someone better than I. May lightning strike me, may all possible curses fall upon me if ever I forget that! You ask me whether I despise you because you gave yourself to me too quickly. Have you really been able to suspect that? *Never, never*: whatever you do, whatever may happen, I am devoted to you for life, to you, to your daughter, to anything and anyone you wish. That is a vow. Remember it. Use it. I make it because I can keep it.

Yes, I desire you and I think of you. I love you more than I loved you in Paris. I can no longer do anything; I keep seeing you in the studio, standing near your bust, your long curls stirring on your white shoulders, your blue dress, your arm, your face—everything. Ah! Now *strength* is beginning to circulate in my blood. You seem to be here; I am on fire, my nerves are trembling . . . you know how . . . you know the heat of my kisses.

Ever since we said we loved each other, you have wondered why I have never added the words "for ever." Why? Because I always sense the future, the antithesis of everything is always before my eyes. I have never seen a child without thinking that it would grow old, nor a cradle without thinking of a grave. The sight of a naked woman makes me think of her skeleton. As a result, joyful sights make me sad and sad ones affect me but little. I do too much inward weeping to be able to shed outward tears; something read in a book moves me more than a real misfortune. When I had a family, I often wished I had none, so that I might be freer, free to live in China or among savages. Now that I no longer have one, I long for it, and cling to the walls that still hold the imprint of its shadow. Others would be proud of the love you lavish on me, their vanity would drink its fill of it, and their male egotism would be flattered by it to its inmost depths. But after our frenzied moments together my heart swoons with sadness; for I say to myself: "She loves me and I love her, but I do not love her enough. If she had never known me, she would have been spared the tears she is shedding now." Forgive me, forgive me in the name of all the rapture you have given me. But I have a foreboding of immense unhappiness for you. I fear lest my letters be discovered, that everything become known. *I am sick and my sickness is you.*

You think that you will love me for ever, my child. For ever! What presumption on human lips! You have loved before, have you not? So have I. Remember that you have said "for ever" before. But I am bullying you, hurting you. You know that my caresses are fierce. No matter: I should rather disturb your happiness now than increase it cold-bloodedly, as others would do, so that when it does end you will suffer more. . . . Who knows? You will thank me later, perhaps, for having had the courage not to be more tender. Ah! If I lived in Paris, if every day of my life could be passed at your side—yes, then I'd let myself go with the current, without crying for help! I should find in you, for my heart, my body and my mind, a daily gratification that would never weary me. But apart, destined to see each other only rarely, how frightful! What a prospect! What can we do? Still—I cannot imagine how I was able to leave you. But that is how I am; there you see my wretched character. If you were not to love me, I should die; but you do love me, and I am writing you to stop. I am disgusted by my own stupidity. But in whatever direction I look I can see only unhappiness! I should like to have come into your life like a cool brook to refresh its thirst, not like a devastating torrent. At the thought of me your flesh would have quivered, your heart smiled. Never curse me! Ah, I shall love you well before loving you no longer. I shall always bless you; your image will stay with me all imbued with poetry and tenderness, as last night was bathed in the milky vapor of its silvery mist.

Sometime this month I'll come to see you and will stay

an entire day. In two weeks or less I shall be with you. When Phidias writes I will come at once; I promise. . . .

You want me to send you something I have written. No, you would find everything too good. Have you not given me enough, without literary praise? Do you want to make me completely fatuous? Nothing I have here is legible; you couldn't decipher it, with all its crossings-out and inserts—I have never made a decent copy of anything. Aren't you afraid of spoiling your style by having too much to do with me? You'd like me to publish something immediately; you'd like to urge me on; you'd end by getting me to take myself seriously (may the Lord preserve me from that!). Formerly the pen ran quickly over my paper; now it runs but scratchily. I cannot write a sentence, I keep changing my pen, because I can express nothing of what I want to say. Come to Rouen with Phidias, pretend to meet me by chance, and come to this house for a visit. That will be more satisfactory than any possible description, and you'll think of my rug and of the great white bearskin I stretch out on during the day, just as I think of your alabaster lamp and the way I watched its dying light flickering on the ceiling. Did you understand, that night, that I was waiting for it to go out? I was timid; I *am* timid, despite my cynicism—or perhaps because of it. I told myself that I'd wait until the candle died. Oh! Such forgetfulness of everything! Such exclusion of the rest of the world! The smoothness of the skin of your naked body! . . . And the hypocritical pleasure I took in my resentment as your other guests stayed, and stayed! I shall always remember your look when you were at my knees, and your ecstatic smile when you opened the door and we parted. I went down through the shadows on tiptoe like a thief. Wasn't I one? And are they all as happy, when they flee with their spoils?

I owe you a frank explanation of myself, to answer a page of your letter which makes me see that you harbor illusions about me. It would be cowardly of me (and cowardice is a vice that disgusts me, in whatever aspect it shows itself) to let them continue any longer.

My basic character is, whatever anyone may say, that of the mountebank. In my childhood and my youth I was wildly in love with the stage. I should perhaps have been a great actor if chance had willed that I be born poorer. Even now, what I love above all else, is form, provided it be beautiful, and nothing beyond it. Women, whose hearts are too ardent and whose minds too exclusive, do not understand this religion of beauty, beauty without feeling. They always demand a cause, an end. I admire tinsel as much as gold: indeed, the poetry of tinsel is even greater, because it is sadder. The only things that exist for me in the world are beautiful verse, well-turned, harmonious, singing sentences, beautiful sunsets, moonlight, pictures, ancient marbles, and strongly marked faces. Beyond that, nothing. I would rather have been Talma than Mirabeau, because he lived in a sphere of purer beauty. I am as sorry for caged birds as for enslaved human beings. In all of politics, there is only one thing that I understand: the riot. I am as fatalistic as a Turk, and believe that everything we can do for the progress of humanity, or nothing, amounts to absolutely the same. As to progress, I have but an obtuse comprehension of muddy ideas. I am completely out of patience with everything pertaining to that kind of language. I despise modern tyranny because it seems to me stupid, weak, and fearful of itself; but I have a deep cult of ancient tyranny, which I regard as the most beautiful manifestation of mankind. I am above all a man of fantasy, caprice, lack of method. I thought long and *very seriously* (do not laugh, it is a memory of my finest hours) of becoming a Mohammedan in Smyrna. The day will come when I will go settle somewhere far away, and nothing more will be heard of me. As to what ordinarily touches men most closely, and for me is secondary—I mean physical love—I have always kept it separate from the other. I heard you jeer at *** on this account the other day: his case is mine exactly. You are the only woman whom I have loved and whom I have possessed. Hitherto the women I chose, I chose merely for the purpose of satisfying desires aroused in me by others. You made me untrue to my system, to my heart, perhaps to my nature, which, incomplete in itself, always seeks the incomplete.

I loved one woman from the time I was fourteen until I was twenty, without telling her, without touching her; [15] and after that I went three years without feeling sexual desire. At one time I thought I should continue so until I died, and I thanked God. I wish I had neither body nor heart, or rather, I wish I might be dead, for the figure I cut on this earth is boundlessly ridiculous. That is what makes me mistrustful and fearful of myself.

You are the only woman whom I have dared to try to please, the only one, perhaps, whom I have pleased. Thank you, thank you for that! But will you understand me to the end? Will you be able to bear the burden of my spleen, my manias, my whims, my prostrations and my wild recoveries? You tell me, for example, to write you every day, and if I do not you will reproach me. But the very idea that you want a letter every morning will prevent me from writing it. Let me love you in my own way, in the way that my nature demands. Let me continue to love you with—since you call it that—originality! Force me to do nothing, and I will do everything. Understand me, do not reproach me. If I thought you frivolous and stupid like other women, I should pay you off with words, promises, vows. That would cost me nothing. But I prefer to express less, not more, than the true feeling of my heart.

15 Madame Schlesinger.

The Numidians, Herodotus says, have a strange custom. They burn the scalps of their infants with coals, so that they may be less sensitive to the action of the sun, which is so fierce in their country. And of all the people on earth they are the healthiest. Assume that I was brought up in Numidia. Wouldn't it have been natural to say to me "You don't feel anything: the sun itself doesn't warm you"? Oh, have no fear: a heart is none the worse for being callused. Don't misunderstand me, however: when I probe myself, I don't think I'm better than my neighbor. Only, I have a certain perspicacity, and a certain delicacy in my manners.

Evening is falling. I have spent my afternoon writing to you. When I was eighteen, back from a trip to the Midi, I wrote similar letters for six months to a woman I didn't love. I did it to force myself to love her, to play a role with conviction. Now it is the exact opposite; the antithesis is complete. One last word: in Paris, there is a man[16] who is at my service, devoted to me unto death; active, bold, intelligent, a great and heroic nature obedient to my every whim. In case of need, count on him as you would on me. Tomorrow I expect your poems, and in a few days your two volumes. Farewell, think of me; yes, kiss your arm for me. Every evening now I read some of your poems. I keep looking for traces of yourself in them; I find them sometimes.

Adieu, adieu; I lay my head on your breasts and look up at you, as at a madonna.

11 P.M.

Adieu, I seal my letter. This is the hour when, alone amidst everything that sleeps, I open the drawer that holds my treasures. I look at your slippers, your handkerchief, your hair, your portrait, I reread your letters and breathe their musky perfume.

16 Maxime Du Camp.

To LOUISE COLET *[1846]*

If you could know what I am feeling at this moment! My heart expands in the night, penetrated by a dew of love!

A thousand kisses, a thousand, everywhere—*everywhere.*

To LOUISE COLET

Saturday-Sunday, midnight, [Croisset, August 9, 1846]

The sky is clear, the moon is shining. I can hear the singing of sailors as they raise anchor, preparing to leave with the oncoming tide. No clouds, no wind. The river is white under the moon, black in the shadows. Moths play around my candles, and the scent of the night comes to me through my open windows. And you, are you asleep? Or at your window? Are you thinking of him who thinks of you? Are you dreaming? What is the color of your dream? A week ago we were taking our beautiful drive in the Bois de Boulogne. What an abyss since that day! For others, those charming hours doubtless went by like those that preceded them and those that followed; but for us it was a radiant moment whose glow will always brighten our hearts. It was beautiful in its joy and tenderness, was it not, poor soul? If I were rich I would buy that carriage and put it in my stable and never use it again. Yes, I will come back, and soon, for I think of you always; I keep dreaming of your face, of your shoulders, of your white neck, of your smile, of your voice that's like a love-cry, impassioned, violent, and sweet all at once. I told you, I think, that it was above all your voice that I loved.

This morning I waited an entire hour on the quay for the postman: he was late. How many heartbeats that red-collared fool must be the cause of, without his knowing it! Thank you for your good letter; but do not love me so much, do not love me so much, you hurt me! Let me love you! Don't you know that to love excessively brings bad luck to lover and beloved?

It's like overfondled children: they die young. Life is not made for that; happiness is a monstrosity; they who seek it are punished.

Yesterday and the day before my mother was in a frightful state; she had delusions of death. I stayed beside her. You don't know what it is, the burden of such despair that has to be borne alone. Remember those last words, if ever you think yourself the unhappiest of women. There is one who is more unhappy than it is possible to be: the step beyond is death or madness.

Before I knew you I was calm; I had become so. I was entering a virile period of moral health. My youth is over. My nervous illness, which lasted two years, was its conclusion, its close, the logical result of what had gone before. For one to have had what I had, something tragic must previously have happened within one's brain. Then everything became itself again; I had a clear vision of things—and of myself, which is rarer. I lived soundly, according to my particular system, made for my special case. I had arrived at an understanding of everything in myself, I had sorted it all, classified it all, with the result that I was more at peace than at any previous period of my existence, whereas everyone was of the opinion that I was now to be pitied. Then you came along, and with the mere touch of a fingertip you threw everything into confusion. The old dregs boiled up again; the lake of my heart began to churn. But only the ocean has tempests; ponds, when they are stirred up, produce nothing but unhealthy smells. I must love you to tell you this. Forget me if you can, tear your soul from your body with your two hands and trample on it, to destroy the traces of me that are in it. Come, don't be angry.

No, I embrace you, I kiss you. I feel wild. Were you here, I'd bite you; I long to do so—I, whom women jeer at for my coldness—I, charitably supposed to be incapable of sex, so little have

I indulged in it. Yes, I feel within me now the appetites of wild beasts, the instincts of a love that is carnivorous, capable of tearing flesh to pieces. Is this love? Perhaps it is the opposite. Perhaps in my case it's the heart that's impotent.

My deplorable mania for analysis exhausts me. I doubt everything, even my doubt. You thought me young, but I am old. I have often spoken with old people about the pleasure of this earth, and I have always been astonished by the brightness that comes into their lackluster eyes; just as they could never get over their amazement at my way of life, and kept saying "At your age! At your age! You! You!" Take away my nervous exaltation, my fantasy of mind, the emotion of the minute, and I have little left. That's what I am underneath. *I was not made to enjoy life.* You must not take these words in a down-to-earth sense, but rather grasp their metaphysical intensity. I keep telling myself that I'll bring you misfortune, that were it not for me your life would have continued undisturbed, that the day will come when we shall part (and I am indignant in advance). Then the nausea of life rises to my lips, and I feel boundless self-disgust and a wholly Christian tenderness for you.

At other times, yesterday for example, when I had sealed my letter, the thought of you sings, smiles, shines, and dances like a joyous fire that gives out a thousand colors and penetrating warmth. I keep remembering the graceful, attractive motion of your mouth when you speak; it is provocative, that rosy, moist mouth; it calls forth kisses and sucks them irresistibly in. . . .

One year, two years, what does it matter? Everything measurable passes, everything that can be counted has an end.

Only three things are infinite: the sky in its stars, the sea in its drops of water, and the heart in its tears. Only in that capacity is the heart large; everything else about it is small. Do I lie? Think, try to be calm. One or two bits of happiness fill it completely, but all the miseries of mankind can enter it together and dwell there as guests.

You speak of work. Yes, you must work; love art. Of all lies art is the least lying. Try to love it with a love that is exclusive, ardent, devoted. It will not fail you. Only the Idea is eternal and necessary. There are no more artists as they once existed, artists whose loves and minds were the blind instruments of the appetite for the Beautiful, God's organs by means of which He demonstrated to Himself His own existence. For them the world did not exist; no one has ever known anything of their sufferings; each night they lay down in sadness, and they looked at human life with astonished gaze, as we contemplate ant-hills.

You judge me as a woman: have I any right to complain? You love me so much that you delude yourself about me; you find that I have talent, intelligence, style. . . . I! I! You'll make me vain, and I was proud not to be so! See: you have already lost something as a result of meeting me. Your critical sense is leaving you, and you think that this person who loves you is a great man. Would that I were, to make you proud of me! (It is I who am proud of you. I keep telling myself: "But she loves me! Is it possible? She!") Yes, I wish that I could write beautiful things, great things, and that you would weep with admiration of them. I think of you at a performance of a play by me, in a box, listening, hearing everyone applaud me. But I fear the contrary—that you will weary of constantly raising me to your level. When I was a child I dreamed of fame like everyone else, no more nor less; in me good sense sprouted late, but it is firmly planted. So it is very doubtful that the public will ever have occasion to read a single line written by me; if this happens, it will not be before ten years, at least.

I don't know what led me to read you something; forgive that weakness. I could not resist the temptation to make you think highly of me. But I was sure of success, wasn't I? What puerility on my part! It was a sweet idea you had, that we should write a book together; it moved me; but I do not want to publish anything. This is a stand I have taken, a vow I have made to myself at a solemn period in my life. I work with absolute disinterestedness and without ulterior motive or concern. I am not a nightingale, but a shrill-voiced warbler, hiding deep in the woods lest I be heard by anyone except myself. If I make an appearance, one day, it will be in full armor; but I shall never have the necessary assurance. Already my imagination is fading, my verve declines, I am bored by my own sentences; and if I keep those that I have written it is because I like to surround myself with memories—just as I never sell my old clothes. I go look at those writings sometimes in the attic where I keep them, and I dream of the time when they were new and of everything I did when I was pregnant with them.

By the way—we'll christen the blue dress together, then. I'll try to arrive some evening about six. We'll have all night and the next day. We'll set the night ablaze! I'll be your desire, you'll be mine, and we'll gorge ourselves on each other to see whether we can be satiated. Never! No, never! Your heart is an inexhaustible spring, you let me drink deep, it floods me, penetrates me, I drown. Oh! The beauty of your face, all pale and quivering beneath my kisses! But how cold I was! I did nothing but look at you; I was surprised, charmed. Now, if I had . . . Come, I'll take another look at your slippers. They are something I'll never give up; I think I love them as much as I do you. Whoever made them, little suspected how my hands would tremble when I touch them. I breathe their perfume; they smell of verbena—and of you in a way that makes my heart swell.

Adieu, my life, adieu my love, a thousand kisses everywhere. Have Phidias write, and I will come. Next winter there will be no way for us to see each other, but I'll come to Paris for at least three weeks. Adieu, I kiss you in the place where I *will* kiss you, where I wanted to; I place my mouth there. I roll on you.

A thousand kisses. Oh, give me some! Give me some!

To LOUISE COLET

Sunday morning, 10 o'clock [*Croisset, August 9, 1846*]

My child, your folly is carrying you away. Calm yourself. You are only becoming irritated against yourself and against life. I told you I was more reasonable than you. And do you think that I am not to be pitied? Be more sparing with your cries; they torture me. What do you want me to do? Can I leave everything here and go live in Paris? Impossible. If I were entirely free I should do it, for with you in Paris I should not have the force to go into exile—a project of my youth, which I shall carry out some day. For I want to live in a place where no one loves me or knows me, where my name means nothing to anyone, where my death or my absence costs no one a tear. I have been too much loved, you see; you love me too much. I am satiated with affection, and I keep wanting it, alas! You tell me that what I needed was a banal kind of love. I reply that I needed either no love at all, or yours, for I cannot imagine one more complete, fuller, more beautiful. It is now ten o'clock; your letter has just come and I have just sent you mine, the one I wrote last night. Scarcely awake, I am writing you again without knowing what I am going to say. At least you see that I think of you. Do not be angry with me when you do not receive a letter from me. It is not my fault. The very days when I do not write you are those when I think of you perhaps most of all. You are afraid that I am ill, dear Louise. People like me can be ill with impunity; they do not die. I have had every kind of illness and accident, horses have been killed under me, carriages have overturned, and I have never been scratched. I am fated to live a long life and to see everything perish around me and in me. In my soul I have already attended a thousand funerals; my friends leave me one after the other, they marry, move away, change; when we meet we barely recognize each other, find scarcely anything to say. What irresistible impulse drove me toward you? For an instant I saw the abyss, I realized its depth, and then vertigo swept me over. But how *not* love you, you who are so sweet, so good, so superior, so loving, so beautiful? I keep thinking of your voice, when you spoke to me the night of the fireworks. They blazed for us, that night, like a flamboyant inauguration of our love.

Your apartment is a little like one I had in Paris for almost two years at 19 rue de l'Est.[17] When you pass that way, look at the second floor. From there too there was a view out over Paris. Summer nights I used to look up at the stars, and in winter at the glowing mist of the great city floating above the houses. Just as from your windows, I saw gardens, roofs, the surrounding hills. It seemed to me, the first time I came to your house, that I was reliving my past, that I had returned to one of those beautiful, sad twilights of 1843, when, bored to death and sick at heart, I used to go to my window for a breath of air. If only I had known you then! Why could that not have been? I was free, alone, without family or mistress, for I have never had a mistress. You will think that I am lying. I have never been more scrupulously truthful, and this is the reason why: the grotesque aspects of love have always prevented me from giving myself over to it entirely. At times I have wanted to give pleasure to a woman, but the idea of the strange spectacle I must be presenting at that moment made me laugh so much that all my desire melted under the fire of an inner glory, which sang a hymn of mockery and derision within me. It is only with you

17 Not the present rue de l'Est, but an old street, since demolished, near the law school and the Luxembourg Gardens.

that I have not yet laughed at myself; but when I see you so intense, so absolutely absorbed in your passion, I am tempted to cry out to you: "No! No! You are making a mistake! Take care! Not this man!" . . .

Heaven made you beautiful, devoted, intelligent; I should like to be other than I am, to be worthy of you. I wish my heart were newer and fresher. Ah! Do not revive me too much: I'll blaze up like straw. You will think that I am selfish, that I fear you. I admit it: I am terrified of your love, because I feel that it is devouring us both, especially you. You are like Ugolino in his prison; you are eating your own flesh to appease your hunger.

Some day, if I write my memoirs—the only thing I shall ever write well, if ever I settle down to it—you will have a place in them, and what a place! For you are making a wide breach in my existence. I had surrounded myself with a wall of stoicism; one look from you blew it to pieces like a cannon ball. Yes, I often think I hear your dress rustling on my rug behind me. I quiver, and turn around, and realize that it was the sound of my curtain rustling in the wind. I keep seeing your fine white forehead; you know, don't you, that your forehead is sublime? Too beautiful, even, to be kissed; pure, noble, eloquent of that which is within. Do you go to Phidias', to that studio where I saw you the first time, among the marbles and the casts?

He should be coming here soon. I await a letter from him which will give me a pretext to go to Paris for a day. Then, toward the first of September, I will find another pretext for going to Mantes or Vernon. Then we shall see. But what is the good of getting accustomed to seeing each other, of loving each other? Why load ourselves with the luxury of affection, if afterwards we have to be miserable? What is the good? But what else can we do?

Adieu, my darling; I have just gone down into the garden and gathered this little rose which I am sending you. I kiss it; put it quickly to your mouth, and then—you know where. . . . Adieu! A thousand kisses. I am yours from night to day, from day to night.

To LOUISE COLET

Wednesday night, [*Croisset, August 12, 1846*]

You must have gone all day without a letter from me. Once again you must have doubted me, poor love. Forgive me. The fault lies not in my will but in my memory; I thought the last mail from Rouen closed at one o'clock, whereas actually it was at eleven. But if you're still holding a grudge against me I hope to make it disappear on Monday—I have great hopes for Monday! Phidias will please write to me. I count on having his note not later than Sunday.

How I love the plan you propose for the celebration! It brought tears of affection to my eyes. Yes, you do love me: it would be a crime to doubt it. And as for me, if I do not love you, what is the name of my feeling for you? Each letter you send me penetrates more deeply into my heart. Particularly the one of this morning; it was of an exquisite charm. It was gay, kind, beautiful, like yourself. Yes, let us love one another, let us love one another, since no one has ever loved us.

I shall arrive in Paris at four or quarter-past. Thus, before half-past four I shall be at your house. Already I see myself climbing your stairs; I hear the sound of the bell. . . . "Is Madame at home?" "Come in." Ah! I am relishing the prospect of those twenty-four hours. But why must every joy bring me pain? I already think of our separation, of your sadness. You will be sensible, won't you? For I feel that I shall be more brokenhearted than the first time.

I am not one of those in whom possession kills love; rather, it kindles it.

To LOUISE COLET [*1846*]

With regard to everything good that has ever happened to me, I am like the Arabs, who, one day a year, still turn in the direction of Granada and lament the beautiful place where they no longer live. Today, a moment ago, I chanced to be walking in the rue du Collège; I saw people on the steps of the chapel; it was prize day; I heard the cries of the pupils, the sound of applause and a band. I went in; I saw everything, just as it was in my time; the same hangings in the same places; I recalled the smell of the wet oak leaves that they used to put on our heads; I thought of the delirium of joy that always gripped me on that day, for two months of complete freedom were before me; my father was there, and my sister, and friends now dead, gone, or changed. And I left, today, with a horrible tightening of the heart. The ceremony, too, was less colorful; there were few people as compared with the crowd that filled the church ten years ago. There was less noise, there was no singing of the *Marseillaise,* which I used to shout out wildly as I banged the benches. The *élite* no longer attend. I remember that formerly it was full of fashionably dressed women; actresses would come, kept women, and women of title. They sat upstairs, in the galleries. How proud we were when they looked at us! Some day I will write about all this. The modern young man, his soul unfurling at sixteen with immense love, lusting for wealth, fame, all the splendors of life—all this overflowing, sad poetry of the heart of an adolescent—this is a new vein which no one has yet explored. Oh Louise! What I am going to say is hard, yet it is born of deep-felt sympathy and pity. If ever you are loved by a poor boy who finds you beautiful, a boy such as I was, timid, gentle, trembling, who fears you and yet seeks you out, who avoids you and yet pursues you, be kind to him, do not reject him; let him only kiss your hand; he will die of ecstasy. Drop your handkerchief, he will take it and sleep with it, drench it with his tears. The spectacle I just saw has reopened the tomb in which my mummified youth has lain sleeping; I have had a whiff of its faded breath; my soul has been haunted by something like those forgotten melodies which re-emerge at twilight, during those slow hours in which remembrance, like a ghost among the ruins, stalks our thoughts. But women will never experience any of this; and certainly they will never express it. They love, they love perhaps more than we, more strongly, but not so boldly. And then, is it enough to be possessed by a feeling, to express it? Has a drinking song ever been written by a drunken man? It is wrong to think that feeling is everything. In the arts, it is nothing without form. All this is to say that women, who have loved a great deal, do not know love because they have been too immersed in it; they do not have a *disinterested* appetite for the beautiful. For them, love must always be linked with something, with a goal, a practical concern. They write to ease their hearts—not because they are attracted by art, which is a self-sufficient principle, no more needful of support than is a star. I know very well that this is not what you think, but it is what I think. Some day I will explain these ideas to you clearly, and I shall hope to convince you, you, a born poet. Yesterday I read your story *Le Marquis d'Entrecasteaux*. It is written in a good, sober, vivid style; it says something, it shows true talent. I especially like the opening, the walk, and the scene with Madame d'Entrecasteaux alone in her room, before her husband comes in. As for myself, I keep studying a little Greek. I am reading Chardin's travels as part of my oriental studies, and to help me with an oriental story I have been planning for a year and a half. But for some time past my imagination has been losing strength. How could it soar, poor little bee? It caught its feet in a pot of jam, and is sinking there up to its neck. Adieu, my beloved; resume your usual life, go out, receive your friends, do not refuse to see the people who were there with me on Sunday. I should like to see them again myself, I don't know why. When I love, my feeling is like a flood that spreads over everything around. . . .

To LOUISE COLET

Friday night, 1 o'clock, [*Croisset, August 15, 1846*]

How beautiful they are, the poems you sent me! Their rhythm is as gentle as the caresses of your voice when you pronounce my name. Forgive me if I think them the best you have done. I did not feel vain when I saw that they had been done for me; I felt love, tenderness. You are a siren, whose seductions would conquer even the hardest-hearted. Yes, my beautiful one, you have enwrapped me in your charm, infused me with your substance. Oh! if I have seemed cold to you, if my sarcasms are harsh and hurt you, I will cover you with love when next I see you, with caresses, with ecstasy. I want to gorge you with all the joys of the flesh, so that you faint and die. I want you to be amazed by me, and to confess to yourself that you had never even dreamed of such transports. I am the one who has been happy; now I want you to be the same. When you are old, I want you to recall those few hours, I want your dry bones to quiver with joy when you think of them. Not yet having received Phidias' letter (I await it with impatience and annoyance) I cannot be with you Sunday. And even if I could, we wouldn't have the night together. Moreover, you will have visitors. I should have to dress, and consequently should need baggage. I want to come without anything, without bundles or bags, to be freer, with nothing to bother me.

I can understand your wish to see me again in the same place, with the same people; I too should like that. Don't we always cling to our past, however recent it may be? In our appetite for life we feast again on past feelings and dream of those of the future. Bound to the present, the soul is stifled; the world is not big enough for it. I often think of your alabaster lamp and the chain on which it hangs. Look at it when you read this, and thank it for lending me its light.

Du Camp (he is the friend I mentioned in one of my earlier letters) arrived today—he is to spend a month. Continue to address your letters to him,[18] as you did your last. He brought me your portrait. The frame is of carved black wood and sets off the engraving very well. It is facing me as I write, leaning gently against a cushion of my divan in the corner between two windows—where you would be if you were here. I often slept on this divan in the rue de l'Est. During the day I would lie on it when I was tired, and refresh my heart with some great poetic dream, or the memory of an old love. I shall leave it there like that; no one will touch it. (The other one is in my drawer, with your bag, on top of your slippers.) My mother has seen it; she likes your face, thinks you are pretty. You have an "animated, open, pleasant expression," she says. (I have pretended to her that proofs of the engraving happened to be delivered one afternoon when I went to see you, and that you presented some of them to your visitors.)

You ask me whether the few lines I sent you were written for you;[19] you would like to know for whom; you are jealous. For no one, like everything that I have written. I have always forbidden myself ever to put anything of myself into my works, and yet I have put in a great deal. I have always tried not to make Art subservient to the requirements of any particular individual. I have written very tender pages without love, and burning pages with no fire in my blood. I imagined, I recollected, and I combined. What you read is a memory of nothing at all. You predict that some day I will write beautiful things. Who knows? (That is my motto.) I doubt it; my imagination is

18 A device to throw Madame Flaubert off the scent.

19 In reply to Louise's request that he show her something he had written, Flaubert had sent her a lyrical passage from *Novembre* about Madame Schlesinger.

withering, I am becoming too fastidious. All I ask is to be able to continue to admire the masters with that innermost rapture for which I would gladly sacrifice everything, everything. But as for becoming a master myself, never; I am sure of it. I have immense deficiencies: I lack originality, to begin with, and perseverance in my work. Style is achieved only by dint of atrocious labor, fanatical and unremitting stubbornness. Buffon's saying is a great blasphemy; genius is not "a long patience." But there is some truth in it, more than is generally believed, especially nowadays.

This morning I read poems from your volume with a friend who came to see me.[20] He is a poor boy who gives lessons here for a living and who is a poet, a true poet, who writes superb and charming things and who will remain unknown because he lacks two requirements: bread and time. Yes, we have read you, we have admired you.

How sweet it is, to be able to say to myself: "Despite everything, she belongs to me!" Next Sunday two weeks will have passed since you knelt beside me and gazed at me with sweetly avid eyes; I was looking at your brow, trying to guess everything it concealed, and staring too with infinite wonder at the lightness and thickness of your hair.

I wouldn't like you to see me now: I am frighteningly ugly. I have an enormous boil on my right cheek, and the swelling has half-closed one of my eyes. I must look ridiculous. If you saw me thus, love might sulk, for it is frightened by the grotesque. But don't worry, I shall be all right when we meet; just as I was, as you love me.

Tell me whether you use the verbena; do you put it on your handkerchiefs? Put some on your slip. But no—do not use perfume; the best perfume is yourself, your own fragrance. Perhaps I shall have a letter tomorrow.

20 Louis Bouilhet.

Adieu, I bite your lip. Is the little red spot still there?

Adieu, a thousand kisses. Till next Monday, perhaps; I'll have another taste of yours.

I belong to you, body and soul.

To LOUISE COLET

Thursday, 1 o'clock in the morning,
[*Croisset,*] *August 21, 1846*

Alone, now! All alone! . . . It's a dream. Oh, how far it all seems, though it was only yesterday! There are whole centuries between a little while ago and now. A little while ago I was with you, we were together. Our pathetic ride in the Bois! How dreary the sky was! That night, when I left you, it was raining. There were tears in the air, the sky was somber.

I keep thinking of our last reunion at the hotel, with your silk dress open, and the lace coiling over your breast. Your entire face was smiling, full of the wonderment of love and ecstasy. How your sweet eyes shone!

Twenty-four hours ago; you remember? Oh! Why can't we recapture any part of something that is gone? Adieu, before I sleep I am going to read the letter you wrote me while waiting for me.

Adieu, adieu, a thousand kisses of love. Were you here, I would kiss you as I did yesterday. I am still thirsty for you; you have not quenched me! Adieu, adieu!

To LOUISE COLET

Friday midnight, [*Croisset, August 21-22, 1846*]

. . . Today I have done nothing. Neither written nor read a line. I unpacked my *Temptation of Saint Anthony*[21] and hung

21 An engraving by Callot.

it on my wall; that is all. I greatly love this picture. I have wanted it for a long time. For me the somber grotesque has immense charm; it corresponds to the inner needs of my nature, bitter like that of a buffoon. It does not make me laugh, but sets me dreaming. I discern it wherever it may be; and since like everyone else I have it within me, I like to analyze myself—this occupation gives me pleasure. What prevents me from taking myself seriously, although I am quite grave by nature, is that I find myself very ridiculous; and my ridiculousness is not relative, as in comedy, but the intrinsic ridiculousness of human life, which manifests itself in the simplest action or the most commonplace gesture. Never, for instance, do I shave without laughing—the process seems so stupid. All this is very difficult to explain; it has to be felt; you will never feel it, you who are all of one piece, like a beautiful hymn of love and poetry. I am an arabesque in marquetry; there are pieces of ivory, of gold, and of iron; there are some of painted cardboard, some of diamond, and some of tin. . . .

To LOUISE COLET

Friday, 10 P.M.

Croisset, [*September 18, 1846*]

. . . You tell me, my angel, that I have not initiated you into my inner life, into my most secret thoughts. Do you know what is innermost, most hidden, in my heart, and what is most authentically myself? Two or three modest ideas about art, lovingly brooded over; that is all. The greatest events of my life have been a few thoughts, a few books, certain sunsets on the beach at Trouville, and talks five or six hours long with a friend who is now married and lost to me. I have always looked on life differently from others, and the result has been that I have always (but not sufficiently, alas!) withdrawn into a harsh solitude, keeping everything to myself. I have so often been humiliated, have so often shocked people and made them indignant, that I have long since come to realize that in order to live in peace one must live alone and seal one's windows lest the air of the world seep in. Despite myself I still retain some of this habit. That is why I deliberately avoided the company of women for several years. I did not want to hinder the development of my innate principle; I wanted no yoke, no influence. In the end I did not desire women's company at all. Stirrings of the flesh, throbbings of the heart, were absent from my life, and I was not even conscious of my sex. As I have told you, I had a grand passion when I was little more than a child. When it ended I decided to divide my life into two parts: to put on one side my soul, which I reserved for Art, and on the other my body, which was to live as best it could. Then you came along and upset everything. Now I am returning to a human existence.

You have awakened all that was slumbering, or perhaps rotting, within me! I had been loved before, and intensely, though I am one of those who are quickly forgotten and more apt to kindle emotion than to keep it aflame. The love I arouse is always that which is felt for something a little strange. Love, after all, is only a superior kind of curiosity, an appetite for the unknown that makes you plunge headlong into the storm.

As I said, I have been loved before, but *never the way you love me;* nor has there ever been between a woman and myself the bond that exists between us. I have never felt for any woman so deep a devotion, so irresistible an attraction; never has there been such a sense of complete communion. Why do you keep saying that I love the tinselly, the showy, the flashy? "Poet of form!" That is the favorite term of abuse hurled by utilitarians at genuine artists. For my part, until someone comes along and separates for me the form and the substance of a given sentence, I shall continue to maintain that those two terms are meaningless. Every beautiful thought has a beautiful form, and vice versa. In the world of Art, form exudes Beauty; just as in our world it exudes temptation and love. Just as you cannot remove from a physical body the qualities that constitute it—color, extension, solidity—without reducing it to a hollow abstraction, without destroying it, so you cannot remove the form from the Idea, because the Idea exists only by virtue of its form. Imagine an idea that has no form—such a thing is impossible, just as a form that does not express an idea. Such concepts are stupidities on which literary criticism feeds. Good stylists are reproached for neglecting the Idea, the moral goal; as though the goal of the doctor were not to heal, the goal of the painter to paint, the goal of the nightingale to sing, as though the goal of Art were not, first and foremost, Beauty!

Sculptors who create real women, with breasts that can hold milk and thighs that suggest fecundity, are accused of sensualism. Whereas were they to carve wads of drapery and figures flat as signboards they would be called idealists, spiritualists. "Yes, he does neglect form, it's true," people would say, "but he is a thinker!" Whereupon the bourgeois would proceed with cries of joy to make themselves admire what really bores them. It is easy, with a conventional jargon, with two or three ideas acceptable as common coin, to pass as a socialist humanitarian writer, a renovator, a harbinger of the evangelical future dreamed of by the poor and the mad. Such is the modern mania: writers blush for their trade. Merely to write verse or a novel, merely to carve marble, is not enough! It was acceptable previously, before the poet had a "social mission." Now every piece of writing must have its moral significance, must teach a lesson, elementary or advanced; a sonnet must be given philosophical implications; a play must rap the knuckles of royalty and a watercolor contribute to moral progress. Everywhere there is pettifoggery, the craze for spouting and orating; the muse becomes a mere pedestal for a thousand unholy desires. Poor Olympus! Such people would think nothing of planting a potato patch on its summit! If it were only the mediocrities who were involved, the whole thing could be forgotten. But no—vanity has banished pride, and caused a thousand little cupidities to spring up where formerly a single, noble ambition prevailed. Even men of parts, great men, ask themselves: "Why not seize the moment? Why not influence the crowd now, every day, instead of being admired by them only later?" Whereupon they mount the tribune. They join the staff of a newspaper, and there we see them lending the weight of their immortal names to theories that are ephemeral.

They intrigue to overthrow some cabinet minister who would topple without them—when with a single line of satire they could make his name a synonym for infamy. They concern themselves with taxes, customs-duties, laws, peace and war! How petty all this is! How transient! How false and relative! All these wretched things excite them; they attack all the crooks, gush over every good action no matter how commonplace, cry their eyes out over every poor fellow who is murdered, every dog that is run over—as though this were the only purpose of their lives. To me it seems far finer to stand at a distance of several centuries, and from that remove to play on the heartstrings of the generations and provide them with purer pleasures. Who can begin to count the divine thrills that Homer has caused, all the tears that the good Horace has changed into smiles? To speak only of myself, I am grateful to Plutarch for evenings he gave me at the lycée, evenings filled with warlike ardor, as though the enthusiasm of whole armies were contained in my soul. . . .

To LOUISE COLET

Tuesday, 10 A.M.
[*Croisset, September 22, 1846*]

... Thank you for your letter of this morning. I was waiting for the postman on the quay, looking unconcerned and smoking my pipe. I love that postman! I've left orders that whenever he stops he's to get a glass of wine in the kitchen, to refresh him. He likes to come here, and is very punctual. Yesterday he brought me nothing, so he got nothing!

You send me everything you can find to gratify my love for you; you pass on to me all the tributes you receive. I read Plato's[22] letter with all the concentration of which I was capable; I found many things in it, very many. Essentially, he is a man whose heart, despite all he may do to make it seem serene, is cold and empty; his life is dreary, without radiance, I am sure. But he greatly loved you, and still loves you with a love that is deep and lonely; he will feed on it for a long time. I found his letter painful; I looked into the very depths of this colorless existence, filled with tasks undertaken without enthusiasm and carried out with a dogged obstinacy which is the only thing that keeps him going. Your love brought him a little joy; he has clung to it with an old man's hunger for life. You were his last passion, and the only thing that reconciled him to himself. He is, I think, jealous of Béranger; the life and fame of this latter can scarcely afford him much pleasure. As a rule the philosopher is a kind of mongrel being, a cross between scientist and poet, envious of both. Metaphysics puts a lot of sourness into the blood; it's a curious and very amusing phenomenon. I was considerably engrossed in it for two years, but it was a waste of time that I now regret.

You wrote something that is very true: "Love is a great comedy, and so is life, when you are not playing one of the roles";

22 Victor Cousin's.

but I won't concede that it is enjoyable. About a year and a half ago I experienced a living illustration of this, something I came upon by mere chance and preferred not to witness to the end. At that time I often visited a family in which there was a charming young girl, marvelously beautiful—of a very Christian, almost Gothic, beauty, if I can put it that way. She had a candid mind, easily susceptible to emotion; one moment she would be crying, the next laughing, like sunshine after a shower. The feelings of this lovely pure creature were entirely at the mercy of my words. I can still see her lying against her pink cushion and looking at me, as I read, with her great blue eyes. One day we were alone, sitting on a sofa; she took my hand, twined her fingers in mine; this I let her do without thinking (most of the time I'm a great innocent), and she gave me a look which still makes me shudder. Just then her mother entered, took in everything, and smiled at what she thought was the acquisition of a son-in-law. I shall not forget that smile—the sublimest thing I have ever seen. It was a compound of indulgent benevolence and genteel vulgarity. I am sure that the poor girl had been carried away by an irresistible affectionate impulse, one of those moments of mawkish sentimentality when everything within you seems to be melting and dissolving—a voluptuous agony that would fill you with delight if only it didn't bring you to the verge of sobs or tears. You cannot conceive the terror I felt. I returned home shattered, reproaching myself for being alive. I don't know whether I exaggerated the situation, but even though I did not love her I should gladly have given my life to redeem that look of hopeless love to which I had not responded.

. . . What a horrible invention the bourgeois is, don't you agree? Why is he in the world? And what is he doing there, poor wretch? For my part, I cannot imagine how people unconcerned with art can spend their time: how they live is a mystery to me. . . . Adieu; it is time for me to leave you. I am yours, dear love,

I who love you and kiss your breasts. Look at them, and say: he dreams of your roundness and his desire leans its head upon you.

To LOUISE COLET

[*Croisset, Sunday, 11 A.M., September 27, 1846*]

. . . Practical life is loathsome to me; the mere necessity of sitting down in a dining-room at fixed hours fills my soul with a feeling of wretchedness. But when I participate in it (in practical life), when I sit down (at table), I know how to behave like anyone else. You would like me to meet Béranger; I should like it too. He is a grand old man; I find him appealing. But—and now I speak of his works—he has a great misfortune: the kind of people who admire him. There are tremendous geniuses who have but one defect, one vice—that of being especially appreciated by the vulgar, by people susceptible to cheap poetry. For thirty years Béranger has been the inspiration for the love-life of students and the erotic dreams of traveling salesmen. I know perfectly well that he does not write for them; but they are the kind who appreciate him. Popularity, which seems to give genius greater scope, actually vulgarizes it; authentic Beauty is not for the masses, especially in France. *Hamlet* will always give less pleasure than *Mademoiselle de Belle-Isle*.[23] Béranger expresses no passions that *I* feel, no dreams that I dream; his poetry is not mine. I read him historically; he is a man of another age. He was right for his time, but he is no longer right for ours. The happy, carefree love that he sings so joyously in his garret window is very foreign to us who are young today; we can admire it as we might admire the hymn of some extinct religion, but it cannot move us. I have heard so many fools, so many narrow-minded bourgeois, praise Béranger's beggars and his "God of the common folk" that he must really be a great poet to have kept my esteem. For my own con-

23 A play by the elder Dumas.

sumption I prefer geniuses a little less agreeable to the touch, more disdainful of the people, more reserved, more haughty in their manner and in their tastes; or else the only man who can take the place of all others, my adored Shakespeare, whom I am now going to start reading again from one end to the other, and whom I shall not abandon this time until the volumes fall apart in my hands. When I read Shakespeare I become greater, wiser, purer. When I have reached the crest of one of his works I feel that I am high on a mountain; everything disappears and everything appears. I am no longer a man, I am an *eye;* new horizons loom up, perspectives extend to infinity; I forget that I have been living like other men in the barely distinguishable hovels below, that I have been drinking from those distant rivers that seem lesser than brooks, that I have been participating in all the confusion of the ant-hill. Long ago, in a burst of happy pride (I should dearly love to recapture it), I wrote a sentence that you will understand. Speaking of the joy caused by the reading of the great poets I said: "I often felt that the enthusiasm they kindled in me made me their equal and raised me to a level with themselves."[24]

To LOUISE COLET

[*Croisset, Monday morning, September 28, 1846*]

. . . As for Madame Foucaud, she is indeed the one I knew. Is your cousin sufficiently reliable to be entrusted with a letter, can I be sure he will deliver it? For I feel like writing to Madame Foucaud. She is an old acquaintance; don't be jealous of her. You shall read the letter if you like, on the condition that you don't tear it up. Your word will be enough. If I thought of you as a commonplace woman I should not tell you all this. But what you dislike, perhaps, is precisely the fact that I treat you as

24 From *Novembre.*

a man and not as a woman. Try to put some of your intelligence into your relations with me. Later your heart will thank your mind for this. I thought at first that I would find in you less feminine personality, a broader conception of life; but no! The heart, the heart! The poor heart, so kind, so charming, with its eternal graces, is always there, even in those women who are noblest and greatest. As a rule men do everything they can to vex the heart, to make it bleed. With refined sensuality they steep themselves in all those tears which they themselves do not shed, in all those little agonies that are to them a proof of their strength. If I had a taste for that pleasure, it would be easy for me to find it in you.

But no, I should like to make of you something entirely apart—neither friend nor mistress. Each of those categories is too restricted, too exclusive—one doesn't love a friend sufficiently, and with a mistress one is too stupid. It is the intermediate term that I am seeking, the essence of these two sentiments fused together. What I want, in short, is that, like a new kind of hermaphrodite, you give me with your body all the joys of the flesh and with your mind all those of the soul.

Will you understand this? I fear it is not clear. . . .

To LOUISE COLET

[*Croisset, Saturday, 8 A.M., October 3, 1846*]

Come, come, my mouse; stop being hurt because I speak to you about Shakespeare instead of about myself. It's just that he seems to me more interesting. And what should one speak about (I ask you once more) if not about what exclusively preoccupies one's mind? As for me, I fail to understand how those people live who are not from morning to night in an aesthetic state. I have enjoyed more than many the pleasures of family, as much as any man of my age the pleasures of the senses, more than many the pleasures of love. But I don't know any delight to compare with that given me by some of the illustrious dead whose works I have read or seen.

The three finest things in creation are the sea, *Hamlet,* and Mozart's *Don Giovanni.* Once again—don't be offended by all this! For your reproach does not represent your true thoughts. It is the result of a moment of nervous irritation, and cannot dwell permanently in the depths of your heart.

To LOUISE COLET

[*Croisset, Wednesday morning, October 7, 1846*]

. . . How rapturous your letter is, how ardent, how eloquent! Because I tell you that I shall soon be coming, you approve everything in me, you shower me with caresses and praise. You no longer reproach me for my whims, my love of rhetoric, the refinements of my selfishness, etc. But should anything arise to prevent my coming, the whole thing would begin all over again, would it not? Oh, my child, my child, how young you still are!

Love is a springtime plant that perfumes everything with its hope, even the ruins to which it clings. I do not mean by this that you are a ruin, my darling. I mean that though you claim to be older than I in years, you are really younger. You think of me a little as Madame de Sévigné thought of Louis XIV: "Oh, what a great king!" because he danced with her. Because you love me you think me handsome, intelligent, sublime; you predict great things for me. No! No! You are mistaken. Once I had those ideas about myself. Every moron has dreamed of being a great man, and every donkey who ever stared at himself in the water of the stream he was crossing has enjoyed the sight and been sure that he looked like a horse. I lack many qualities, many of the very best, that are needed if one is to do something good. I have written some fine pages here and there, but no complete work. I am planning a book, which will show me how good I am. But this book may never be written. . . .

There are sailors who discover worlds, who add new continents to the earth and new constellations to the heavens: they are the great masters, eternally splendid. Others belch terror from their vessels' guns and sail about waxing rich and fat from their plunder. Still others leave home to seek gold and silk under foreign skies. And still others merely let down their nets to catch salmon for epicures and cod for the poor. I am the obscure and patient pearl-fisher, who returns from his dive empty-handed and blue in the face. Some fatal attraction draws me down into the depths of thought, down into those innermost recesses which never lose their fascination for the strong of heart. I shall spend my life gazing at the Ocean of Art, while on it others navigate or do battle; and from time to time I shall entertain myself by plunging to the bottom in search of bright-hued shells that no one will want. I shall keep them for myself alone, and use them to cover the walls of my hut.

To LOUISE COLET

[*Late April, 1847*]

I have never before been so conscious of how little talent is vouchsafed me for expressing ideas in words. You ask me for a frank, clear explanation. But haven't I given you just that a hundred times, and, if I may say so, in every letter for many months? What can I say now that I have not said before?

You want to know whether I love you, so that everything can be cleared up once and for all. Isn't that what you wrote me yesterday? It is too big a question to be answered by a "Yes" or a "No." Still, I will try to do that, so that you will no longer accuse me of being always evasive. I hope that today you'll at least be fair: you don't spoil me in that respect.

For me, love is not and should not be in the foreground of life; it should remain in the back room. Other things in the soul have precedence over it; things which seem to me nearer the light, closer to the sun. So, if you look upon love as the main dish of existence, the answer is no. As a seasoning, yes. If you mean by "loving" to be exclusively preoccupied with the loved one, to live only through him, to see, of everything there is to see in the world, only him, to be full of the idea of him, just as a little girl's apron is filled with flowers that keep spilling out on all sides even though she holds the corners in her mouth and squeezes it tightly with both hands—to feel, in a word, that your life is tied to his life and that this tie has become an integral organ of your soul—then: NO.

If you mean by loving the desire to take, from this contact of two persons, the foam that floats on the surface, without stirring the dregs that may be below; a union combining affection and pleasure; meetings filled with delight and partings devoid of despair (even when I kissed my best-beloved in their coffins I did not despair) ; the ability to live without one another—since it is quite possible to live severed from everything one desires, orphaned of all one's loves, bereft of all one's dreams, while nevertheless smilingly relapsing into moments of passion; in short, the feeling that this happened because it had to happen and that it will end because everything ends with no blame attached to either side, and the determination, as long as this joy lasts, to go on living as before, or perhaps a little better than before, with an additional resting-place for your heart when it is tired (not that this makes you feel any happier at facing the world each morning) ; —if you grant that it is possible to be in love and yet realize how immensely pitiful are the rewards of love as compared with the rewards of art, and feel an amused and bitter scorn for everything that drags you down to earth; —if you admit that it is possible to be in love and yet feel that a line of Theocritus is more intoxicating than your most precious memories, and feel too that you are quite willing to make big sacrifices (I mean of the things generally considered the most precious: life, money) whereas you would refuse to make small compromises—then: YES.

Ah, when I saw you, poor pretty darling, setting sail on this Ocean (remember my first letters), didn't I warn you: "No! Stay where you are! Stay on shore, arid though your existence may be!"

. . . If this letter wounds you, if it is the "blow" that you have been expecting, it seems to me not so harsh as all that. You have *begged* me to strike you! Blame only yourself. You have asked me, on your knees, to insult you. But no! I send you my affection. . . .

To LOUISE COLET

[*Rouen,*] *1847*

. . . You reproach me for speaking of art with you, "as though we had nothing more important in common." Am I to gather that you are in the habit of speaking about art with people you care nothing about? For you the subject of art is of minor importance, a kind of entertainment, something between politics and the day's news? Not for me! The other day I saw a friend who lives outside France. We were brought up together; he reminisced about our childhood, my father, my sister, the lycée, etc. Do you think that I spoke to him about the things that are closest to me, or at least that I have the highest regard for—about my loves and my enthusiasms? I was careful not to, I assure you, for he would have trampled them underfoot. The spirit observes the proprieties too, you know. He bored me to death, and at the end of two hours I was longing for him to go—which doesn't mean that I'm not devoted to him, and don't love him, if you call it loving. What is there worth talking about except Art? But who is there to talk about Art with? The first person who happens along? You are luckier than I, if such is the case with you, for I never meet anyone with whom I can discuss it.

You wish me to be frank? Very well then, I will be. One day, our day together in Mantes, under the trees, you told me that you "would not exchange your happiness for the fame of Corneille." Do you remember that? Is my memory correct? If you knew how those words shocked me, how they chilled the very marrow of my bones! Fame! Fame! What is fame? Nothing, a mere noise, the external accompaniment of the joy Art gives us. "The fame of Corneille" indeed! But—to *be* Corneille! To feel *one's self* Corneille!

But then I have always seen you lump art together with a lot of other things—patriotism, love, what you will—a lot of things which to my mind are alien to it and, far from adding to its stature, diminish it. This is one of the chasms that exists between you and me. It was you who opened it and you who revealed it to me.

Yes, when I met you I immediately conceived love for you and did love you. After possessing you I felt none of the weariness that is said to be the inevitable sequel, and everything in my heart and my body impelled me toward you. But every time I went to you there was a dispute, a quarrel; you were sulky, something I said offended you; something always came between us, like a double-edged sword which each of us used to wound the other. Whenever I think of you, even when I evoke my most cherished memories of you, one or another of your lamentations comes to my mind and spoils everything. During the time I used to visit you in Paris, you wept whenever I left; now you reproach me because I don't come. Through loving me you have come to hate me, or at least you would like to. Do hate me, if it will make you any less miserable. Had we met earlier and under different circumstances we might perhaps have drunk the cup without making it so bitter. But when we met our hearts were already well past their springtime, and we were unhappy together, like people who marry late. Who is to blame? Not you, not I; both, perhaps. You made no effort to understand me, and I may not have understood you. I have wounded many of your feelings, and you have often hurt me deeply. But I am so accustomed to being hurt that I should never have noticed it if you had not complained about my wounding you. It's a pity, for I love your face, and everything about you is sweet. But, but—I am so weary! So bored, so fundamentally incapable of making anyone happy! Make you happy! Ah, poor Louise, *I* make a woman *happy!* I don't even know how to play with a child. My mother snatches away her little granddaughter when I touch her, for I make her cry, and she is like you, always calling me and wanting to be near me. . . .

So use your critical sense, and concentrate on my ridiculous aspects: there are plenty of them. Will you do this? I will help you; I'll get fun out of it myself. It will be the counterpart of all my hymns of self-glorification. And when I cease to mean anything to you, write me and tell me so openly and bluntly; on that day a new phase will begin.

To MAXIME DU CAMP

Croisset, April 7, 1848

Alfred died on Monday at midnight. I buried him yesterday. It was I who wrapped him in his shroud, I who gave him the last kiss, I who saw the coffin nailed down. I passed two long days and nights beside him, reading Creuzer's *Religions of Antiquity* as I watched.

The window was open, the night splendid. I could hear a cock crowing, and a night moth circled round and round the taper. I shall never forget it, or the look on Alfred's face, or the distant sound of a hunting-horn which came from the forest that first night at midnight. On Wednesday I walked all the afternoon, with a dog that followed me without being called. It had become attached to Alfred and always went with him when he walked alone. The night before his death this same dog howled frightfully and could not be quieted. From time to time I rested on mossy banks, smoking and looking up at the sky, and behind a heap of brushwood I lay down and slept a little.

During the last night I read *Feuilles d'automne.* I kept coming either upon his favorite passages or upon something appropriate to my present circumstances. Now and then I went over to him and lifted the veil covering his face. I was wrapped in a cloak that had belonged to my father but which he wore only once—the day of Caroline's wedding.

At daybreak, about four o'clock, the attendant and I began our task. I lifted him, turned him, covered him. All the next day I kept feeling in my fingertips the coldness and stiffness of his limbs. He was horribly decomposed; we wrapped him in two shrouds. When it was done he looked like an Egyptian mummy in its bandages, and I was filled with an indescribable sense of joy and relief on his account. Outside there was a whitish mist. As the sky lightened I began to see against it the line of the trees in the forest; the two tapers burned dimly in the dawning whiteness; birds began to sing, and I recited to myself this line from his *Bélial: "Il ira, joyeux oiseau, saluer dans les pins le soleil levant"*—or rather I could hear his voice reciting it, and for the rest of the day I was exquisitely obsessed by it.

We laid him in the entry, where the doors had been removed and where the morning air poured in, freshened by the rain. He was carried to the cemetery on men's shoulders—an hour's walk. As I walked behind the coffin it seemed to sway with the movements of a boat. The service was atrociously long. In the cemetery the earth was muddy. I stood beside the grave and watched each shovelful as it fell; I thought there must be a hundred thousand of them.

I returned to Rouen on the box of a carriage with Bouilhet under a beating rain. The horses went at a gallop, and I cried out to urge them on. The air did me good. I slept all last night and most of today.

That is what I have passed through since Tuesday evening. I have had marvelous intimations and intuitions and flashes of untranslatable ideas. A host of things have been coming back to me, with choirs of music and clouds of perfume.

As long as he was capable of doing anything, he read Spinoza in bed until one in the morning. On one of his last days, when the window was open and the sun pouring in, he cried out: "Shut it! It is too beautiful—too beautiful!"

At certain moments, dear Max, you were strangely present to me, and my mind was a confusion of mournful images.

Adieu! I embrace you, and long to see you, for I have unutterable things to say to you.

To ERNEST CHEVALIER

Croisset, Sunday, July 4, [*1848*]

Dear Ernest

Every time I write you I seem fated to have to report sad news. You have read in the newspapers of the atrocious events that have been taking place in Paris:[25] Du Camp was struck by a bullet in the calf of his right leg and will be laid up for at least a month; I am told that his wound is slight but am not entirely reassured.

[25] This letter contains the only contemporary references in the extant correspondence to the "June Days." Maxime Du Camp had joined the National Guard.

While that was taking place the rest of us were coping with a different kind of onslaught.

Hamard returned from Paris a month ago announcing his intention of becoming an actor and of making his debut at the Comédie Française in two weeks. In the last four months he has spent thirty thousand francs, not to mention his silver and his diamonds, which he gave to the Republic, etc. etc. In short, he is completely insane. His purpose in returning here was to claim his daughter. But my mother was advised to keep her away from him because of his condition, and we left hurriedly for Forges, the first place that occurred to us. There my mother trembled at the sound of every carriage that arrived in the town, and she begged shelter from Monsieur and Madame Beaufils, who welcomed her in a way I shall never forget—perfectly. Meanwhile his family wanted to have him committed and his uncle petitioned that he be declared incompetent. But unfortunately the outbreak in Paris kept the police from doing anything. When he learned that action was being taken against him he temporarily regained his sanity. He petitioned that my mother be forced to return his child; but the judge decided that she should keep her until the hearing on the issue of incompetence. An amicable settlement was arrived at and now he has consented that my mother keep the child until January and the hearing concerning his incompetence has been postponed. Six months from now he will be, I hope, completely insane and the case against him will be watertight. I spare you countless details, horrible for my mother. . . .

And you, what has become of you? Have you a little peace? As for me, as you may imagine, I am living in hell; all conceivable blows are falling on my head; at each new misfortune I think the limit has been reached, but they keep coming and coming! And I haven't told you everything. . . .

To LOUISE COLET

[*no date*]

It is impossible for me to continue any longer a correspondence that is becoming epileptic. Change it, I beg. What have I done to you that you should unfold before me, with all the pride of grief, the spectacle of a despair for which I know no remedy? If I had betrayed you, exposed you, sold your letters, etc., you could not write me things more atrocious or more distressing.

What have I done, good God? What have I done?

You know quite well that I cannot come to Paris. Are you trying to make me answer you brutally? I am too well brought up to do that, but it seems to me that I have said this often enough for you to remember it.

I had formed quite a different idea of love. I thought it was something independent of everything, even of the person who inspired it. Absence, insult, infamy—all that does not affect it. When two persons love, they can go ten years without seeing each other and without suffering any ill effects therefrom.[26]

You claim that I treat you like "the lowest kind of woman." I don't know what "the lowest kind of woman" is, or the highest kind, or the next-highest. Women are relatively inferior or superior by reason of their beauty and the attraction they exert on us, that's all. You accuse me of being an aristocrat, but I have very democratic ideas about this. It is possible, as you say, that moderate affections are always lasting. But in saying that, you condemn your own, for it is anything but moderate. As for myself, I am weary of grand passions, exalted feelings, frenzied loves, and howling despairs. I love good sense above all, perhaps because I have none.

I don't understand why you constantly pick quarrels and sulk. You should not do this, for you are kind, good, and charming,

26 "What is one to make of this sentence?" Louise scribbled in the margin of Flaubert's letter.

and one cannot help holding it against you that you wantonly spoil all those qualities.

Calm yourself, work, and when we meet again welcome me with a good laugh and tell me you've been silly.

To LOUISE COLET[27]

Friday night, August 11, 1848

Thank you for the gift.

Thank you for your very beautiful poem.

Thank you for the remembrance.

Yours, G.

To LOUIS BOUILHET

[*Cairo, end of December, 1849, or beginning of January, 1850*]

De Saltatoribus. We haven't yet had any dancing-girls; they are all in exile in Upper Egypt. The party we were planning to have on the Nile the last time I wrote you didn't come off. However, nothing is lost. We have had male dancers. Oh! Oh! Oh!

How we longed for you! I was indignant and very sad that you were not here. Three or four musicians playing curious instruments (we shall bring some home) stood at the end of the hotel dining-room while one gentleman was having his dinner and the rest of us were sitting on the divan smoking our pipes. As dancers, imagine two rascals, quite ugly, but charming in their corruption, in the deliberate degradation of their glances and the femininity of their movements, their eyes painted with antimony and dressed as women. For costume, they had loose trousers and an embroidered jacket. The latter came down to the epigastrium, whereas the trousers, held up by an enormous

27 In this note Flaubert addresses Louise with the formal *vous* instead of the familiar *tu* found in previous letters. The affair broke off about now, to be resumed only after Flaubert's return from his Near-Eastern journey, in 1851.

cashmere girdle folded double several times, began only at the bottom of the stomach, so that the entire stomach, the loins, and the beginning of the buttocks are naked, seen through a black gauze held tight against the skin by the upper and lower garments. At every movement, this gauze ripples with a mysterious, transparent undulation. The music never changed or stopped during the two hours. The flute is shrill, you feel the throb of the tambourines in your breast, the voice of the singer dominates everything. The dancers advance and retreat, moving the pelvis with a short convulsive movement. A quivering of the muscles is the only way to describe it; when the pelvis moves, the rest of the body is motionless; when the breast shakes, nothing else moves. In this manner they advance toward you, their arms extended and rattling a kind of metal castanet, and their faces, under the rouge and the sweat, remain more expressionless than a statue's. By that I mean they never smile. The effect is produced by the gravity of the head in contrast to the lascivious movements of the body. Sometimes they lie down flat on their backs, like a woman in bed, then rise up with a movement of the loins similar to that of a tree which swings back into place after the wind has stopped. In their bowings and salutations their great trousers suddenly inflate like oval balloons, then seem to melt away, expelling the air that swells them. From time to time, during the dance, the impresario who brought them plays around with them, kissing them on the stomach and the loins, and makes obscene remarks in an effort to put additional spice into a thing which is already quite clear in itself. It is too beautiful to be exciting. I doubt whether we shall find the women as good as the men; the ugliness of the latter adds greatly to the thing as Art. I had a headache for the rest of the day.

The other day I took a bath. I was alone in the depths of the hot-room, watching the daylight fade through the great glass bull's-eyes in the dome. Hot water was flowing everywhere;

stretched out indolently I thought of a quantity of things as my pores tranquilly dilated. It is very voluptuous and sweetly melancholy to take a bath like that quite alone, lost in those dark rooms where the slightest noise resounds like a cannon shot, while the naked Kellaks call out to one another as they massage you, turning you over like embalmers preparing you for the tomb. . . .

We chat with priests of all religions. The poses and attitudes which the people take are sometimes really beautiful. We have them translate songs, tales, folklore—the most genuinely popular and oriental things possible. We hire scholars for this—that is literally true. We act with considerable swank, and permit ourselves much insolence and enormous liberty of language. The proprietor of our hotel thinks that we sometimes go a little too far.

One of these days we are to have a visit from some sorcerers—always in the hope of seeing more beautiful oriental movements. . . .

Go to see my mother often; keep up her courage; write to her when she is away; the poor woman needs it. You would be doing a highly charitable action, and it would interest you to observe the timid unfolding of a nature that is good and upright. Ah, dear fellow, were it not for her and you I would think not at all of my homeland, I mean my home. Around me here are to be seen fine examples of baseness: it's straight out of antiquity. Long live despotic government, which flouts human dignity! My God, what scoundrels all these people are!

And in the evening, when you come home and the verses do not come and you think of me, and are bored, take a sheet of paper and write me everything, everything that comes into your head. I devoured your letter when it came, and have reread it several times.

To His Mother

Cairo, January 5, 1850

. . . A few days ago I spent a fine afternoon. Max remained at home to do I forget what, and I took Hassan (a second dragoman we have temporarily hired) and went to have a talk with the bishop of the Copts. I entered a square courtyard surrounded by columns, in the center of which was a little garden—that is, a few large trees and borders of dark greenery around which ran a kind of latticework divan. My dragoman, with his loose trousers and his large-sleeved jacket, walked ahead; I behind. On one of the corners of the divan was sitting a scowling, evil-looking old personage with a white beard, wearing a heavy pelisse; books in a baroque kind of handwriting were strewn all about him. At a certain distance were standing three doctors in black robes, younger and also with long beards. The dragoman said: "This is a French gentleman (*cawadja fransaoui*) who is traveling all over the world in search of knowledge, and who has come to you to converse of your religion." . . . The bishop received me with many courtesies; coffee was brought, and soon I began to ask questions concerning the Trinity, the Virgin, the Gospels, the Eucharist—all my old erudition of *Saint Antoine* came back in a flood. It was superb, the sky blue above us, the trees, the quantities of books, the old fellow ruminating in his beard before answering me, myself sitting cross-legged beside him, gesticulating with my pencil and taking notes, while Hassan stood motionless, translating aloud, and the three other doctors, seated on their stools, nodded their heads and interpreted an occasional word. I enjoyed it deeply. That was indeed the ancient Orient, land of religions and flowing robes. When the bishop gave out, one of the doctors replaced him; and when finally I saw that they were all somewhat flushed, I left. I am going back, for there is much to learn in that place. The Coptic religion is the most ancient of existing Christian sects, and little or nothing is known about it in Europe (so far as I know). I am going likewise to talk with the Armenians, the Greeks, the Sunnites, and especially the Mohammedan scholars.

We are still waiting for the return of the caravan from Mecca; it is too good an event to miss, and we shall not leave for Upper Egypt until the pilgrims have arrived. There are some droll things to see, we have been told: the horses of the priests walking over the prostrate bodies of the faithful, all kinds of dervishes, singers, etc.

When I think of my future (that happens rarely, for I generally think of nothing at all, despite the elevated thoughts one is supposed to have in the presence of ruins!), when I ask myself: "What shall I do when I return? What shall I write? What will I be good for? Where shall I live? What path shall I follow?" and the like, I am full of doubts and indecisions. At every stage of my life I have shirked, in just this way, facing my problems, and I shall die at sixty before having formed any opinion concerning myself or, perhaps, written anything that would have shown me my capabilities. Is *Saint Antoine* a good book or a bad one? That is something I often ask myself. Was I really mistaken in it, or was it perhaps the others who were wrong? However, I do not worry about any of this; I live like a plant, filling myself with sun and light, with colors and fresh air. I keep eating, so to speak; later the problem of digestion will have to be solved, and that is the important thing.

You ask me whether the Orient is up to what I imagined it to be. Yes, it is, and more than that it extends far beyond the narrow idea I had of it. I have found, clearly delineated, everything that was hazy in my mind. Facts have taken the place of suppositions—so excellently that it is often as though I were suddenly coming upon old and forgotten dreams.

To LOUIS BOUILHET

March 13, 1850
On board our Nile boat
12 leagues beyond Syene

In six or seven hours we are going to pass the tropic of that well-known personage Cancer. It is 30 degrees [Réaumur] in the shade at this moment, we are barefoot and clad in nothing but shirts, and I am writing to you on my divan, to the sound of the darabukkas of our sailors, who are singing and clapping their hands. The sun is beating down mercilessly on the awning over our deck. The Nile is flat as a river of steel. On its banks are clumps of tall palms. The sky is blue as blue. *How I miss you!* . . .

As for work, every day I read the *Odyssey* in Greek. Since we have been on the Nile I have done four books; we are coming home by way of Greece, so it may be of use to me. The first days on board I began to write a little, but I was not long, thank God, in realizing the ineptitude of such behavior: just now it is best for me to be all eyes. We live, therefore, in the grossest idleness, stretched out on our divans, watching everything that goes by: camels, herds of oxen from the Sennar, boats floating down to Cairo laden with Negresses and elephants' tusks. We are now, my dear sir, in a land where women go naked—one might say with the poet "naked as the hand," for by way of costume they wear only rings. I have seen daughters of Nubia, whose necklaces of golden coins descended below their waist, and whose black stomachs were encircled by strings of colored beads. And their dancing! But let us proceed in proper order.

From Cairo to Beni Suef, nothing very interesting. . . . From Beni Suef we took a five-day trip to Lake Moeris . . . and at Medinet el-Faiyum spent the night in the home of a Christian from Damascus, who offered his hospitality. With him, evidently as boarder, there was a Catholic priest. Under the pretext that the Mohammedans drink no wine, these brave Christians gorge themselves with brandy: the number of glasses tipped off in sign of religious confraternity is incredible. Our host was a man of a little learning, and since we were in the country of Saint Anthony we spoke of him, of Arius, of Saint Athanasius, etc., etc. The poor fellow was delighted. Do you know what was hanging on the walls of the room where we slept? An engraving of a view of Quillebœuf and another one of a view of the abbey at Granville! . . .

Traveling that way, by land, you spend your nights in houses of dried mud, looking up at the stars through chinks in the sugarcane roofs. On your arrival the sheikh at whose home you are staying has a sheep killed, and the notables of the town come to pay you a visit and kiss your hands. You let them do it with the aplomb of a sultan, and then you take your place with them at table; that is, you all sit down on the ground around a common dish into which you dip your hands, tearing, chewing, and belching to outdo one another. The custom of the country demands that you belch after meals: I do it badly.

At a place called Gebel-el-Teir we had an amusing sight. On the summit of a mountain overlooking the Nile there is a convent of Copts, who have the habit, as soon as they see a boatload of tourists, of running down, throwing themselves in the water, and swimming out to ask for alms. Everyone who passes is assailed by them. You see these monks, totally naked, rushing down their perpendicular cliffs and swimming toward you as fast as they can, shouting: *"Baksheesh, baksheesh, cawadja christiani!"* And since there are many caverns in the cliff at this particular spot, echo repeats: *"Cawadja, cawadja!"* loudly as a cannon. Vultures and eagles were flying overhead, the boat was darting through the water, its two great sails bulging. To drive off the Christian monks one of our sailors, the clown of the crew, began to dance a naked, lascivious dance, offering them his behind as they clung to the sides of the boat. The other sailors screamed insults at them, repeating the names of Allah and of Mohammed. Some hit them with sticks, others with ropes; Joseph rapped their knuckles with his kitchen tongs. It was a chorus of blows, yells, and laughter. As soon as they were given money they put it in their mouths and returned home via the route they had come. If they weren't received with a good beating, the boats would be assailed by such hordes of them that capsizing would be almost inevitable.

At Qena . . . we had landed to buy provisions and were walking peacefully and dreamily in the bazaars, inhaling the odor of sandalwood which floated about us, when suddenly, at a turn in the street, we found ourselves in the quarter of the prostitutes. Picture to yourself, my friend, five or six curving streets lined with hovels about four feet high, built of dry grey mud. At the doors, women standing or sitting on straw mats. The Negresses had dresses of sky-blue; others were in yellow, in white, in red—loose garments fluttering in the warm wind. Odors of spices. On their bare breasts long necklaces of golden coins, so that when they move they rattle like country carts. They call after you in drawling voices: "*Cawadja, cawadja,*" their white teeth gleaming between their red or black lips, their metallic eyes rolling round like wheels. I walked through these streets and walked through them again, giving baksheesh to all the women, letting them call me and catch hold of me; they took me round the waist and tried to pull me into their houses. Think of the sun beating down on all this. I resisted, quite deliberately, having made up my mind not to destroy the mood of melancholy induced by the scene. I left completely dazzled, and have remained so. There is nothing more beautiful than the sight of such women calling you. If I had gone with them another image would have taken its place, lessened its splendor.

I have not, however, always been so stoically artistic; at Esna

I visited Kuchiouk Hanem, a very celebrated courtesan. When we arrived at her house at two in the afternoon she was waiting for us; her confidante had come to the boat in the morning, escorted by a pet sheep all spotted with yellow henna and with a black velvet muzzle on its nose, which followed her like a dog; very droll. Kuchiouk Hanem was just leaving her bath. She wore a large tarboosh topped with gold and green and with a tassel falling to her shoulders; her front hair was braided in thin braids that were drawn back and tied together; the lower part of her body was hidden in immense pink trousers; her torso was entirely naked under purple gauze. She was standing at the top of her staircase, with the sun behind her, sharply silhouetted against the blue background of the surrounding sky. She is a regal-looking creature, large-breasted, fleshy, with slit nostrils, enormous eyes, and magnificent knees; when she danced there were formidable folds of flesh on her stomach. She began by perfuming our hands with rose water. Her bosom gave off a smell of sweetened turpentine, and on it she wore a three-strand golden necklace. Musicians were summoned and she danced. . . .

That night we visited her again. There were four women dancers and singers, almahs (the word almah means learned woman, blue-stocking; used, however, as we would use the word whore—which goes to show, Monsieur, that women of letters in all countries—!). The party lasted from six to half past ten, with interludes of love-making. Two squatting rebec players made continual shrill music. When Kuchiouk undressed to dance, folds of their turbans were lowered over their eyes, so that they could see nothing. This modesty gave a shocking effect. I spare you any description of the dance, I'd write it too poorly. To be understood it has to be illustrated with gestures—and even this would be inadequate.

When it was time to leave, I did not go. Kuchiouk was not too eager to have us spend the night with her, out of fear of thieves who are apt to come when they know strangers are there. Maxime stayed alone on the divan and I went downstairs with Kuchiouk to her room. A wick was burning in an antique-style lamp hanging on the wall. In an adjoining room guards were talking in a low voice with a serving woman, an Abyssinian Negress whose arms were scarred by plague-sores. Kuchiouk's little dog was sleeping on my silk jacket. Her body was sweaty; she was tired from dancing, and cold. I covered her with my fur coat and she fell asleep. As for myself, I didn't close an eye. Throughout the night I had experiences of dream-like intensity. . . .

To LOUIS BOUILHET

Damascus, September 4, 1850

You too, Brutus!—which doesn't mean that I'm a Caesar!

You too, my fine friend, whom I so admired for your immovable faith! . . . In the midst of my lassitudes, my discouragements and my nausea you were always the seltzer water which enabled me to digest life. I used to soak myself in you as in a tonic bath. When I was alone and full of self-pity I used to say to myself: "Look at him!" and then I would return, vigor renewed, to my work. You were my most moral example, my continual edification. Is the saint now to fall from his niche? I beg you—do not abandon your pedestal!

Are we fools, perhaps? Maybe so, but it is not up to us to say so, still less to believe it. However, we should by now have finished with our migraines and our nervous despairs. One thing is our ruin, one stupid thing shackles us: "taste"—good taste. We have too much of it—or rather, we worry about it more than we should. Fear of bad taste engulfs us like a fog (a foul December fog that suddenly appears, freezes your guts, stinks, and stings your eyes), and not daring to advance, we stand still.

Think how captious we are becoming, how endless our criteria, our principles, our preconceived ideas, our rules. . . . What we lack is daring. Our scruples make us like those poor believers who scarcely live for fear of hell and who wake up their confessor at dawn in order to accuse themselves of having had amorous dreams during the night. Let us worry less about the results of our efforts. Let us love the muse and love her and love her. The child that may be born is of minor importance: the purest pleasure is in the kissing.

If we do badly, if we do well—what is the difference? I have stopped thinking of posterity—a wise move. My stand is taken. Unless some excessively literary wind begins to blow in a few years, I have resolved not to "make the presses groan" with any elucubration of my brain. You and my mother and others (for it is a wonderful thing, how no one will allow anyone to live as he likes) used to scold me for my manner of life. Just wait a bit till I come back, and see whether I don't resume it. I'll dig into my hole, and—though the world crumble—I will not budge. Activity—unless it be truly frenzied—is becoming more and more distasteful to me. I have just sent back without even looking at them several silk scarves which were brought me to choose from; I had only to raise my eyes and decide, but the thought of the effort so overpowered me in advance that I sent away the merchants without buying anything. Had I been a sultan, I should have thrown them out of the window: I was full of rancor toward anyone who was seeking to force me into any activity whatever. But let's get back to our bottles, as old Michel says.

If you think that your troubles bore me, you are mistaken. I have shared greater burdens of the same nature; I am afraid of nothing in that line. If my room in the hospital could tell of all the boredom and worry that two young men used to give vent to within it, I believe it would collapse on the heads of the bourgeois who now inhabit it.[28] My poor Alfred! Astonishing how much I think of him, and how numerous the unshed tears in my heart with regard to him! How we used to talk! How complete our confidence and our understanding! We flew high.

But watch out for one thing: take care lest you *enjoy* being bored, for that is dangerous. What is your trouble? How I should like to be there to implant a kiss on your brow and a kick on your behind! What you are feeling now is the result of the long effort you have made for *Melaenis.* Do you think that the brain of a poet is like a loom for weaving cotton, able to keep on producing indefinitely without fatigue or intermission? . . .

You do well to think of my idea for a *Dictionnaire des idées reçues.* Such a book, fully and amply executed, and preceded by a good preface in which we would indicate just how the work was intended to reconcile the French public to tradition, to order, and to conventional morality, and written in such a way that the reader couldn't tell whether or not we were pulling his leg—that would perhaps be a strange book, and it might very well have some success, for it would be very timely. . . .

To LOUIS BOUILHET

Constantinople, November 14, 1850

Of Constantinople, where I arrived yesterday morning, I shall tell you nothing today, except to say that I have been struck by the idea of Fourier, that some day it will be the capital of the world. It is really fantastic as a human ant-hill. You know that feeling of being crushed and overwhelmed that one has on a first visit to Paris: here you are penetrated by that feeling, elbowing so many unknown men, from the Persian and the Indian to the American and the Englishman, so many separate individualities

28 The family of his brother Achille.

which, in their frightening total, humble your own. And then, the city is immense. One gets lost in the streets, which seem to have no beginning or end. The cemeteries are like forests in the middle of the city. . . .

The oriental cemetery is one of the most beautiful things about the East. It does not have that profoundly exasperating quality of cemeteries at home—no wall, no ditch, no separation or enclosure of any kind. It is situated anywhere, in the country or in a town, here and there and everywhere, like death itself alongside of life, and given no attention whatever. You walk through a cemetery as you walk through a bazaar. All the graves are alike; they differ only in age, and as they grow old they sink and disappear, like one's memory of the dead. The cypresses planted in the cemeteries are gigantic, and give the places a green light full of peace. . . .

Where have you got with the muse? I expected a letter from you here with something in verse enclosed. What are you reading? How I should love to see you!

As for me, literally speaking, I don't know where I'm at. At times I feel annihilated (the word is weak) ; at other times my unborn style circulates within me with intoxicating heat. Then it leaves me. I meditate very little, daydream occasionally. My type of observation is preponderantly moral. I should never have suspected that side of the journey. The psychological, human, comic side abounds. One meets splendid specimens. . . .

From time to time, in a town, I open a newspaper. Things seem to be going at a dizzy rate. We are dancing not on a volcano but on the rather rotten seat of a latrine. I am engrossed by the idea of studying the question. After my return I should like to burrow into the socialists and do, in theatrical form, something very brutal, very farcical, and—of course—impartial. I have the words on the tip of my tongue, and the tone of the thing at the tips of my fingers. Many subjects for which I have more definite plans are less eager to be born than that one.

As for subjects, I have three; perhaps they are all the same, a thought that bothers me considerably. One: *Une Nuit de Don Juan,* which I thought of in quarantine in Rhodes. Two: the story of Anubis, the woman who wished to be loved by a god. That is the loftiest of the three, but is full of atrocious difficulties. Three: my Flemish novel of the young girl who dies a virgin and mystic, having lived with her father and mother in a small provincial town in a garden of cabbages and fruit trees, beside a stream the size of the Robec. What worries me is the kinship of idea of these three plans. In the first, insatiable love in the two forms: earthly and mystical. In the second, the same story, but the character gives herself, and the earthly love is less exalted because it is more precise. In the third they are both united in the same person, and the one leads to the other; only, my heroine dies of religious rapture after experiencing sensual rapture. Alas! It seems to me that when one is as good as this at dissecting children which are to be born, one is not sufficiently vigorous to create them. My metaphysical clarity fills me with terrors of which I must rid myself. I need to know my own measure. In order to be able to live at peace, I must have an opinion of myself, a definite opinion which will regulate me in the use of the powers which I possess. I have to know the quality and the limits of my land before beginning to plough it. I am experiencing a need, with relation to my personal literary problem, that everyone in our age feels to some extent with relation to the life of society: I feel the need of "getting established."

In Smyrna, during a rain which kept me indoors, I took Eugène Sue's[29] *Arthur* from the reading-room. It's indescribable, enough to make you vomit. You have to read this to realize the pitifulness of money, success, and the public. Literature has be-

29 Best-selling author of *The Wandering Jew* and *The Mysteries of Paris.*

come consumptive. It spits and slobbers, covers its blisters with salve and sticking-plaster, and has grown bald from too much hair-slicking. It would take Christs of art to cure this leper.

To return to the antique in literature has been done already. To return to the Middle Ages has also been done already. Only the present remains. But the present offers shaky ground: where is one to lay the foundation? And yet there is no other way of building something vital and durable. All this troubles me so much that I have come to dislike being spoken to about it. I am irritated by it sometimes, like an ex-convict listening to a discussion of the penal system; especially in conversation with Maxime, who strikes hard and is not one to be encouraging—and I badly need to be encouraged. On the other hand, my vanity is not yet resigned to receiving encouragement prizes only!

I am about to reread the whole of the *Iliad*. In a fortnight we are to be in the Troad, and in January we shall be in Greece. I fret at my ignorance: if only I knew Greek! And I wasted so much time over it! "*La sérénité m'abandonne!*" The man who retains the same self-esteem when he travels that he had as he looked at himself every day in the mirror in his room at home is either a very great man or a very sturdy fool. I don't know why, but I am becoming very humble.

Passing Abydos, I thought of Byron. That is his Orient, the Turkish Orient, the Orient of the curved sword, the Albanian costume, and the grilled window looking on the blue sea. I prefer the baked Orient of the bedouin and the desert, the depths of Africa, the crocodile, the camel, the giraffe.

I lament not having gone to Persia (money! money!). I keep dreaming of Asiatic journeys, of going overland to China, of impossibilities, of the Indies or of California—the latter always excites me on the human side. At other times I become so choked up with emotion that I could weep, thinking of my study at Croisset, of our Sundays. Ah, how I shall miss my days of travel, how I shall keep reliving them, how I shall keep repeating the eternal monologue: "Fool! You did not enjoy it enough!" . . .

Why has the death of Balzac affected me so strongly? One is always saddened by the death of a man one admires. I had hoped to know him later, hoped he would like me. Yes, he was a stout fellow, one who completely understood his age. He, who had studied women so well, died just after he had married—and when the society which he knew had begun its denouement. With Louis Philippe, something disappeared which we shall not see again. Now we must dance to a different tune.

Why have I a melancholy desire to return to Egypt, to go back up the Nile and see Kuchiouk Hanem? All the same, it was a rare night that I spent there, and I tasted it to the full. How I missed you!

Tomorrow I am going to have your name, *Loue Bouilhette* (Turkish pronunciation), written on a sheet of blue paper in letters of gold—a present which I expect you to hang on your wall. It will remind you that you have been with me every day of my journey.

I feel that I am not telling you anything very interesting. Now I'll go to bed, and tomorrow will tell you about my trip. That will be more entertaining for you than my perpetual self, of which I am getting devilishly tired.

To His Mother

Constantinople, November 14, 1850

. . . There are many things in the world that in your innocence you know nothing of, poor darling. I am turning into a very great moralist—indeed the study of man has always been my great passion—and I have lately caught glimpses of many a hidden turpitude. It is horrible, the way women are taught to lie. Their training in this never ends. From their first chambermaid to their last lover everyone does his best to turn them into cheats, and then everyone blames them for being so. Puritanism, hypocrisy, bigotry, the system of segregation and confinement—these have corrupted and destroyed in the bud the most charming of God's creations. In a word, I fear the moral strait-jacket. As you know, our first impressions are indelible. We carry our pasts within us; throughout our lives we bear our nurses' imprint. When I analyze myself I find within me, still fresh and effective, numerous elements from my early years (although the influence of each has been modified by that of the others) : old Langlois, Mignot, *Don Quixote,* my childish reveries in the garden near the window of the dissecting-room. My advice is that you should engage someone to teach her[30] English and the first rudiments. Supervise everything yourself as much as you can, and pay special attention to the character and the "good sense" (in the broadest meaning of the term) of the governess.

Speaking of moral observation, I should never have suspected how much opportunity travel offers for this sort of thing. You run up against so many different kinds of people that in the end you actually do acquire a certain knowledge of the world. The earth abounds in marvelous characters. Travel is an immense, unexploited mine of comedy. I don't know why no one has ever said this, it seems to me so obvious. And then people open up so quickly, and make you such strange confidences! A man has been traveling for a year with no one to talk to; he runs into you one night in a hotel or a tent; first you talk about politics, then about Paris, then the cork comes out gently, the wine flows, and in two hours you have it all, or nearly all. The next day you say good-bye forever to your intimate friend of the previous night; often, at such moments of farewell, you even feel strangely melancholy.

30 Flaubert is speaking of his niece Caroline, now in her fifth year.

To his mother [*1850*]

We came on the Lloyd with an American, his wife, and his son, nice people traveling for their own amusement. The son is a strapping boy of fourteen, red-faced, silent, gawky, passionately attached to a spyglass from which he is never separated. The husband is a fat little man, vigorous, blunt, gay. The wife, fortyish, speaks French with a very nice little accent; she is expressionless, blond, wears silk dresses, uses lots of cold cream, looks very distinguished and gracious. For three days I have been making a scientific study of this transatlantic household (very respectable people, incidentally) and here is the result of my work. The son has been or will soon be taken to a brothel by his father's courier, who is conniving with the dragoman to rob his employers. Monsieur is rough with Madame, who bathes her red eyes before coming to table. I have also discovered that this good American is a frightful skirt-chaser; he is pursuing a little Greek woman, wife of an interpreter at the consulate, unworthy of tying the American lady's shoes. This fine fellow neglects his wife and son and spends his time enjoying mythological conversations with the daughter of Greece. He drags her around everywhere with them. We have come upon them watching the dervishes and visiting mosques. The other night we were walking alone with him in a street in Pera when close to us there passed a hideous pink hat with a black veil. The American stopped short and exclaimed *"Oh! le petit fâme grec!"* There's a lot in all this to laugh about and especially to think about, don't you agree? . . .

To His Mother

Constantinople, December 15, 1850

When am I to be married, you ask me, apropos of the news of Ernest's marriage. When? Never, I trust. As far as man can answer for what he will do, I reply in the negative. Contact with the world, with which I have been steadily rubbing shoulders now for fourteen months, makes me feel more and more like returning to my shell. Uncle Parain, who claims that travel changes a man, is wrong. As I set out so shall I return, except that there are a few less hairs on my head and considerably more landscapes within it. That is all. As far as my ideas of behavior are concerned, I will keep the ones I have always had until I see a reason to change. And, seriously, if I had to say how I really feel, deep down, and if I am not presumptuous in saying it, I will tell you that I feel I am too old to change. I have passed the age. When one has lived as I have, a life so inward and secret, full of turbulent analyses and repressed impulses, when one has so frequently excited and calmed one's self by turns, and employed all one's youth in learning to manage one's soul, as a horseman manages the horse which he forces to gallop, to walk, to jump, to trot, and to amble—all simply to provide himself with entertainment and to learn more about such things; well, what I was going to say is, if one doesn't break one's neck at the beginning the chances are one won't break it later. Like a married man I, too, am "established," in that I have found my equilibrium in life. And I don't imagine that there will be any internal disturbance to make me change my mind. For me, marriage would be an apostasy which it appalls me to think of. Alfred's death has not erased the memory of the irritation which his marriage caused me. It was as though pious folk were to hear the news of some great scandal caused by their bishop. When, in a big way or a small one, one wishes to meddle with God's works, one must begin—if only from the hygienic point of view—by putting one's self in such a position that one cannot be made a fool of. You can depict wine, love, women, and great exploits on the condition that you are not a drunkard, a lover, a husband, or a hero. If you are involved in life, you see it badly; your sight is affected either by suffering or by enjoyment. The artist, in my way of thinking, is a monstrosity, something outside nature. All the woes with which Providence showers him come from the stubbornness with which he denies that axiom. His refusal to admit it brings suffering not only to him, but to those with whom he is in contact. Ask women who have loved poets, or men who have loved actresses. So (and this is my conclusion) I am resigned to living as I have lived; alone, with a throng of great men instead of a social circle, with my bear-rug (being a bear myself), etc. I care nothing for the world, for the future, for what people will say, for any kind of established position, or even for literary fame, which in my early days I used to stay awake so many nights dreaming about. That is what I am like: that is my character.

God knows why I've written you these two pages of tirade, poor dear. No, no; when I think of your sweet face, so sad, so loving, and of the joy I have in living with you, who are so full of serenity, so full of a serious, grave kind of charm, I know very well that I shall never love another as I do you. You will never have a rival, never fear! The senses or the fancy of a moment will not take the place of that which lies enclosed in triple sanctuary. Some will perhaps mount to the threshold of the temple, but none will enter. . . .

To LOUIS BOUILHET

Patras, February 10, 1851

. . . What has become of you? What are you doing? In the physical sense, I mean. *Quid de Venere?* It's a long time since you've told me of your exploits. As for me, my hair is disappearing. When you see me again I'll be wearing a skull cap; I'll be bald like an office clerk or a worn-out notary—the stupidest kind of premature senility. It depresses me. Maxime makes fun of me; he may be right. Such depression is a feminine feeling, unworthy of a man and a republican, I know. But I see my baldness as the first symptom of a decline that humiliates me and that I feel keenly. I am getting fat and paunchy and am beginning to be repulsive. Perhaps I shall soon lament my youth, and, like the grandmother in Béranger, my wasted time. Where art thou, luxuriant locks of my eighteenth year, falling with such hope and pride to my shoulders!

Yes, I am growing old; it seems to me that I am no longer capable of producing anything good. I am afraid of everything having to do with style. What am I going to write when I return? That is what I keep asking myself. These last days, on horseback, I have been thinking a good deal about my *Nuit de Don Juan*. But this subject seems to me very commonplace and outworn; it would be just another treatment of the nun theme. To sustain it an uncommonly vigorous style would be needed, without a single weak line. Add to all this the fact that it's raining, that we are in a filthy little inn where we have to wait several days for the steamer, that my trip is over and that I am depressed. I want to return to Egypt. I keep thinking of India. What a foolish creature man is, especially this man!

Even after the Orient, Greece is beautiful. I was deeply moved by the Parthenon. It's better than the Gothic, whatever anyone may say to the contrary, and above all, I think, it is harder to understand.

As we gazed at Parnassus, we thought of the exasperation that the sight would have caused a romantic poet of 1832, and of the harangue he would have addressed to it.

The Parthenon is the color of brick, with, in spots, tones of bitumen and ink. The sun shines on it almost constantly; whatever the weather, it gleams gloriously. Birds come and perch on the dismantled cornice—falcons, crows. The wind blows between the columns; goats browse amid the broken pieces of white marble underfoot. Here and there, in the hollows, heaps of human bones, reminders of war. Small Turkish ruins amid the great Greek ruin; and then, in the distance and always, the sea!

Among the pieces of sculpture found on the Acropolis I noticed especially a small bas-relief representing a woman fastening her shoe. There is only a fragment of the torso, just the two breasts, from the base of the neck to above the navel. One of the breasts is draped, the other uncovered. What breasts! Good God! What a breast! It is apple-round, solid, abundant, detached from the other: you can feel the weight of it in your hand; the fecund maternity and the sweetness of the love it invokes make you almost swoon. The rain and the sun have turned the white marble to yellow, a tawny color, almost like flesh. It is so tranquil, so noble! It seems to be about to swell; one feels that the lungs beneath it are about to expand and breathe. It knew how to wear its sheer pleated drapery! How one would have lain upon it, weeping! How one would have fallen on one's knees before it, hands joined in worship! A little more and I should have prayed. . . .

To His Mother

Rome, April 8, 1851

Nothing new to report: we never emerge from the museums. The Vatican and the Capitol take up all our time, especially the Vatican, which really has some pretty little things. The quantity of masterpieces in Rome is enough to frighten and flatten you: you feel even smaller than in the desert. The city is filling up for Holy Week. Hotels are crowded, and late-comers are having trouble finding rooms.

I am going to write to Bouilhet, from whom I hear no more than if he were dead, which annoys me. Poor fellow—how he would enjoy it here! How he would relish the ruins and the campagna. For the Roman campagna is the most ancient thing in Rome. As for the city itself, despite the number of ancient remains it hides its ancient character under a Jesuit garb. Rome should be thought of as a vast museum containing only things of the sixteenth century. The other day I saw a Murillo *Virgin* that's enough to make you lose your mind, as Uncle Parain would say; anyone who tried to equal it would sweat blood more than once.

I had a thought yesterday after seeing Michelangelo's *Last Judgment.* It is this: that there is nothing viler on earth than a bad artist, a poor wretch who all his life sails just offshore from beauty without ever making a landing and planting his flag. To practice art in order to earn money, flatter the public, spin facetious or dismal yarns for reputation or cash—that is the most ignoble of professions, just as by the reverse of the same token the artist seems to me master among men. I should rather have painted the Sistine Chapel than won many a battle, including Marengo. The former will endure longer and was perhaps more difficult of achievement. And I consoled myself for my wretchedness by thinking that my intentions, at least, are honorable. Everyone can't get to be Pope.

II

"LES AFFRES DE L'ART"

1851-1857

THE year and a half in Egypt, the Near East, Greece and Italy had been a kind of catharsis for Flaubert: catharsis by exposure to one of the chief ingredients of the romanticism in which he had been raised—the exotic color of the East, of which Hugo's *Les Orientales* (a volume Flaubert had with him on his travels) is only one of many French romantic reflections.[1] In the East, where he had often thought he longed to dwell, or at least to dally, Flaubert learned what he wrote to Louise Colet: ". . . we are all so wretchedly constituted that once there we languish and long to come home. We miss everything French—the look of French houses, even Frenchmen we care nothing about. No! For us the only way is to shut ourselves up and keep our noses to our work, like moles."

On his return to France in 1851 he did two things rather rapidly: he resumed relations with Louise Colet, and he began to write *Madame Bovary.*

There is little information as to his manner of going about either of these things. How the reconciliation with Louise was effected is not known; nor are any external influences that may have led the author of the "mythological and theological fireworks of *Saint Antoine*" to devote himself to the chronicle of a Norman bourgeoise. Maxime Du Camp, in his memoirs, credits Louis Bouilhet with the

[1] Other reflections: *Mademoiselle de Maupin* and other works by Gautier; Delacroix's Algerian pictures; Ingres's odalisques; Meyerbeer's *L'Africaine;* Bizet's *Les Pêcheurs de perles;* Delibes's *Lakmé;* Pierre Loti, etc.

deciding voice in the choice of subject; and whether or not this is correct, Bouilhet visited Croisset almost every week-end (except for absences in Paris) during the four and a half years of the book's composition. Flaubert later referred to Bouilhet as his "midwife," and from the letters it is clear that the entire manuscript was gone over by him more than once.

Flaubert's life at Croisset after the oriental journey was one of ascetic discipline, external and internal. He shut himself off almost entirely from the world. The day was divided into rigid compartments: aside from reading and the tutoring of his niece his entire time was devoted to his manuscript. Having decided to abandon the lyrical extravagance of his earlier work, he went to the other extreme: impersonality became his ideal. The passion for self-expression is now harnessed to serve objective goals: fidelity to local color, exact rendition of dialogue, documentation covering every detail, accurate characterization of Norman bourgeois types, utmost precision of language and style. The romanticism which was so integral a part of himself is shown to be a destructive force in the life of his heroine, who, however, precisely because of her romanticism, is displayed as superior to her grubby bourgeois milieu. The book attacks both the romantic and the bourgeois values—those two antitheses which together defined the intellectual and social climate of the France of his day. The result is extreme pessimism, almost nihilism, tempered only by his conception of Art (he almost always wrote the word with a capital A).

Concerning this conception, and concerning the progress of his work, he wrote at length to Louise, one of the few people who were his links with secular life at this time. Once again, however, she was unable to tolerate an almost completely epistolary relationship; her complaints about his "monstrous personality" became ever shriller and more frequent, and there was a second—this time, final—rupture.

Meanwhile Maxime Du Camp, immediately after his return from his travels with Flaubert, had purchased a part-interest in the *Revue de Paris,* and he urged his friend to make a public appearance in it with excerpts from *La Tentation de Saint Antoine.* Flaubert's refusal to do this, and his obstinate insistence on composing a long work slowly, rather than preparing something for immediate magazine publication, and his insistence also on remaining at Croisset rather than leading a social "literary" life in Paris—all this brought him warnings from Max that he was neglecting opportunities to make himself known. The increasingly evident vulgarity of his friend cooled Flaubert's affection and lessened his esteem.

When the book was finished in April, 1856, Flaubert was conscious of having performed a tour de force: of having given to his "anti-plastic" material enduring form, which he called Beauty (this word, too, he usually wrote with a capital letter).

The reaction of his friends and the world at large to this work which he had accomplished at the cost of the most exacting self-denial, veritable agonies of creation—*"les affres de l'Art"*—was such that he was definitively confirmed in his rejection of the values of his society. After considerable hesitation he had accepted Maxime Du Camp's suggestion that the book make its first appearance in installments in the *Revue de Paris* beginning August 1, but shortly after the manuscript was delivered to the *Revue* Du Camp wrote him that many cuts were imperative, and saying:

> Let us take full charge of the publication of your novel in the *Revue;* we will make the cuts that we think are indispensable; and later you can superintend the book publication yourself, restoring anything you choose. My private opinion is that if you do not do this you will be compromising your entire career and making your first appearance with a work which is confused and muddled and to which the style alone does not give sufficient interest. Be brave, close your eyes during the operation, and have confidence—if not in our talent, at least in the experience which we have acquired in such things and also in our affection for you. You have buried your novel underneath a heap of details which are well done but utterly superfluous; they hide the essentials, and must be removed—an easy task. We shall have it done under our supervision by someone who is experienced and clever; not a word will be added to your manuscript, it will merely be cut down; the job will cost you about a hundred francs, which will be deducted from your cheque, and you will have published something really good, instead of something imperfect and padded.

This supreme irony, that the artist who had spent four and a half years putting his book together, sometimes spending weeks in search of a word or a phrase, should be asked to pay a hack rewrite man a hundred francs for butchering it—this caused Flaubert simply to scrawl the word *"Gigantesque!"* on the letter and retort to Du Camp that the novel was to be published as it was or not at all. After some delay it was agreed that only one passage would be omitted, and publication began on October 1.

Meanwhile the editors of the *Revue*—which had a vague aura of "liberalism" about it and had displeased the imperial censor by some of its contents in earlier issues—learned on good authority that the government was planning to prosecute the magazine and Flaubert as well for "outrage of public morals and religion": certain passages in *Madame Bovary* were the pretext, and suppression of the *Revue* was the goal. When Flaubert opened his copy of the issue of December 1, he found the newest installment of his novel headed by an editorial note:

> The editors find themselves obliged to omit from this installment a passage which they consider unsuitable for publication in the *Revue de Paris.* They hereby advise the author of their action and assume full responsibility for it.

Flaubert's protests against this, and against the editors' demands for further cuts in the last installment, were useless: the *Revue,* it appeared, had the legal right to suppress any passage it chose, and Du Camp informed Flaubert that in an attempt to save him and the *Revue* from prosecution the editors intended to exercise that right. The *Revue* also refused Flaubert's request that the last installment be canceled entirely, and it appeared with the following heading:

> Considerations which it is not in my province to judge compelled the *Revue de Paris* to omit a passage from the issue of December 1; its scruples having been again aroused on the occasion of the present issue, it has thought proper to omit several more. In consequence, I hereby decline responsibility for the lines which follow. The reader is therefore asked to consider them as a series of fragments, not as a whole.
>
> Gustave Flaubert.

But as Flaubert had prophesied, the *Revue* accomplished nothing by its cuts. The government proceeded with its prosecution. Only with difficulty did Flaubert and the *Revue* win their case, and even in handing down his verdict of not guilty the judge expressed grave moral disapprobation of parts of *Madame Bovary.*

After the verdict Flaubert sold the rights to his novel for five years to the publisher Michel Lévy for five hundred francs, and it appeared in book form in April, 1857. Its immediate commercial success was in large part a *succès de scandale,* and Flaubert's pessimism about mankind and society became more ferocious than ever.

* * *

In this section, when portions of letters to Louise Colet are printed in series, each portion is not separately headed with her name.

To LOUISE COLET

Croisset, July 26, 1851

I write you because "my heart prompts me to speak kindly to you," dear friend. If I could make you happy I should joyfully do so; it would be only fair. I feel guilty at the thought of having made you suffer so; don't you understand that? However, neither I, nor you, but only the circumstances, can be held responsible for this—and for all the rest.

At Rouen the other day you must have found me very cold, though I assure you I was as warm as I found it possible to be. I made every effort to be kind. Tender, no; that would have been wretchedly hypocritical, and a kind of insult to the sincerity of your feelings.

Read, do not dream. Plunge into long studies; there is nothing continually good but the habit of stubborn work. It releases an opium which lulls the soul. I have gone through periods of bleak despair, and have turned endlessly in a void, desperate with boredom. This can be overcome by force of persistence and pride: try.

I should like you to be in such a state that we could see each other calmly. I like your company when it is not *stormy*: the tempests we love in our youth weary us in our maturity. It is like horseback riding; there was a time when I loved to gallop; now I walk my horse with a loose rein. I am growing very old; the slightest jolt disturbs me, and I enjoy feeling no more than acting.

You tell me nothing of what interests me most, your plans. You have not yet settled on anything, I gather. The advice I gave you was good; first make sure of your bread and butter, as Phidias used to say.

I shall see you again soon in Paris, if you are there. (Weren't you to stay in England a month?) I shall be in Paris the end of next week, I presume. I shall go to England toward the end of August; my mother wants me to accompany her. I don't enjoy the thought of traveling, but—— If you are still there I will come to see you. We will try to be happy with each other. In Paris I will leave at your house the two manuscripts you let me see. I shall also return to you, but only in person, a bronze medal I once accepted from you in a moment of weakness and which I must not keep. It belongs to your daughter.

Farewell. God bless you, poor child!

Croisset, [*September, 1851*]

My dear friend, I leave for London next Thursday. I will take your letters and will write you on my return what I have been able to do for you. I don't really know why I should call on Mazzini; still, if there is anything you want him to do for you I will be glad to ask him.

I began my novel yesterday evening. Now I foresee terrifying difficulties of style. It is no small thing to be simple. I am afraid of turning into a Paul de Kock or a kind of Chateaubriandized Balzac.

To MAXIME DU CAMP

[*Croisset,*] *Monday, October 21, 1851*

I am impatient to have you here so that we can have a long, detailed talk before I make my decision. Last Sunday we read over parts of *Saint Antoine*:[2] Apollonius, a few of the gods, and the second half of the second part, that is the Courtesan, Thamar, Nebuchadnezzar, the Sphinx, the Chimera, and all the animals. It would be very difficult to publish excerpts: you'll see for yourself. There are some quite good things, but—but—but! They leave one essentially unsatisfied, and the word "curious," I think, would be the verdict of the most indulgent, indeed the most intelligent, readers. Of course I'd have on my side a lot of people who wouldn't understand a word and would admire it for fear that their neighbors might understand it better than they. Bouilhet's objection to publication is that I have put into this work all my defects and only a few of my good qualities. According to him, it would give an unfair picture of me as a man. Next Sunday we shall read all the speeches of the gods; perhaps they would make the best selection. I have no more feeling of my own about this matter of choice than about the main question of publication. I don't know what to think. I am completely neutral. So far I have never been accused of lacking individuality or of being unaware of my little self. Well, in this question, perhaps the most important in the life of an artist, I lack individuality completely, I am obliterated, non-existent; although I do everything I can to form some sort of opinion, I find myself utterly without one. The arguments for and against seem to me equally good. I'll toss up for it, and I'll not regret the decision whatever it may be.

If I do publish, it will be for the stupidest of reasons—because I am told to, because I choose to imitate or obey others, not from any initiative of my own. I feel neither the need nor

2 Primitive version.

the desire to publish. And don't you think that we should do only as our hearts urge us? The idiot who goes to a duel because his friends urge him and tell him that he must, even though he himself has no desire to go and thinks it stupid, etc., is, at bottom, much more wretched than the self-confessed coward who swallows the insult without even noticing it and stays calmly at home. Yes, I repeat: what I dislike is that the idea comes not from me but from another, from others—proof, perhaps, that I am wrong.

And then let us look further: if I publish I won't do it by halves—when one does a thing it must be done well. I'll go to Paris for the winter. I'll be a man like other men, I'll lead a life of passions and intrigues. I'll have to do many things that will revolt me and that I can find lamentable in advance. Well—am I made for all that? If you knew all the invisible nets that keep me inactive, all the mists that float in my brain! I often feel the most killing and stupefying fatigue at the idea of having to perform the slightest action, and I grasp even the clearest idea only by dint of great effort. My youth (you knew only its last phase) steeped me in the opiate of boredom, and I shall feel its effects to the end of my days. I have a hatred of life. There: I have said it; I will not take it back. Yes, of life, and of everything that reminds me that life must be borne. It bores me to eat, to dress, to stand on my feet, etc. I have dragged this hatred everywhere, wherever I have been: at school, in Rouen, in Paris, on the Nile, throughout our travels. You, with your clear-cut, precise nature, always rebelled against these vague Normandisms which I tried so clumsily to excuse. You used to respond with a harshness that often hurt. I always forgave you, but it was painful at the time.

Do you think that it has been out of stubbornness, without long deliberations, that I have lived to the age of thirty in this way of which you disapprove? Why have I not had mistresses?

Why have I preached chastity? Why have I stayed in this provincial backwater? Do you think I don't have erections like other men, and that I wouldn't enjoy cutting a fine figure in Paris? Indeed I should enjoy it considerably. But take a good look at me and tell me whether it's possible. I am no more cut out for that sort of thing than to be a good dancer. Few men have had fewer women than I. That is the punishment for my cult of "plastic beauty," as Theo calls it; and if I remain unpublished, that will be my chastisement for all my youthful dreams of glory. Must not each of us follow his own path? If I dislike moving about, maybe I'm right not to. Sometimes I even think that I should not try to write a rational book, but should rather completely abandon myself to lyricism, to bombast, to any fantastic philosophical extravagance that may enter my head. Who knows? Some day I may give birth to a work that will be at least my own.

Suppose I do publish. Will I be able to stand up against the consequences? They have been the ruin of stronger men than I. Who can tell whether in four years I might not become an ignoble fool. Is Art really my only goal? I have thought so up until now; but if I need something in addition it is proof that I am deteriorating; and if this additional something gives me pleasure it is proof that I have deteriorated already. Were it not for the fear of speaking in pride, I should at once say "No! A thousand times no!" Like a snail afraid of touching something unclean or of being crushed underfoot, I retreat into my shell. I don't say that I am incapable of any kind of activity, but it must be of short duration and must give me pleasure. I jumped into the fray on two occasions, to help Achille and to help you, and both times I was successful. I have physical strength, but not patience, and patience is everything. Were I a strong man at a fair I could lift the weights, but not walk about brandishing them. Recklessness, adaptability, hypocrisy—

the necessary knowledge of how to get on in the world—all this is a closed book to me; and I would commit many blunders. The two changes you made in your story *Tagahor* . . . shocked me as being a humiliating concession. They angered me. I am not sure that I forgive you even now. You see what I am like.

The Muse reproaches me for being tied to my mother's apron strings. I followed these strings to London, earlier they had come to join me in Rome, and they will come with me to Paris. Ah, if you could rid me of my brother-in-law and my sister-in-law,[3] how little the apron strings would bother me! Yesterday I had a talk with my mother. She was like me; she had no opinion. Her final word was: "If you have written something you think good, publish it." A great help!

I assign you everything that precedes as a theme for meditation. Only, when you meditate, consider my whole self. Despite what I wrote in the *Education sentimentale*[4]—that even in the most intimate confidences there is something that remains unsaid—I have told you everything. In so far as a man can be honest with himself it seems to me that I am honest. I am showing you my very bowels. I am putting my trust in you, in your instinct, which I sense is sure, and in your intelligence, which is keen when it is not impeded by irrelevant considerations. I will do whatever you wish, whatever you tell me. I entrust you with my individuality, for I am weary of it. I had no idea, when I began my letter, that I was going to write all this. It came of itself, and I send it off. It may make things easier when we meet two weeks from now.

3 Emile Hamard was still a source of annoyance. Achille Flaubert's bourgeois wife was never popular with Gustave.

4 Primitive version.

To LOUISE COLET

[*Croisset, January 12 or 14, 1852*]

I am hideously worried, mortally depressed. My accursed Bovary is harrying me and driving me mad. Last Sunday Bouilhet criticized one of my characters and the outline. I can do nothing about it: there is some truth in what he says, but I feel that the opposite is true also. Ah, I am tired and discouraged! You[5] call me Master. What a wretched Master!

No—it is possible that the whole thing hasn't had enough spadework, for distinctions between thought and style are a sophism. Everything depends on the conception. So much the worse! I am going to continue, and as quickly as I can, in order to have a complete picture. There are moments when all this makes me wish I were dead. Ah! No one will be able to say that I haven't experienced the agonies of Art![6]

Friday night, [*Croisset, January 16, 1852*]

There are in me, literally speaking, two distinct persons: one who is infatuated with bombast, lyricism, eagle flights, sonorities of phrase and the high points of ideas; and another who digs and burrows into the truth as deeply as he can, who likes to treat a humble fact as respectfully as a big one, who would like to make you feel almost *physically* the things he reproduces; this latter person likes to laugh, and enjoys the animal sides of man. . . .

What seems beautiful to me, what I should like to write, is a book about nothing, a book dependent on nothing external, which would be held together by the strength of its style, just as the earth, suspended in the void, depends on nothing external for its support; a book which would have almost no subject, or

5 In this letter the *tu* form of address is resumed.

6 Such, at least, would seem to be the least inadequate translation of Flaubert's famous phrase, *"les affres de l'Art."*

at least in which the subject would be almost invisible, if such a thing is possible. The finest works are those that contain the least matter; the closer expression comes to thought, the closer language comes to coinciding and merging with it, the finer the result. I believe that the future of Art lies in this direction. I see it, as it has developed from its beginnings, growing progressively more ethereal, from the Egyptian pylons to Gothic lancets, from the 20,000-line Hindu poems to the effusions of Byron. Form, as it is mastered, becomes attenuated; it becomes dissociated from any liturgy, rule, yardstick; the epic is discarded in favor of the novel, verse in favor of prose; there is no longer any orthodoxy, and form is as free as the will of its creator. This emancipation from matter can be observed everywhere: governments have gone through similar evolution, from the oriental despotisms to the socialisms of the future.

It is for this reason that there are no noble subjects or ignoble subjects; from the standpoint of pure Art one might almost establish the axiom that there is no such thing as subject, style in itself being an absolute manner of seeing things.

[*Croisset,*] *Saturday night, February 1, 1852*

Bad week. Work didn't go; I had reached a point where I didn't know what to say. It was all shadings and refinements; I was completely in the dark: it is very difficult to clarify by means of words what is still obscure in your thoughts. I made outlines, spoiled a lot of paper, floundered and fumbled. Now I shall perhaps find my way again. Oh, what a rascally thing style is! I think you have no idea of what kind of a book I am writing. In my other books[7] I was slovenly; in this one I am trying to be impeccable, and to follow a geometrically straight line. No lyricism, no comments, the author's personality absent.

7 Flaubert refers particularly to the first *Education sentimentale* and the first *Tentation de Saint Antoine.*

It will make sad reading; there will be atrociously wretched and sordid things. Bouilhet, who arrived last Sunday at three just after I had written you, thinks the tone is right and hopes the book will be good. May God grant it! But it promises to take up an enormous amount of time. I shall certainly not be through by the beginning of next winter. I am doing no more than five or six pages a week.

[Croisset,] February 8, [1852]

So you are decidedly enthusiastic about *Saint Antoine!* Well, that makes one, at least! That's something. Though I don't accept everything you say about it, I think my friends refused to see what there was in it. Their judgment was superficial; I don't say unfair, but superficial. . . .

Now I am in an entirely different world, a world of attentive observations of the most humdrum details. I am delving into the damp and moldy corners of the soul. It is a far cry from the mythological and theological fireworks of *Saint Antoine*. And, just as the subject is different, so I am writing in an entirely different manner. Nowhere in my book must the author express his emotions or his opinions.

I think that it will be less lofty than *Saint Antoine* as regards ideas (a fact that I consider of little importance) , but perhaps it will be more intense and unusual, without being obviously so.

Wednesday, 1 A.M., [Croisset, March 3, 1852]

Thank you, thank you, my darling, for all the affection you send me. It makes me proud that you should feel happy about me; how I will embrace you next week!

I have just reread several children's books for my novel. I am half crazy tonight, after all the things I looked at today—from old keepsakes to tales of shipwrecks and buccaneers. I came upon old engravings that I had colored when I was seven or eight and that I hadn't seen since. There are rocks painted blue and trees painted green. At the sight of some of them (for instance a scene showing people stranded on ice floes) I re-experienced feelings of terror that I had as a child. I should like something that would put it out of my mind; I am almost afraid to go to bed. There is a story of Dutch sailors in ice-bound waters, with bears attacking them in their hut (this picture used to keep me awake), and one about Chinese pirates sacking a temple full of golden idols. My travels and my childhood memories color off from each other, fuse, whirl dazzlingly before my eyes, and rise up in a spiral. . . .

For two days now I have been trying to live the dreams of young girls, and for this purpose I have been navigating in milky oceans of books about castles and troubadours in white-plumed velvet caps. Remind me to speak to you about this. You can give me exact details that I need.

Saturday, 1 A.M., [*Croisset, March 20-21, 1852*]

The entire value of my book, if it has any, will consist of my having known how to walk straight ahead on a hair, balanced above the two abysses of lyricism and vulgarity (which I seek to fuse in analytical narrative). When I think of what it can be I am dazzled. But then, when I reflect that so much beauty has been entrusted to me, I am so terrified that I am seized with cramps and long to rush off and hide—anywhere. I have been working like a mule for fifteen long years. All my life I have lived with a maniacal stubbornness, keeping all my other passions locked up in cages and visiting them only now and then, for diversion. Oh, if ever I produce a good book I'll have worked for it! Would to God that Buffon's blasphemous words were true.[8] I should certainly be among the foremost.

8 *Le génie est une longue patience.*

To LOUISE COLET [*1852*]

Saturday, 12:30 A.M. [*Croisset, March 27, 1852*]

Tonight I finished scribbling the first draft of my young girl's dreams. I'll spend another fortnight sailing on these blue lakes, after which I'll go to a ball and then spend a rainy winter, which I'll end with a pregnancy. And about a third of my book will be done.

Saturday night, [*Croisset, April 24, 1852*]

If I haven't written sooner in reply to your sorrowful and discouraged-sounding letter, it is because I have been in a great fit of work. The day before yesterday I went to bed at five in the morning and yesterday at three. Since last Monday I have put everything else aside, and have done nothing all week but sweat over my *Bovary,* disgruntled at making such slow progress. I have now reached my ball, which I will begin Monday. I hope that may go better. Since you last saw me I have written 25 pages in all (25 pages in six weeks). They were tough. Tomorrow I shall read them to Bouilhet. As for myself, I have gone over them so much, recopied them, changed them, handled them, that for the time being I can't make head or tail of them. But I think they will stand up. You speak of your discouragements: if you could see mine! Sometimes I don't understand why my arms don't drop from my body with fatigue, why my brains don't melt away. I am leading a stern existence, stripped of all external pleasure, and am sustained only by a kind of permanent rage, which sometimes makes me weep tears of impotence but which never abates. I love my work with a love that is frenzied and perverted, as an ascetic loves the hair shirt that scratches his belly. Sometimes, when I am empty, when words don't come, when I find I haven't written a single sentence after scribbling whole pages, I collapse on my couch and lie there dazed, bogged in a swamp of despair, hating myself and blaming myself for this demented pride which makes me pant after a chimera. A quarter of an hour later everything changes; my heart is pounding with joy. Last Wednesday I had to get up and fetch my handkerchief; tears were streaming down my face. I had been moved by my own writing; the emotion I had conceived, the phrase that rendered it, and the satisfaction of having found the phrase—all were causing me to experience the most exquisite pleasure. At least I believe that all those elements were present in this emotion, which after all was predominantly a matter of nerves. There exist even higher emotions of this same kind: those which are devoid of the sensory element. These are superior, in moral beauty, to virtue—so independent are they of any personal factor, of any human implication. Occasionally (at great moments of illumination) I have had glimpses, in the glow of an enthusiasm that made me thrill from head to foot, of such a state of mind, superior to life itself, a state in which fame counts for nothing and even happiness is superfluous. If everything around us, instead of permanently conspiring to drown us in a slough of mud, contributed rather to keep our spirits healthy, who can tell whether we might not be able to do for aesthetics what stoicism did for morals? Greek art was not an art; it was the very constitution of an entire people, of an entire race, of the country itself. In Greece the profile of the mountains was different from elsewhere, and they were composed of marble, which was thus available to the sculptors, etc.

The time for Beauty is over. Mankind may return to it, but it has no use for it at present. The more Art develops, the more scientific it will be, just as science will become artistic. Separated in their early stages, the two will become one again when both reach their culmination. It is beyond the power of human thought today to foresee in what a dazzling intellectual light the works of the future will flower. Meanwhile we are in a shadowy corridor, groping in the dark. We are without a lever; the ground is slipping under our feet; we all lack a basis—literati and scribblers that we are. What's the good of all this? Is our chatter the answer to any need? Between the crowd and ourselves no bond exists. Alas for the crowd; alas for us, especially. But since there is a reason for everything, and since the fancy of one individual seems to me just as valid as the appetite of a million men and can occupy an equal place in the world, we must (regardless of material things and of mankind, which disavows us) live for our vocation, climb into our ivory tower, and dwell there along with our dreams. At times I have feelings of great despair and emptiness—doubts that taunt me at my moments of naïvest satisfaction. And yet I would not exchange all this for anything, because my conscience tells me that I am fulfilling my duty, obeying a decree of fate—that I am doing what is Good, that I am in the Right.

To MAXIME DU CAMP

Croisset, [June 19,] 1852

Dear Max

You seem to be suffering, where I am concerned, from a tic or a congenital malady. It does not bother me—have no fear of that—I have long since made up my mind on the matters you mention.

I shall tell you merely that all the words you use—"hurry," "this is the moment," "it is high time," "your place will be taken," "become established," "outside the law"—are for me a vocabulary devoid of sense. It is as though you were talking to an Algonquin. I don't understand.

"Get somewhere"—where? To the position of Murger, Feuillet, Monselet, Arsène Houssaye, Taxile Delord, Hippolyte Lucas, and six dozen others? Thank you.

"To be known" is not my chief concern—that can give complete gratification only to very mediocre vanities. Besides, is there ever any certainty about this? Even the most widespread fame leaves one longing for more, and seldom does anyone but a fool die sure of his own reputation. Fame, therefore, can no more serve us as a gauge of our own worth than obscurity.

I am aiming at something better—to please myself. Success seems to me a result, not a goal. Now it is this goal that I am trying to attain; and it seems to me that for a long time I have not strayed from the path to make love to the ladies or take a nap on the grass. If I must chase will-o'-the-wisps I may as well chase the most exalted.

May the United States perish, rather than a principle! May I die like a dog, rather than hasten the ripening of a sentence by a single second!

I have conceived a certain manner of writing and a certain beauty of language which I wish to achieve. When I think that I have gathered my fruit I shall not refuse to sell it, nor shall I forbid hand-clapping if it is good. In the meantime I do not wish to fleece the public. That's all there is to it.

If by the time it's done it's too late and nobody wants it, too bad. I assure you I wish I had more facility, much less labor, and greater profits. But I see no remedy for this.

It may well be that there are favorable opportunities from a commercial point of view, a good market for one kind of article or another, a passing public taste which raises the price of rubber or cotton. Let those who wish to manufacture these things hasten to set up their factories: I well understand that they should. But if your work of art is good, if it is authentic, it will be recognized and will find its place—in six months, six years, or after you're gone. What difference does it make? You tell me that it is only in Paris that one breathes the breath of life. In my opinion your Parisian "breath of life" often has the odor of rotting teeth. In that Parnassus one is visited more often by a miasma than by divine madness, and you'll agree that laurels gathered there are apt to be somewhat spattered with shit.

I am sorry to see a man like you go one better than the Marquise d'Escarbagnas in Molière, who thought that "outside of Paris there is no salvation for gentlemen." This judgment itself seems to me provincial, in other words, narrow. Humanity exists everywhere, my dear sir, though there is more nonsense in Paris than elsewhere.

And there is unquestionably one thing that one does acquire in Paris—and that is impertinence; but at the cost of a little virility.

Anyone who becomes a man of real consequence in the face of a Parisian upbringing must have been born a demi-god. To assert himself he has had to struggle without respite against the pressure of his milieu; whereas only someone born destitute of natural endowments can fail to develop something like originality if he lives alone and works hard and continuously.

As for deploring so bitterly my sodden way of life, it is as though you were to reproach a shoemaker for making shoes or a blacksmith for striking his iron or a painter for living in his studio. Since I work from one o'clock in the afternoon until one o'clock in the morning every day, except from six to eight in the evening, I scarcely see how I could make use of the remaining time. If I led a genuinely provincial or rural existence, devoting myself to dominoes or melon-raising, I could understand the reproach. But if I am becoming brutish you will have to lay the blame on Lucian, Shakespeare, and novel-writing.

I told you that I shall move to Paris when my book is done and that I shall publish it if I am satisfied with it. My resolution has not changed in the slightest. That is what I can say, and I can say nothing more.

And believe me, dear friend, don't excite yourself about trifles. As for the waxing and waning of literary quarrels I don't give a damn. As to whether or not Augier has a success I don't give a double damn; and as to whether Vacquerie and Ponsard inflate themselves and occupy the place that should be mine I don't give a triple damn, and I have no intention of troubling them to give it back to me.

Whereupon I embrace you.

To MAXIME DU CAMP

[*Croisset, June 25 or 26, 1852*]

Dear Max

I am sorry you should be so sensitive. Far from wanting to make my letter offensive, I tried to make it the opposite. To the extent that I could I kept within the limits of the subject, as they say in rhetoric. But why do you begin all over again? Are you always going to preach diet to a man who insists that he is in good health? I find your distress on my account comical, that's all. Do I reproach you for living in Paris, for having published, etc.? Even when you wanted, once, to move to a house in the country near mine, did I applaud this project? Have I ever advised you as to how to lead your life? . . . Each of us must live in the way that suits him. All plants don't require the same care. And besides, if destiny is not with us, you will strive in vain in Paris and I shall strive in vain here; if we haven't the vocation nothing will come of our efforts, and if on the contrary we have it why torment ourselves about the rest?

Everything that you can tell me, I assure you, I have already told myself—whether it be blame or praise, bad or good. Everything added by you will be merely a repetition of a mass of monologues that I know by heart. But there is one thing I must say. I deny absolutely the existence of the literary renascence which you announce. I see no new writers, no original books, no ideas that aren't outworn. Everyone is trailing at the backsides of the masters, as in the past. The same old humanitarian or aesthetic saws are repeated over and over again. I don't deny that the young men of today really want to create a school, but I challenge them to do it. I should be glad to find myself mistaken—I should profit from the discovery.

As for my "position," as you call it, of man of letters, I abandon it to you willingly. . . . I decline the honor of such a title and of such a mission. I am simply a bourgeois living quietly in the country, occupying myself with literature, and asking nothing of others, neither consideration nor honor nor even esteem. . . .

You and I are no longer following the same route, we are no longer sailing in the same skiff. May God lead each of us where he wishes to go! I am not seeking port, but the high seas. If I am shipwrecked, you have my permission not to mourn.

Yours,

To LOUISE COLET

Tuesday, [*Croisset, July 6, 1852*]

Musset has never separated poetry from the sensations of which it is the consummate expression. Music, according to him, was made for serenades, painting for portraits, and poetry for consoling the heart. But if you put the sun inside your trousers, all you do is burn your trousers and wet the sun. That is what has happened to him. Nerves, magnetism: for him poetry is those things. Actually, it is something less turbulent. If sensitive nerves were the only requirement of a poet, I should be superior to Shakespeare and to Homer, whom I picture as a not very nervous individual. Such confusion is blasphemy. I know whereof I speak: I used to be able to hear what people were saying in low voices behind closed doors thirty paces away; all my viscera could be seen quivering under my skin; and sometimes I experienced in the space of a single second a million thoughts, images, associations of all kinds which exploded in my mind like a grand display of fireworks. But all this, closely related though it is to the emotions, is mere parlor talk.

Poetry is by no means an infirmity of the mind; whereas these nervous susceptibilities are. Extreme sensitivity is a weakness. Let me explain:

If my mind had been stronger, I shouldn't have fallen ill as a result of studying law and being bored. I'd have turned those circumstances to good account instead of being worsted by them. My unhappiness, instead of confining itself to my brain, affected the rest of my body and threw me into convulsions. It was a "deviation." One often sees children whom music hurts physically: they have great talent, retain melodies after but one hearing, become over-excited when they play the piano; their hearts pound, they grow thin and pale and fall ill, and their poor nerves writhe in pain at the sound of notes—like dogs. These are never the future Mozarts. Their vocation has been misplaced: the idea has passed into the flesh, and there it remains sterile and causes the flesh to perish; neither genius nor health results.

It is the same with art. Passion does not make poetry, and the more personal you are, the weaker. I have always sinned in that direction myself, because I have always put myself into what I was doing. Instead of Saint Anthony, for example, *I* am in my book; and I, rather than the reader, underwent the temptation. *The less you feel a thing, the fitter you are to express it as it is* (as it *always* is, in itself, in its essence, freed of all ephemeral contingencies). But you must have the capacity to *make yourself feel it.* This capacity is what we call genius: the ability to *see,* to have your model constantly posing in front of you.

That is why I detest so-called poetic language. When there are no words, a glance is enough. Soulful effusions, lyricism, descriptions—I want all these embodied in Style. To put them elsewhere is to prostitute art and feeling itself.

Thursday, 4 A.M., [*Croisset, July 22, 1852*]

I am in the process of copying and correcting the entire first part of *Bovary*. My eyes are smarting. I should like to be able to read these 158 pages at a single glance and grasp them with all their details in a single thought. A week from Sunday I shall read the whole thing to Bouilhet, and a day or two later you will see me. What a bitch of a thing prose is! It is never finished; there is always something to be done over. Still, I think it is possible to give it the consistency of verse. A good prose sentence should be like a good line of poetry—*unchangeable,* just as rhythmic, just as sonorous. Such, at least, is my ambition (I am sure of one thing: no one has ever conceived a more perfect type of prose than I; but as to the execution, how weak, how weak, oh God!) . Nor does it seem to me impossible to give psychological analysis[9] the swiftness, clarity, and impetus of a strictly dramatic narrative. That has never been attempted, and it would be beautiful. Have I succeeded a little in this? I have no idea. At this moment I have no definite opinion about my work.

Monday, 1 A.M., [*Croisset, July 27, 1852*]

Yes, it is a strange thing, the relation between one's writing and one's personality. Is there anyone more in love with antiquity than I, anyone more haunted by it, anyone who has made a greater effort to understand it? And yet in my books I am as far from antiquity as possible. From my appearance one would think me a writer of epic, drama, brutally factual narrative; whereas actually I feel at home only in analysis—in

9 Flaubert's words are "*l'analyse psychologique.*"

anatomy, if I may call it such. By natural disposition I love what is vague and misty; and it is only patience and study that have rid me of all the white fat that clogged my muscles. The books I most long to write are precisely those for which I am least endowed. *Bovary,* in this sense, is an unprecedented tour de force (a fact of which I alone shall ever be aware) : its subject, characters, effects, etc.—all are alien to me. It should make it possible for me to take a great step forward later. Writing this book I am like a man playing the piano with leaden balls attached to his fingers. But once I have mastered my technique, and find a piece that's to my taste and that I can play at sight, the result will perhaps be good. In any case, I think I am doing the right thing. What one does is not for one's self, but for others. Art is not interested in the personality of the artist. So much the worse for him if he doesn't like red or green or yellow: all colors are beautiful, and his task is to use them. . . .

I have read the Gautier:[10] lamentable! Here and there a fine strophe, but not a single good poem. It is strained, contrived; he has pulled all the old strings. You feel that it's a mind that has taken aphrodisiacs. An inferior kind of erection—the man is weak. Ah, how old all these great men are! They drool: and for the state they're in they have only themselves to blame.

Saturday, 5 o'clock, [*Croisset, September 4, 1852*]

I am turning toward a kind of aesthetic mysticism (if those two words can be used together), and I wish it were stronger. When you are given no encouragement by others, when you are disgusted, frustrated, corrupted, and brutalized by the outside world, so-called decent and sensitive people are forced to seek somewhere within themselves a more suitable place to live. If society continues on its present path I think we shall see a return of such mystics as have existed in all the dark ages of the

10 Théophile Gautier's volume of poems, *Emaux et Camées.*

world. Unable to expand, the soul will withdraw into itself. The time is not far off when we shall see the return of universal yearnings, beliefs in the approaching end of the world and in the advent of a Messiah. But in the absence of any theological foundation, what will be the basis of this enthusiasm, which is ignorant of its own name? Some will seek it in the flesh, others in the ancient religions, still others in Art; and mankind, like the Jewish tribes in the desert, will adore all kinds of idols. People like us were born a little too soon; twenty-five years from now, the point of intersection of all these quests will provide superb subjects for a master. Then prose—prose especially, the youngest form—may serve to orchestrate a symphony with an extraordinarily rich human content. We may once again have books like the *Satyricon* and the *Golden Ass,* but bubbling over with intellect as those bubble over with sensuality.

This is the very thing that the socialists, with their incessant materialistic preaching, consistently refuse to see. They have denied the necessity of suffering; they have decried three-quarters of modern poetry, the blood of Christ that stirs within us. Nothing will extirpate suffering, nothing will eliminate it. Our purpose is not to dry it up, but to create outlets for it. If the sense of man's imperfection, of the meaninglessness of life, were to perish—as would follow from their premise—we should be stupider than the birds, who at least perch on trees. The human soul is at present sleeping, drunk with the words it has heard; but some day it will awake in a frenzy and give itself over to an orgy of Freedom; for there will no longer be anything to restrain it, neither government, nor religion, nor any formula. Republicans of every stripe seem to me the most primitive pedagogues in the world—they dream of organization, legislation, a society made in the image of a convent. I believe, on the contrary, that all rules are on their way out, that barriers are crumbling, that a general work of demolition is in progress.

This great confusion will perhaps bring freedom in its train. Art, which is always in the van, has certainly followed their course. What poetic standards are alive today? Plastic form is becoming increasingly impossible as our languages become increasingly limited and rigid and our ideas vague, confused, and elusive. All we can do, then, is to use our brains; we must tauten the strings of our battered instruments, and above all we must become virtuosos, since in the present age naïveté is a chimera. Moreover, the picturesque has almost disappeared. Even so poetry will not die; but what will be the poetry of the things of the future? I cannot conceive it. Who can tell? Beauty will perhaps become a feeling useless to mankind, and Art something halfway between algebra and music.

Sunday, 11 P.M., [*Croisset, September 19, 1852*]

What trouble my *Bovary* is giving me! Still, I am beginning to see my way a little. Never in my life have I written anything more difficult than what I am doing now—trivial dialogue. . . . I have to portray, simultaneously and in the same conversation, five or six characters who speak, several others who are spoken about, the scene, and the whole town, giving physical descriptions of people and objects; and in the midst of all that I have to show a man and a woman who are beginning (through a similarity in tastes) to fall in love with each other. If only I had space! But the whole thing has to be swift without being dry, and well worked out without taking up too much room; and many details which would be more striking here I have to keep in reserve for use elsewhere. I am going to put the whole thing down quickly, and then proceed by a series of increasingly drastic revisions; by going over and over it I can perhaps pull it together. The language itself is a great stumbling-block. My characters are completely commonplace, but they have to speak in a literary style, and politeness of language takes away so much picturesqueness from any speech!

Night of Friday-Saturday, 2 A.M.,
[*Croisset, October 1-2, 1852*]

The other day I learned that a young man I knew at school had been interned at Saint-Yon (the Rouen insane asylum). A year ago I read a book of stupid poems by him; but I was moved by the sincerity, enthusiasm, and faith expressed in the preface. I was told that like me he lived in the country, secluded and working as hard as he could. The bourgeois had the greatest contempt for him. He complained of being constantly slandered and insulted; he suffered the common ordeal of unrecognized geniuses. Eventually he lost his mind, and now he is raving and screaming and treated with cold baths. Who can assure me that I am not on the same path? What is the line of demarcation between inspiration and madness, between stupidity and ecstasy? To be an artist is it not necessary to *see everything* differently from other men? Art is no mere game of the intellect; it is a special atmosphere that we breathe. But if in search of more and more potent air we descend ever deeper into art's subterranean recesses, who knows that we may not end by breathing deadly miasmas? It would make a nice book—the story of a man whose mind is sound (quite possibly my young friend is sane) locked up as insane and treated by stupid doctors.

Monday night, [*Croisset, November 22, 1852*]

I am going to read *Uncle Tom* in English. I admit that I am prejudiced against it. Literary merit alone doesn't account for that kind of success. A writer can go far if he combines a certain talent for dramatization and a facility for speaking everybody's language, with the art of exploiting the passions of the day, the concerns of the moment. Do you know what books sell best year after year? *Faublas* and *l'Amour conjugal,*[11] two inept productions. If Tacitus were to return to earth he would sell less well than M. Thiers. The public respects monuments, but has little love for them. They are given conventional admiration and no more. The bourgeoisie (which today comprises all of mankind including the "people") has the same attitude toward the classics as toward religion: it knows that they exist, would be sorry if they didn't, realizes that they serve some vague purpose, but makes no use of them and finds them very boring.

I have had the *Chartreuse de Parme* brought to me from the lending-library and shall read it carefully. I know *Le Rouge et le noir,* which I find badly written and incomprehensible as regards characters and intentions. I am quite aware that people of taste are not of my opinion; but people of taste are a queer caste: they have little saints of their own whom nobody knows. It was our friend Sainte-Beuve who launched this fashion. People swoon with admiration before parlor wits, before talents whose only recommendation is that they are obscure. As for Beyle, after reading *Le Rouge et le noir* I fail completely to understand Balzac's enthusiasm for such a writer. Speaking of reading, I read Rabelais and *Don Quixote* every Sunday with Bouilhet and never tire of them. What overwhelming books! The more one contemplates them the bigger they grow, like the pyramids, and in the end they almost frighten you. What is stupendous about *Don Quixote* is the absence of art, and that perpetual fusion of illusion and reality which makes the book so comic and so poetic. What dwarfs all others are beside it! How small one feels, oh Lord, how small one feels!

I am working quite well, I mean quite heartily; but it is difficult to give adequate expression to something one has never

[11] *Tableau de l'amour conjugal* by Dr. Nicolas Venette (1686) and *Amours du Chevalier Faublas* by J. B. Louvet de Couvray (one of the three parts of his novel *Les Aventures du Chevalier Faublas,* 1787-89).

felt: one has to expend much care and rack one's brains devilishly in order not to go too far and yet go far enough. The psychological development of my characters is giving me a lot of trouble; and everything, in this novel, depends on it: for in my opinion ideas can be as entertaining as actions, but in order to be so they must flow one from the other like a series of cascades, carrying the reader along midst the throbbing of sentences and the seething of metaphors.

[*Croisset,*] *Saturday, 1 o'clock, December 11, 1852*

I begin by devouring you with kisses, for I am transported with joy. Your letter of this morning has lifted a terrible weight from my heart. It was time, too: yesterday I was unable to work all day; every time I moved (literally) my brain throbbed and pounded in my skull, and by eleven o'clock I had to go to bed. I had fever and felt prostrated. For three weeks I have been suffering horribly from worry, and have not stopped thinking of you for a second—but in a way that has been scarcely agreeable. . . . I should need a whole book to develop my feelings in a comprehensible manner. The idea of causing the birth of someone horrifies me. I should curse myself were I to become a father. I, have a son! Oh, no! No! No! I desire my flesh to perish, and have no wish to transmit to anyone the troubles and ignominies of existence. . . .

I also had a superstitious thought. Tomorrow I shall be thirty-one. I have just passed that fatal thirtieth year, the year that ranks a man. It is the age when a man takes his future shape, settles down, marries, chooses a trade. There are few people who do not become bourgeois at thirty. Paternity would have confined me within those ordinary ways of living. . . .

Why did you desire this bond between us? . . .

I breathe again! The day is fine, the sun is shining on the river, at this moment a brig is passing with all sails unfurled;

my window is open, my fire blazing. Adieu! I love you more than ever, and I kiss you to suffocation in honor of my birthday.

Saturday night, 3 o'clock, [*Croisset, January 15, 1853*]

The beginning of the week was frightful, but things have been going better since Thursday. I still have six to eight pages to do before reaching a break, and then I'll come to see you. I think that will be in a fortnight. Bouilhet will probably come with me. His reason for not writing you more often is that he has nothing to report or has no time. Do you realize that the poor devil has to give eight hours of lessons a day? . . .

Last week I spent *five days writing one page,* and I dropped everything else for it—my Greek, my English; I gave myself up to it entirely. What worries me in my book is the element of *entertainment.* That side is weak; there is not enough action. I maintain, however, that *ideas* are action. It is more difficult to hold the reader's interest with them, I know, but this is a problem for style to solve. I now have fifty pages in a row without a single event. It is an uninterrupted portrayal of a bourgeois existence and of a love that remains inactive—a love all the more difficult to depict because it is timid and deep, but alas! lacking in inner turbulence, because my gentleman has a sober nature. I had something similar in the first part: the husband loves his wife in somewhat the same fashion as her lover. Here are two mediocrities in the same milieu, and I must differentiate between them. If I bring it off it will be a great achievement, I think, for it will be like painting in monotone without contrasts—not easy. But I fear that all these subtleties will be wearisome, and that the reader will long for more movement. But one must be loyal to one's conception. If I tried to insert action I should be following a rule and would spoil everything. One must sing with one's own voice: and mine will never be dramatic or attractive. Besides, I am convinced that everything is a question of style, or rather of form, of presentation.

A bit of news: our young friend Du Camp has been promoted to *officier* in the Légion d'Honneur! How pleased he must be! When he compares himself with me and surveys the distance he has traveled since we separated, he must certainly think that he has left me far behind and done well for himself (in a worldly sense). You'll see, he'll end by getting himself a good post and turning his back on literature. He makes no distinctions: women, decorations, art, fashion—for him all these things are on the same level, and whatever advances his career is important. These are fine times we are living in (curious symbolisms, as old Michelet would say)—we decorate photographers and exile poets;[12] how many good pictures do you suppose a painter would have to produce to be made an *officier?* Of all the writers in the Légion d'Honneur only one has the rank of *commandeur,* and that is Monsieur Scribe! How immensely ironic it all is! And what a shower of honors descends on those who are without honor!

Sunday night, half-past one, [*Croisset, February 27-28, 1853*]

You should write more coldly. We must be on our guard against that kind of over-heating called inspiration, which often consists more largely of nervous emotion than of muscular strength. At this very moment, for example, I am keyed up to a high pitch—my brow is burning, sentences keep rushing into my head; for the past two hours I have been wanting to write to you and haven't been able to wrench myself away from work for an instant. Instead of one idea I have six, and where the most simple type of exposition is called for I find myself writing similes and metaphors. I could keep going until tomorrow noon without fatigue. But I know these masked balls of the imagina-

12 Victor Hugo was living in exile on the island of Jersey.

tion! You emerge from them in a state of exhaustion and despair, having seen only falsity and uttered nothing but nonsense. Everything should be done coldly, with poise.

Sunday, 4 o'clock, Easter Day
[*Croisset, March 27, 1853*]

As for me, the more I realize the difficulties of writing, the more daring I become; this is what keeps me from pedantry, into which I should otherwise doubtless fall. I have plans for writing that will keep me busy till the end of my life, and though I sometimes have moments of bitterness that make me almost scream with rage (so acutely do I feel my own impotence and weakness) I have others when I can scarcely contain myself for joy. Something deep and extra-voluptuous gushes out of me, like an ejaculation of the soul. I feel transported, drunk with my own thought, as though a hot gust of perfume were being wafted to me through some inner conduit. I shall never go very far; I know my limitations. But the goal I have set for myself will be achieved by others: thanks to me someone more talented, more instinctive, will be set on the right path. It is perhaps absurd to want to give prose the rhythm of verse (keeping it distinctly prose, however) and to write of ordinary life as one writes history or epic (but without falsifying the subject). I often wonder about this. But on the other hand it is perhaps a great experiment, and very original too. I know where I fail. (Ah, if only I were fifteen!) No matter: I shall always be given some credit for my stubbornness. And then, who can tell? Some day I may find a good motif, an air completely suited to my voice, neither too high nor too low. In any case I shall have lived nobly and often delightfully.

There is a saying by La Bruyère that serves me as a guide:

"A good author likes to think that he writes sensibly."[13] That is what I ask—to write sensibly; and it is asking a good deal. Still, one thing is depressing, and that is to see how easily the great men achieve their effects by means extraneous to Art. What is more badly put together than much of Rabelais, Cervantes, Molière, and Hugo? But such quick punches! Such power in a single word! We have to pile up a lot of little pebbles to build our pyramids; theirs, a hundred times greater, are made with a single block. But to seek to imitate the method of those geniuses would be fatal. They are great for the very reason that they have no method.

Thursday, half-past four, [*Croisset, March 31, 1853*]

Nothing great is ever done without fanaticism. Fanaticism is religion: and the eighteenth-century *philosophes* who decried the former actually overthrew the latter. Fanaticism is faith, the essence of faith, burning faith, active faith, the faith that works miracles. Religion is a relative conception, a thing invented by man—an idea, in sum; the other is a feeling. What has changed on earth is the dogmas, the *stories* of Vishnu, Ormuzd, Jupiter, Jesus Christ. But what has never changed is the amulets, the sacred springs, the votive offerings, etc., the brahmins, the santons, the hermits—in a word the belief in something superior to life and the need to put one's self under the protection of this force.

In Art too the creative impulse is essentially fanatical. Poetry is only a way of perceiving external objects, a special sense through which matter is strained and transfigured without being changed. Now, if you see the world solely through this lens, the color of the world will be the color of the lens and the words you use to express your feeling will thus be inevitably related to the

[13] La Bruyère's words: "*Un esprit médiocre croit écrire divinement, un bon esprit croit écrire raisonnablement.*" (*Les Caractères. Des Ouvrages de l'esprit,* 18.)

facts that produce it. To be well done, a thing must accord with your constitution. A botanist's hands, eyes, and head must not be like those of an astronomer; and he must see the stars only in reference to plants. From this combination of innateness and education result sureness of touch, individual manner, taste, spontaneity—in short, illumination. How often have I heard people tell my father that he diagnosed illnesses without knowing how or why! The same feeling that made him instinctively decide on the remedy must enable us to hit on the right word. One doesn't achieve this unless one has—first—been born to one's calling, and—second—practised it long and stubbornly.

We marvel at the men of the age of Louis XIV, and yet they were not men of great genius. Reading them we experience none of that awe which makes us feel that Homer, Rabelais, and above all Shakespeare are more than human; certainly not. But what conscientious workmen! How they strained to find the exact expression for their thought! Such labor! Such tireless revision! How they asked each other's advice! How well they knew Latin! How slowly they read! That is why we have their thought in its entirety; that is why their form is whole, crammed full of substance to the bursting-point. In this domain there are no degrees: one work well done is equal in value to any other. La Fontaine will live as long as Dante, and Boileau as long as Bossuet or even Hugo.

Wednesday night, midnight, [*Croisset, April 6, 1853*]

What is making me go so slowly is that nothing in this book is derived from myself; never has my personality been of less use to me. Later I may be able to produce things that are better (I certainly hope so) ; it is difficult for me to imagine that I will ever write anything more carefully calculated. Everything is deliberate. If it's a failure, it will at least have been good practice. What is natural for me is unnatural for others—I am at home in the realm of the extraordinary and the fantastic, in flights of metaphysics and mythology. *Saint Antoine* didn't demand a quarter of the mental tension that *Bovary* is causing me. It was an outlet for my feelings; I had only pleasure in writing it, and the eighteen months spent writing its five hundred pages were the most deeply voluptuous of my entire life. Think of me now: having constantly to be in the skins of people for whom I feel aversion. For six months I have been a platonic lover, and at this very moment the sound of church bells is causing me Catholic raptures and I feel like going to confession!

Tuesday night, an hour after midnight,
[*Croisset, April 26-27, 1853*]

In our day I believe that a thinker (and what is an artist if not a triple thinker?) should have neither religion, country, nor even any social conviction. Absolute doubt now seems to me so completely substantiated that it would be almost silly to seek to formulate it. Bouilhet told me the other day that he felt the need to proclaim himself publicly, in writing, setting down all his reasons, an apostate Christian and an apostate Frenchman, and then to leave Europe and if possible never hear of it again. Yes, it would be a relief to vomit out all the immense contempt that fills the heart to overflowing. What good cause is there these days to arouse one's interest, let alone one's enthusiasm?

Wednesday, midnight, [*Croisset, June 1, 1853*]

There are certain things that tell me immediately with what manner of man I have to deal: (1) admiration for Béranger; (2) dislike of perfumes; (3) liking for thick cloth; (4) a fringe beard; (5) aversion to brothels. How many worthy young men I have known who had a pious horror of "houses" and yet picked up the most beautiful cases of clap you can imagine from their so-called mistresses. The Latin Quarter is full of this doctrine and such happenings. It is perhaps a perverse taste, but I like prostitution—and for its own sake, quite apart from what lies underneath. My heart has never failed to miss a beat at the sight of one of those provocatively dressed women walking in the rain under the gas lamps, just as the sight of monks in their robes and knotted girdles touches some ascetic, hidden corner of my soul. Prostitution is a meeting-point of so many elements—lechery, frustration, negation of human relationship, physical frenzy, the clink of gold—that a glance into its depths makes one giddy and teaches one all manner of things. It fills you with such sadness! And makes you dream so of love! Ah, elegy-makers, it is not on ruins that you should lean, but on the breasts of these light women.

Yes, that man has missed something who has never awakened in an anonymous bed beside a face he will never see again, and who has never left a brothel at sunrise feeling like throwing himself into the river out of pure disgust for life. And just their shameless way of dressing—the temptation of the chimera—the aura of the unknown, of the *maudit*—the old poetry of corruption and venality! During my first years in Paris, I used to sit in front of Tortoni's on hot summer evenings and watch the streetwalkers stroll by in the last rays of the sun. At such moments I overflowed with biblical poetry. I thought of Isaiah, of "fornication in high places," and I walked back along the rue de la Harpe saying to myself: "And her mouth is smoother than oil."[14] I swear that I was never more chaste. My only complaint about prostitution is that it no longer exists. The kept woman has invaded the field of debauchery, just as the journalist has invaded poetry; everything is becoming mongrelized. There are no more courtesans, just as there are no more saints; there are only varieties of semi-prostitutes, each more sordid than the last.

14 Flaubert is probably thinking of Jeremiah 3:6 or 13:27, and of Proverbs 5:3.

To VICTOR HUGO

Croisset, June 2, 1853

I think, Monsieur, that I should inform you that your communication dated April 27 arrived here badly damaged. The outer envelope was torn in several places and bits of your handwriting exposed. The inner envelope (addressed to Madame C.) [15] had been torn along the end, and its contents were visible —two other letters and a printed sheet. Was it the customs who opened the envelope, hoping to find a bit of lace? It would be naïve, I think, to suppose that: the indiscretion must be laid at the door of the saviors of society. If you have something of importance to transmit to me, Monsieur, I believe that the following procedure would be the most sure: you could address your letters from Jersey to a family of honest merchants, whom I know in London; they would open the outer envelope and enclose the inner in one which would thus bear their English handwriting and a London postmark. I should then forward enclosures to Madame C. Your later envelope, dated May, has arrived intact.

I beg of you, Monsieur, to allow me to thank you for all the thanks you have sent me, and to accept none of them. The man who has occupied the greatest and best place in my restricted life may indeed expect some service of me, if what I have done you choose to call service. The shyness which one feels in declaring a genuine passion will not allow me, despite your exile, to tell you at length of the bond that links me to you. In brief, it is my gratitude for all the enthusiasm you have afforded me. But I do not wish to become entangled in phrases which would serve me but badly in attempts to enlarge upon it.

I have seen you in person; we have met several times—you unaware of me, I gazing eagerly at you. It was in the winter of

[15] With Louise Colet, Flaubert was helping the exiled Hugo correspond surreptitiously with friends in France.

1844, in the studio of poor Pradier. There were five or six of us; we drank tea and played a game; I even remember your big gold ring, with its etching of a rampant lion, which we used as a forfeit. Since then you have played for higher stakes, and in more fearsome games; but in whatever you do, the rampant lion plays its part. *He* bears on his brow the mark of its claws, and when he passes into history, the centuries will know him by that red scar.

As for you, who knows? Future makers of aesthetic will perhaps thank Providence for this monstrousness, for this consecration. For is it not by martyrdom that virtue is brought to perfection? Is it not by outrage that grandeur is rendered yet more grand? And in you there is lacking neither inherent grandeur nor that conferred by circumstances.

I send you, Monsieur, together with all my admiration for your genius, the assurance of my entire devotion to you.

To LOUISE COLET

Saturday night, 1 A.M., [*Croisset, June 25-26, 1853*]

At last I have finished the first section of my second part. I have now reached the point I should have reached before our last meeting at Mantes—you see how far behind I am. I shall spend another week reading it over and copying it, and a week from tomorrow shall spew it all out to Bouilhet. If it is all right it will be a great worry off my mind and a considerable accomplishment, I assure you, for I had very little to go on. But I think that this book will have a great defect: namely, a want of proportion between its various parts. I have so far 260 pages containing only preparations for action—more or less disguised expositions of character (some of them, it is true, more developed than others), of landscapes and of places. My conclusion, which will be the account of my little lady's death and funeral and of her husband's grief, will be sixty pages long at least. That leaves, for the body of the action itself, 120 to 160 pages at the most. Isn't this a real defect? What reassures me (though not completely) is that the book is a biography rather than a fully developed story. It is not essentially dramatic; and if the dramatic element is well submerged in the general tone of the book the lack of proportion in the development of the various parts may pass unnoticed. But then isn't life a little like this? An act of coition lasts a minute, and it has been anticipated for months on end. Our passions are like volcanoes; they are continually rumbling, but they erupt only from time to time.

Tuesday, 1 A.M., [*Croisset, June 28-29, 1853*]

I find Musset's remarks on *Hamlet* utterly bourgeois, and this is why. He criticizes as an inconsistency the fact that Hamlet is skeptical even after seeing his father's soul with his own eyes. But in the first place it was not the soul that he saw. He saw a ghost, a shade, a *thing,* a material living thing, which was in no way popularly or poetically related, at that period, to the abstract idea of the soul. It is we, metaphysicians and moderns that we are, who use such language as that. And Hamlet does not *doubt* at all in the philosophical sense; rather, he wonders. I think that Musset's observation is not original with him; that he took it from Mallefille's preface to his *Don Juan.* In my opinion it is superficial. A peasant of our own day can perfectly well see a ghost, and next morning in the crude light of day he will not ponder on the flesh and the soul, though he may think generally about life and death. Hamlet thinks in terms not of scholastic concepts, but of human attitudes. His perpetual state of fluctuation, his constant uncertainty, his irresolution and his inability to solve his problems—these, far from being inconsistent, are what make the play sublime. But our clever friends want characters to be all of a piece, consistent—as they are in books only.

The truth is that Shakespeare's conception of Hamlet reaches into the remotest corners of the human soul. Ulysses is perhaps the greatest type in all ancient literature, and Hamlet in all modern.

If I weren't so weary, I should develop my idea at greater length. It is so easy to chatter about the Beautiful. But it takes more genius to say, in proper style: "close the door," or "he wanted to sleep," than to give all the literature courses in the world.

Criticism occupies the lowest place in the literary hierarchy: as regards form, almost always; and as regards moral value, incontestably. It comes after rhyming-games and acrostics, which at least require a certain inventiveness.

To VICTOR HUGO

Croisset, July 15, [*1853*]

How am I to thank you, Monsieur, for your magnificent gift?[16] What am I to say—unless perhaps I echo the dying Talleyrand when visited by Louis Philippe: "This is the greatest honor ever conferred upon my house!"? There that parallel ends, for all kinds of reasons, but I shall not hide from you that you have profoundly "touched the proud weakness of my heart," as Racine would have said. Noble poet! How many monsters he would find now to depict, all of them a hundred times worse than his dragon-bull!

Exile, at least, spares you that sight. Ah, if you knew into what filth we are plunged! Private infamies proceed from political turpitude, and it is impossible to take a step without treading on something unclean. The atmosphere is heavy with nauseous vapors. Air! Air! I open my window and turn toward you. I hear the powerfully beating wings of your muse as she passes by,

16 Hugo had sent Flaubert a photograph of himself.

and I breathe, as the perfume of forests, the incense that rises from the depths of your style.

All my life, Monsieur, you have been for me a charming obsession, a long love that has never weakened. I have read you during sinister wakes and on beaches beside the sea in the summer sun. I carried you with me to Palestine, and it was you who consoled me, ten years ago, when I was dying of ennui in the Latin Quarter. Your poetry became a part of me, like my nurse's milk. Some of your poems will remain in my memory for ever, for they have been the great adventures of my life.

Here I shall stop. If sincerity exists, it is in what I have just written. From now on, I shall molest you no longer, and you may make use of the correspondent without fear of his correspondence. But since you stretch out your hand across the ocean, I take it and grasp it. I grasp it proudly, the hand that wrote *Notre-Dame* and *Napoléon le Petit,* the hand that has hewn colossi and fashioned poison cups for traitors, that has culled the most glorious delights from the loftiest reaches of the intellect, and that now, like the hand of Samson, alone remains raised amid the double ruins of Art and Liberty!

I am, Monsieur, yours, with once again a thousand thanks.

To LOUISE COLET

Friday night, 1 A.M., [*Croisset, July 15, 1853*]

What artists we should be if we had never read, seen, or loved anything that was not beautiful; if from the outset some guardian angel of the purity of our pens had kept us from all contamination; if we had never known fools or read newspapers! The Greeks were like that. . . . But classic form is insufficient for our needs, and our voices are not made to sing such simple tunes. Let us be as dedicated to art as they were, if we can, but differently. The human mind has broadened since Homer. Sancho Panza's belly has burst the seams of Venus' girdle. Rather than persist in copying old modes we should exert ourselves to invent new ones. I think Leconte de Lisle is unaware of all this. He has no instinct for modern life; he lacks heart. By this I do not mean personal or even humanitarian feelings, no—but *heart,* almost in the medical sense of the word. His ink is pale; his muse suffers from lack of fresh air. Thoroughbred horses and thoroughbred styles have plenty of blood in their veins, and it can be seen pulsing everywhere beneath the skin and the words. Life! Life! . . . That is the only thing that counts! That is why I love lyricism so much. It seems to me the most natural form of poetry—poetry in all its nakedness and freedom. All the power of a work of art lies in this mystery, and it is this primordial quality, this *motus animi continuus* (vibration, continual movement of the mind—Cicero's definition of eloquence), which gives conciseness, distinctness, form, energy, rhythm, diversity. It doesn't require much brains to be a critic: you can judge the excellence of a book by the strength of its punches and the time it takes you to recover from them. And then the excesses of the great masters! They pursue an idea to its furthermost limits. In Molière's *Monsieur de Pourceaugnac* there is a question of giving a man an enema, and a whole troop of actors carrying syringes pour down the aisles of the theatre. Michelangelo's figures have cables rather than muscles; in Rubens' bacchanalian scenes men piss on the ground; and think of everything in Shakespeare, etc., etc., and the most recent representative of the family, old Hugo. What a beautiful thing *Notre-Dame* is! I lately reread three chapters in it, including the sack of the church by the vagabonds. That's the sort of thing that's strong! I think that the greatest characteristic of genius is, above all, *energy*. Hence, what I detest most of all in the arts, what sets me on edge, is the *ingenious,* the clever. This is not at all the same as bad taste, which is a good quality gone wrong. In order to have what is called bad taste, you must have a sense for poetry; whereas cleverness, on the contrary, is incompatible with genuine poetry. Who was cleverer than Voltaire, and who less a poet? In our darling France, the public will accept poetry only if it is disguised. If it is given to them raw they protest. They have to be treated like the horses of Abbas-Pasha, who are fed a tonic of meat balls covered with flour. That's what Art is: knowing how to make the covering! But have no fear: if you offer this kind of flour to lions, they will recognize the smell twenty paces away and spring at it.

I have written a monumental letter to the Grand Crocodile.[17] I won't pretend that it hasn't given me a good deal of trouble (I think it a little grandiloquent, too grandiloquent, perhaps)— so much in fact that I now know it by heart. If I still remember it when we meet, I will repeat it to you. The parcel leaves tomorrow.

I have been in excellent form this week. I have written eight pages, all of which I think can stand pretty much as they are. Tonight I have just outlined the entire big scene of the Agricultural Show. It will be colossal—thirty pages at least. Against the background of this rustico-municipal celebration, with all its details (all my secondary characters will be shown in action), there will be continuous dialogue between a gentleman and the lady he is doing his best to seduce. Moreover, somewhere in the middle I have a solemn speech by a counselor of the prefecture, and at the end (this I have already finished) a newspaper article written by my pharmacist, who gives an account of the celebration in fine philosophical, poetical, progressive style. You see it is no small chore. I am sure of my local color and of many of my effects; but it's a hideous job to keep it from getting too long— especially since this sort of thing shouldn't be skimpy. Once this is behind me I shall soon reach my scene of the lovers in the

[17] Victor Hugo.

autumn woods, with their horses cropping the leaves beside them; and then I think I'll have clear sailing—I'll have passed Charybdis, at least, even though Scylla still remains to be negotiated.

Sunday, 4 o'clock, [*Trouville, August 14, 1853*]

I spent an hour yesterday watching the ladies bathe. What a sight! What a hideous sight! The two sexes used to bathe together here. But now they are kept separate by means of signposts, preventive nets, and a uniformed inspector—nothing more depressingly grotesque can be imagined. However, yesterday, from the place where I was standing in the sun, with my spectacles on my nose, I could contemplate the bathing beauties at my leisure. The human race must indeed have become absolutely moronic to have lost its sense of elegance to this degree. Nothing is more pitiful than these bags in which women encase their bodies, and these oilcloth caps! What faces! What figures! And what feet! Red, scrawny, covered with corns and bunions, deformed by shoes, long as shuttles or wide as washerwomen's paddles. And in the midst of everything, scrofulous brats screaming and crying. Further off, grandmas knitting and respectable old gentlemen with gold-rimmed spectacles reading newspapers, looking up from time to time between lines to savor the vastness of the horizon with an air of approval. The whole thing made me long all afternoon to escape from Europe and go live in the Sandwich Islands or the forests of Brazil. There, at least, the beaches are not polluted by such ugly feet, by such foul-looking specimens of humanity.

The day before yesterday, in the woods of Touques, in a charming spot beside a spring, I found old cigar butts and scraps of paté. People had been picnicking. I described such a scene in *Novembre,* eleven years ago; it was entirely imagined, and the other day it came true. Everything one invents is true, you may be sure. Poetry is as precise as geometry. Induction is as accurate as deduction; and besides, after reaching a certain point one no longer makes any mistake about the things of the soul. My poor Bovary, without a doubt, is suffering and weeping at this very instant in twenty villages of France.

Sunday, 11 o'clock
[*Trouville, August 21-22, 1853*]

Yes, I maintain (and in my opinion this should be a rule of conduct for an artist) that one's existence should be in two parts: one should live like a bourgeois and think like a demigod. Physical and intellectual gratifications have nothing in common. If they happen to coincide, hold fast to them. But do not *try* to combine them: that would be factitious. And this idea of "happiness," incidentally, is the almost exclusive cause of all human misfortunes. We must store up our hearts' marrow and give of it only in small doses; and the innermost sap of our passions we must preserve in precious flasks. These essences of ourselves must be reserved as sublime nourishment for posterity. Who can tell how much is wasted every day in emotional outpourings?

We marvel at the mystics, but what I have just said explains their secret. Their love, like mountain streams, ran in a single bed—narrow, deep, and steep; that is why it carried everything before it.

If you seek happiness and beauty simultaneously, you will attain neither one nor the other, for the price of beauty is self-denial. Art, like the Jewish God, wallows in sacrifices. So tear yourself to pieces, mortify your flesh, roll in ashes, smear yourself with filth and spittle, wrench out your heart! You will be alone, your feet will bleed, an infernal disgust will be with you throughout your pilgrimage, what gives joy to others will give none to you, what to them are but pinpricks will cut you to the quick, and you will be lost in the hurricane with only beauty's faint glow visible on the horizon. But it will grow, grow like the sun, its golden rays will bathe your face, penetrate into you, you will be illumined within, ethereal, all spiritualized, and after each bleeding the flesh will be less burdensome. Let us therefore seek only tranquillity; let us ask of life only an armchair, not a throne; only water to quench our thirst, not drunkenness. Passion is not compatible with the long patience that is a requisite of our calling. Art is vast enough to take complete possession of a man. To divert anything from it is almost a crime; it is a sin against the Idea, a dereliction of duty. But we are weak, the flesh is soft, and the heart, like a branch heavy with rain, trembles at the slightest tremor of the earth. We pant for air like a prisoner, an infinite weakness comes over us, we feel that we are dying. Wisdom consists in jettisoning the smallest possible part of the cargo, that the vessel may keep safely afloat. . . .

You have been reproaching me, these last days, with my "Trouville ghosts";[18] but since coming here I have written you frequently, and my longest interval between letters has been six days (ordinarily I write you only once a week) . Have you really not noticed, then, that here of all places, in this private, personal solitude that surrounds me, I have turned to you? All the memories of my youth speak to me as I walk, just as the sea shells crunch under my feet on the beach. The crash of every wave awakens far-distant reverberations within me. I hear the rumble of bygone days, and in my mind the whole endless series of old passions surges forward like the billows. I remember my spasms, my sorrows, gusts of desire that whistled like wind in the rigging, and vast vague longings that swirled in the dark like a flock of wild gulls in a storm cloud. On whom should I lean, if not on you? My weary mind turns for refreshment to the

18 Once again the reference is chiefly to his youthful passion for Madame Schlesinger.

thought of you as a dusty traveler might sink onto a soft and grassy bank.

Friday night, 11 o'clock, [*Trouville, August 26, 1853*]

Try to write me a letter that will be waiting for me when I return to Croisset on Saturday, or rather Sunday morning. That will insure me a good home-coming. What a dose of work I'm going to give myself when I get back! This vacation hasn't been a waste of time; I feel refreshed. During the past two years I have scarcely given myself a breath of air: I needed one. I have drawn fresh strength from the sight of the sea, the meadows and the trees. We writers, always absorbed in Art, communicate with nature only by means of our imaginations. But sometimes it is good to look the moon or the sun in the face. As we stare stupidly at the trees, their sap flows into our hearts. Just as the tastiest mutton comes from sheep that graze on thyme, our minds become pungent from feasting on nature's riches. . . .

While I have been here I have taken stock of myself, and this is the conclusion I have come to at the end of these four idle weeks: adieu, adieu for ever to everything personal, intimate, relative! I have abandoned any idea of ever writing my memoirs. Nothing pertaining to myself interests me. Youthful attachments, beautiful though they may be in the perspective of memory, no longer seem attractive to me as subjects, even when I think of how they might lend themselves to stylistic treatment. Let all those things die, and may they never revive. What would be the good? A man is no more than a flea. Our joys, like our sorrows, must be sublimated in our works. The clouds are not recognizable as dewdrops drawn up by the sun. Evaporate, then, O earthly rain, tears of bygone days, and in the heavens form yourselves into gigantic scrolls all glowing with light! . . .

What seems to me the highest and the most difficult achievement of Art is not to make us laugh or cry, or to rouse our lust or our anger, but to do as nature does—that is, fill us with wonderment. The most beautiful works have indeed this quality. They are serene in aspect, incomprehensible. The means by which they act on us are various: they are as unmoving as cliffs, stormy as the ocean, leafy, green, and murmuring as forests, sad as the desert, blue as the sky. Homer, Rabelais, Michelangelo, Shakespeare, and Goethe seem to me *pitiless.* They are bottomless, infinite, multiple. Through small openings we glimpse abysses whose dark depths make us giddy. And yet over the whole there hovers an extraordinary gentleness. It is like the brilliance of light, the smile of the sun, and it is calm, calm, and strong. . . .

How insignificant a creation, for example, is Figaro, as against Sancho! How one pictures Sancho on his donkey, eating raw onions, urging the steed on, all the while talking with his master. How vividly we see the roads of Spain, though nowhere are they described. But Figaro—where is he? At the Comédie Française. Parlor literature.

Wednesday, 12:30 A.M., [*Croisset, September, 1853*]

So our friend Leconte de Lisle is dreaming of going to India and staying there the rest of his days. It's a lovely dream. But it's no more than that. He is like the rest of us—we are all so wretchedly constituted that once there we languish and long to come home. We miss everything French—the look of French houses, even Frenchmen we care nothing about. No! For us the only way is to shut ourselves up and keep our noses to our work, like moles. Unless things change during the next few years free minds will form a brotherhood more exclusive than any secret society. Withdrawn from the crowd, a new mysticism will develop. Great ideas grow in the shade and on the edge of precipices, like firs.

One truth, however, seems to me to have emerged from all

this: the populace, numbers, majorities, approval, official recognition—these do not matter. Seventeen eighty-nine demolished royalty and nobility, 1848 the bourgeoisie, and 1851 the "people." Nothing is left except the vulgar and stupid mob. All of us are equally mired in mediocrity. Social equality has spread to the mind. Our books, our Art, our science, are designed for everybody, like railroads and public shelters. Mankind is frenziedly seeking moral abasement, and I resent being a part of it.

I worked well today. In a week I shall be in the midst of my agricultural show, which I am now beginning to see clearly. I have a jumble of lowing cattle and chattering people, and above it all the dialogue of my two lovers—it will be good, I think. . . .

Here is winter arriving; the leaves are turning yellow, and already many have fallen. I have a fire now and work with my lamp lit and curtains drawn, as in December. Why do I like the first days of autumn more than those of spring? Certainly I have passed beyond my love for the pallid poetry of falling leaves and moonlit mists! But this golden color enchants me. There is a sad, intoxicating perfume everywhere. I keep thinking of great feudal hunts, of life as it was lived in the châteaux. There is the sound of stags belling beside a lake; the wind blows through the woods; flames leap high in the vast fireplaces. . . .

Friday night, 2 A.M., [*Croisset, December 23, 1853*]

I must love you to write you tonight, for I am *exhausted.* My head feels as though it were being squeezed in an iron vise. Since two o'clock yesterday afternoon (except for about twenty-five minutes for dinner), I have been writing *Bovary.* I am in the midst of love-making; I am sweating and my throat is tight. This has been one of the rare days of my life passed completely in illusion from beginning to end. At six o'clock this evening, as I was writing the word "hysterics," I was so swept away, was bellowing so loudly and feeling so deeply what my little Bovary was going through, that I was afraid of having hysterics myself. I got up from my table and opened the window to calm myself. My head was spinning. Now I have great pains in my knees, in my back, and in my head. I feel like a man who has ——ed too much (forgive me for the expression)—a kind of rapturous lassitude. And since I am in the midst of love it is only proper that I should not fall asleep before sending you a caress, a kiss, and whatever thoughts are left in me. Will what I write be good? I have no idea—I am hurrying a little, to be able to show Bouilhet a complete section when he comes to see me. What is certain is that my book has been going at a lively rate for the past week. May it continue so, for I am weary of my usual snail's pace. But I fear the awakening, the disillusion that may come from the recopied pages. No matter; it is a delicious thing to write, whether well or badly—to be no longer yourself but to move in an entire universe of your own creating. Today, for instance, man and woman, lover and beloved, I rode in a forest on an autumn afternoon under the yellow leaves, and I was also the horse, the leaves, the wind, the words my people spoke, even the red sun that made them half-shut their love-drowned eyes. Is this pride or piety? Is it a silly overflow of exaggerated self-satisfaction, or is it really a vague and noble religious instinct? But when I think of these marvelous pleasures I have enjoyed I am tempted to offer God a prayer of thanks—if only I knew he could hear me! Praised be the Lord for not creating me a cotton merchant, a vaudevillian, a wit, etc.! Let us sing to Apollo like the ancient bards, and breathe deeply of the cold air of Parnassus; let us strum our guitars and clash our cymbals, and whirl like dervishes in the eternal pageant of Forms and Ideas.

Monday night, 1 o'clock, [*Croisset, January 2, 1854*]

[Bouilhet] was satisfied with my love scene. However, before said passage I have a transition of eight lines which took me three days; it doesn't contain a superfluous word, yet I must do it over once again because it is too slow. It is a piece of direct discourse which has to be changed into indirect, and in which I haven't room to say everything that should be said. It all has to be swift and casual, since it must remain inconspicuous in the ensemble. After this I shall still have three or four other infinitesimal corrections, which will take me one more entire week. How slow I am! No matter; I am getting ahead. I have taken a great step forward, and feel an inner relief that gives me new vigor, even though tonight I literally sweated with effort. It is so difficult to undo what is done, and well done, in order to put something new in its place, and yet hide all traces of the patch. . . .

How true it is that concern with morality makes every work of the imagination false and stupid! I am becoming quite a critic. The novel I am writing sharpens this faculty, for it is essentially a work of criticism, or rather of anatomy. The reader will not notice, I hope, all the psychological work hidden under the form, but he will sense its effect. At the same time I am also tempted to write big, sumptuous things—battles, sieges, descriptions of the fabulous ancient East. Thursday night I spent two wonderful hours, my head in my hands, dreaming of the bright walls of Ecbatana. Nothing has been written about all that. How many things still hover in the limbo of human thought! There is no shortage of subjects, but only of men.

Speaking of men, allow me to tell you now, lest I forget them, two charming little anecdotes. First: there was recently brought to the Rouen morgue the body of a man who had drowned himself with his two children tied to his belt. There is terrible hardship here. Gangs of paupers are beginning to roam the countryside at night. At Saint-Georges, a league from here, they killed a gendarme. Our good peasants are beginning to shiver in their skins. If they are given a good fright I shall not be sorry for them. This caste deserves no pity. It is vicious and savage in every respect. But to proceed—second anecdote, illustrative of the brotherhood of man: recently, at Provins, there took place the execution of a young man who had murdered a property-owner and his wife, then raped their maidservant and drunk their entire cellar. To witness the guillotining of this eccentric, more than ten thousand persons from the surrounding country arrived in Provins the day before. Since the inns could not hold them all, many spent the night in the open and *slept in the snow*. There were such crowds that the bread supply gave out. Oh universal suffrage! Sophists! Charlatans! Continue to fulminate against the gladiators, and talk about progress! Moralize, make laws, draw up plans! Go ahead—reform the savage beast. Even when you have pulled the tiger's teeth, and he can eat only gruel, he will remain bloodthirsty at heart. Work clothes don't conceal the cannibal, nor can the black skull cap of the bourgeois hide his Carib skull. What's all that to us? Let us stick to our last, and may Providence do the same!

[*Croisset, January 9-10, 1854*]

I have something intimate to say to you. You will be indignant, but I should be a swine were I to hide what I think. It is this: this poem[19] is not publishable *as it is,* and I beg you not to publish it. Why insult Musset? What has he done to you? . . . Does his personal conduct concern you? Who has made us censors? . . . Do you hope to reform him? Why do him a greater wrong than he did you? Think of posterity, and meditate on the sorry figure cut there by the insulters of great men. When Musset is dead, who will know that he drank too much? Poster-

19 Louise Colet, indignant at Alfred de Musset for slighting her in various ways, had written a poem entitled *La Servante,* in which he was portrayed as a drunkard and seducer of servant girls.

ity is very indulgent toward such crimes as that. It has practically forgiven Rousseau for having put his children in an orphanage. And after all how do such things concern us? *This poem is a bad deed, and you have already been punished for it because it is a bad poem as well.* Try to read coldly what I say. If it makes you too angry, keep these pages and reread them in six months, a year (wait that long before publishing), and you will see that I am right. You wrote *La Servante* with a personal emotion that distorted your outlook and made it impossible to keep before your eyes the fundamental principles that must underlie any imaginative composition. It has no aesthetic. You have turned art into an outlet for passion, a kind of chamberpot to catch an overflow. It smells bad; it smells of hate! In short, I find this poem improper in its purpose, poor, and badly executed. And if Musset were to reply? If he did nothing but write a tiny squib that covered you with ridicule? Remember the unlucky story of the knife[20] and how it hurt you. One has to say all these things to you, though by now I blush to do so. But nothing anyone says does you any good. You take life against the grain; you are perpetually confusing life and art, your emotions and your imagination, each of which does harm to the other. You may be sure that others think as I do, and don't dare to tell you so. . . .

[*Croisset, January 13, 1854*]

As to when I shall be finished with *Bovary,* I have already set so many dates, and had to change them so often, that I refuse not only to speak about it any more, but even to think about it. I can only trust in God; it's beyond me. It will be finished when it is finished, even though I die of boredom and impatience—as I might very well do were it not for the fury that keeps me going. Till then I will visit you every two months, as I promised.

Now, poor dear Louise, shall I tell you what I think—or

[20] See p. xxiv.

rather what you feel? I think that your love for me is wavering. Your dissatisfactions, your sufferings on my account, can have no other cause, for as I am now I have always been. But now you see me more clearly, and you judge me correctly, perhaps. I cannot tell. However, when we love completely we accept the loved one as he is, with his defects and his deformities; even festering sores seem adorable to us, we cherish a hunchback for his hump, and a foul breath fills us with delight. It is the same with moral qualities. Now you say I am twisted, infamous, selfish, etc. Do you know that I'm going to end by being unbearably proud as a result of being so constantly criticized? I do not think that there is a mortal on earth less approved of than I am, but I will not change. I will not reform. I have already scratched out, amended, suppressed, or gagged so many things in myself that I am tired of doing it. Everything has its limit, and I am a big enough boy now to consider my training completed. I have other things to think about. I was born with all the vices. I completely suppressed many of them, and have indulged the rest but slightly. God alone knows the martyrdom I suffered during that psychological breaking-in; but I have finished with it. That is the way of death, and I want to remain alive for three or four more books; therefore I am set, immovable. You say I am made of granite. Yes, my feelings are of granite. But if my heart is hard it is at least sturdy, and never gives way. Betrayals and unjust accusations will not change what is engraved on it. Everything will remain, and the thought of you, whatever you do or I do, will not be effaced.

Adieu, a long kiss . . .

Saturday night, 1 o'clock, [*Croisset, February 25, 1854*]

You complain so much about my "morbid character" (oh,

Du Camp, great man, how we have slandered you!)[21] and about my lack of devotion that I have come to consider this whole subject ludicrous. The more you reproach me for my selfishness, the more selfish I become. What do you mean by selfishness? I should like very much to know whether you too are not selfish, and quite impressively so. But I am not even "intelligently" selfish, you say. In other words, I am not only a monster, but a fool. Charming words of love! If during the past year (no! six months) the circle of our affection, as you put it, has been shrinking, who is to blame? Neither my conduct nor my language toward you has changed. Never (think back on my previous visits) did I stay with you longer than the last two times. Formerly when I came to Paris I occasionally dined out with others. But in November, and again two weeks ago, I declined all invitations in order that we might be more completely together; and I never went out purely for my own pleasure.

I think that we are growing old and rancid; we are souring, and between us there is an interchange of bitterness. When I probe myself, this is what I find I feel for you: first, great physical attraction; then a spiritual bond, calm virile affection, and loving respect. I place love above anything afforded by life as we know it, and no longer speak of it in connection with myself. The last night we were together you jeered like a bourgeoise at the pathetic dream I had when I was fifteen,[22] accusing it once again of "not being intelligent." Don't I know it! Haven't you ever understood, then, *anything* in my writings? Haven't you realized that all the irony I let loose against emotion in my works was nothing but a cry of the vanquished—unless it was a paean of victory? You ask for love, and complain that I don't

21 Flaubert refers to similar charges earlier made against him by Du Camp, to which the letters on pages 133-137 are in reply, and which had made Louise indignant at the time.

22 Probably his adolescent passion for Madame Schlesinger.

send you flowers? Flowers indeed! Why don't you find some nice budding boy, or a man with fine manners and all the right ideas? *I* am like the tiger—its member has tufts of stiff hair at the end, which lacerate the female. All my feelings have sharp points that wound others—and sometimes myself. . . . I do not like my emotions to be made public, and to have my passions made a subject for conversation when I am present. Until I was over twenty I used to grow red as a beet when I was asked: "You write, don't you?" From this you can gauge my reserve concerning other feelings. I should love you more ardently, I know, if no one suspected that I loved you. I am vexed with Delisle because you called me *"tu"* in his presence, and I now dislike seeing him. That is how I am, and I have enough to keep me busy as it is without undertaking the job of my own sentimental reformation. You, too, will "understand, when you are older" that it is the hardest woods which decay most slowly. And no matter what happens there is one feeling for me that you must retain: your esteem. I insist on this.

You display but little of it, however, in coming back so constantly to the eight hundred francs I loaned you. Really, one would think that I was dunning you. Have I ever mentioned them to you? There is no reason why I should. Keep the money or return it, it is the same to me. But you sound as though you were saying: "Be patient, my good man, don't worry; you'll get your money back, don't cry." I'd give sixteen hundred francs not to hear about it any more. But isn't it really you who love the less, now? Look into your heart and tell yourself what you see. Of course don't tell *me*; it would be bad form to admit the truth —for the fashion you follow requires emotion to be unchanging, always strong, always shrill. But mine, which is tiny, imperceptible, and mute, always remains the same also.

To LOUISE COLET [*1854*]

Croisset, March 19, 1854

I was about to forget the most important thing I had to tell you, namely that your charges against me are ill-founded. I positively did *not* disavow you at Madame X's, and here is exactly what was said:

"I hear that you come to Paris often."

"No; not at all often. Why?"

"I was even told that you have a great passion."

"I? That is something I am incapable of. For whom?"

"For Madame Colet. I am told that you and she are very intimate indeed."

"Ah, yes, that is true. I am very fond of her; I see her very often; but I assure you that anything more is slander."

And I went on talking nonsense *about myself* and accusing myself of being *physically* incapable of love, thus greatly arousing the hilarity of Monsieur and Madame. I assure you I was half-evasive, half-impudent. Let them believe what they like; my only preference is for not discussing such things at all.

Indeed I imagine that now they consider their suspicions confirmed. But to such questions as theirs one never answers "Yes" unless one is a cad or a conceited ass: society considers it ungallant or boastful. I certainly did not disavow you. If you knew the depth of the pride of a man like me you would not have suspected that. My only concessions to society take the form of silence, not of talk. I bow my head low in the presence of foolishness, but I don't take off my hat to it.

Friday night, midnight, [*Croisset, April 7, 1854*]

I have just made a fresh copy of what I have written since New Year, or rather since the middle of February, for on my return from Paris I burned all my January work. It amounts to thirteen pages, no more, no less, thirteen pages in seven weeks.

However, they are in shape, I think, and as perfect as I can make them. There are only two or three repetitions of the same word which must be removed, and two turns of phrase that are still too much alike. At last something is completed. It was a difficult transition: the reader had to be led gradually and imperceptibly from psychology to action. Now I am about to begin the dramatic, eventful part. Two or three more big pushes and the end will be in sight. By July or August I hope to tackle the denouement. What a struggle it has been! My God, what a struggle! Such drudgery! Such discouragement! I spent all last evening frantically poring over surgical texts. I am studying the theory of clubfeet. In three hours I devoured an entire volume on this interesting subject and took notes. I came upon some really fine sentences. "The maternal breast is an impenetrable and mysterious sanctuary, where . . . etc." An excellent treatise, incidentally. Why am I not young? How I should work! One ought to know everything, to write. All of us scribblers are monstrously ignorant. If only we weren't so lacking in stamina, what a rich field of ideas and similes we could tap! Books that have been the source of entire literatures, like Homer and Rabelais, contain the sum of all the knowledge of their times. They knew everything, those fellows, and we know nothing. Ronsard's poetics contains a curious precept: he advises the poet to become well versed in the arts and crafts—to frequent blacksmiths, goldsmiths, locksmiths, etc.—in order to enrich his stock of metaphors. And indeed that is the sort of thing that makes for rich and varied language. The sentences in a book must quiver like the leaves in a forest, all dissimilar in their similarity.

Saturday night, 1 o'clock, [*Croisset, April 22, 1854*]

I am still struggling with clubfeet. My dear brother failed to keep two appointments with me this week, and unless he comes tomorrow I shall be forced to make another trip to Rouen. No matter; my work progresses. I have had a good deal of trouble these last few days over a religious speech. From my point of view, what I have written is completely impious. How different it would have been in a different period! If I had been born a hundred years earlier how much rhetoric I'd have put into it! Instead, I have written a mere, almost literal description of what must have taken place. The leading characteristic of our century is its historical sense. This is why we have to confine ourselves to relating the facts—but *all* the facts, the *heart* of the facts. No one will ever say about me what is said about you in the sublime prospectus of the *Librairie Nouvelle*: "All her writings converge on this lofty goal" (the ideal of a better future). No, we must sing merely for the sake of singing. Why is the ocean never still? What is the *goal* of nature? Well, I think the goal of mankind exactly the same. Things exist because they exist, and you can't do anything about it, my good people. We are always turning in the same circle, always rolling the same stone. Weren't men freer and more intelligent in the time of Pericles than they are under Napoleon III? On what do you base your statement that I am losing "the understanding of certain feelings" that I do not experience? First of all, please note that I *do* experience them. My heart is "human," and if I do not want a child "of my own" it is because I feel that if I had one my heart would become too "paternal." I love my little niece as though she were my daughter, and my "active" concern for her is enough to prove that those are not mere words. But I should rather be skinned alive than "exploit" this in my writing. I refuse to consider Art a drain-pipe for passion, a kind of chamberpot, a slightly more elegant substitute for gossip and confidences. No, no! Genuine poetry is not the scum of the heart. Your daughter deserves better than to be portrayed in verse "under her blanket,"[23] called an angel, etc. . . . Some day much of contemporary literature will be regarded as puerile and a little silly, because of its sentimentality. Sentiment, sentiment everywhere! Such gushing and weeping! Never before have people been so softhearted. We must put blood into our language, not lymph, and when I say blood I mean heart's blood; it must pulsate, throb, excite. We must make the very trees fall in love, the very stones quiver with emotion. The story of a mere blade of grass can be made to express boundless love. The fable of the two pigeons has always moved me more than all of Lamartine, and it's all in the subject matter. But if La Fontaine had expended his amative faculties in expounding his personal feelings, would he have retained enough of it to be able to depict the friendship of two birds? Let us be on our guard against frittering away our gold. . . .

How impatient you all are in Paris to become known, to rent your houses before the roofs are built! Where are those who follow the teaching of Horace—that a work should be kept hidden for nine years before it is shown?[24]

To LOUIS BOUILHET

Wednesday night, [*Croisset, May 30, 1855*]

I am too subject to weaknesses and discouragements myself

23 Flaubert, always severe about Louise's poetry, had particularly disliked some lines in a poem called *A ma fille:*

De ton joli corps sous la couverture
Plus souple apparaît le contour charmant;
Telle au Parthénon quelque frise pure
Nous montre une vierge au long vêtement.

He considered the first two lines "obscene." "And then," he wrote Louise, "what is the Parthenon doing there, so close to your daughter's blanket?"

24 This is the latest available letter from Flaubert to Louise Colet, though the affair still had several tumultuous months to run. Louise is said to have precipitated its end herself by violating Flaubert's privacy—bursting in upon him, one day, in his study at Croisset. She was ejected from the house. Madame Flaubert, a witness of the scene, is said to have reproached her son for his mercilessness, declaring that she felt as though she had seen him "wound her own sex."

not to understand yours, so you need make no excuses on this score. Tell me everything you wish about your troubles; I am sure in advance that I shall sympathize. Yes, this is a wretched century and everything is a filthy mess. What makes me indignant is the *bourgeoisisme* of our fellow-writers. Such businessmen! Such vulgar idiots! . . .

There is something on my mind that I must try once again to tell you, as clearly as I can. You will accuse me of giving sermons, of being a pedant, a man who likes to hear himself talk, but so much the worse—I must do what I consider my (yes, I will use the word) duty.

I want merely to comment on these words from your letter: "Nothing I attempt succeeds, everything falls to pieces in my hands—*merde.*"

Question: What pains have you taken to ensure that *anything* you attempt should succeed? Proposition: If you don't mend your ways, and if you succeed nevertheless, it will be a miracle.

Now for the demonstration.

You arrived in Paris[25] under favorable, even exceptionally favorable, conditions; no other man of letters has ever been so fortunate. Before appearing on the scene you had already published a considerable work in a magazine. This was a passport; you were not unknown; you were qualified to "present yourself," as the saying goes. Thanks to this you immediately, and without having to pull any strings, secured a hearing at the Comédie Française.

I ask you whether *since then* you have paid a single visit, made the slightest effort or even semblance of an effort for the purpose of—I don't say acquiring sponsors, but at least establishing contacts. You'd like to write for the Comédie Française,

25 After publication of his poem, *Melaenis,* in the *Revue de Paris,* Bouilhet had left his tutoring job in Rouen and gone to Paris, hoping to further his literary career.

and yet you don't even set foot in the place! The most elementary common sense demanded that before submitting your manuscript you should have made friends with all the men there and slept with all the women. . . .

I know quite well that you go to see people when you have immediate need of them. Do you think this the proper way of doing things?

You know all this as well as I do. But you deceive yourself with high-sounding words—"I can't help it; it goes against my nature, etc."—and then you complain about the unkindness of people to whom you are a complete stranger. . . .

As for your play, if it is refused again write another—a second, a third—*you must keep after people,* don't give up, don't let go. Follow the dictates of your vocation. You will tell me that you were not "born for the theatre"—empty talk. Besides, what do you know about it? Molière was no longer a beginner when he wrote his first good play. You will object: "How am I going to live in the meantime?"—and indeed there is that little necessity to be considered. You know very well what my answer is, and I also know your rejoinder and reject it. Are you saving your money to build yourself a mausoleum? Your mother would not "die of grief," as you claim. No one dies of grief, you may be sure of it. Confess, rather, that you lack courage and are merely rationalizing your own cowardice. Besides, even if you were right, it is preferable that she should die rather than you. Murder is a lesser crime than suicide. You are sufficiently moral to grant the truth of that axiom.

. . . You have the financial means to live in Paris for several years. When you are down to your last five-franc piece—and when, having done (socially speaking) everything necessary for success, you are still unsuccessful—then shout, do something, come back to your job here if you like. In the meantime you are not doing yourself justice.

That is what I had to tell you. Think it over. Try to be objective; look at yourself from the outside and you will admit that I am right. And if I have offended you in the slightest, forgive me; my intentions were good—the fool's excuse.

By now it has probably occurred to you to compare me to Du Camp. Four years ago he made me approximately the same reproaches I am now making you. (His sermons were longer, and his tone was different, alas!) But the situations are not the same. He thought of me as a kind of person I had no wish to be. Participation in practical life was far from my mind; he kept insisting that I was straying from a path on which, actually, I hadn't even set foot. . . .

Bovary is going *pianissimo*. . . .

To LÉON LAURENT-PICHAT

Croisset, Thursday night, [*October 2,*] *1856*

Dear Friend

I have just received *Bovary* and first of all wish to thank you for it (I may be vulgar, but I am not ungrateful); you did me a service by taking it as it is and I will not forget it.

Confess that you thought me and still think me (more than ever, perhaps) wildly ridiculous. Some day it would give me pleasure to admit that you were right; I promise you faithfully that if that time comes I will make you the most humble apologies. But you must understand that this was a test which I felt I must make; let us hope that what I learn from it will not be too much of a jolt. Do you think that this ignoble reality, so disgusting to you in reproduction, does not oppress my heart as it does yours? If you knew me better you would know that I abhor ordinary existence. Personally, I have always held myself as aloof from it as I could. But aesthetically, I desired this once—and only this once—to plumb its very depths. Therefore I plunged into it heroically, into the midst of all its minutiae, accepting everything, telling everything, depicting everything, pretentious as it may sound to say so.

I am expressing myself badly, but well enough, I think, for you to understand the general trend of my resistance to your criticisms, judicious as they may be. You were asking me to turn it into another book. You were asking me to violate the inner poetics that determined the pattern (as a philosopher would say) after which it was conceived. Finally, I should have failed in my duty to myself and to you, in acting out of deference and not out of conviction.

Art requires neither complaisance nor politeness; nothing but faith—faith and freedom.

To LÉON LAURENT-PICHAT

[*Croisset, between December 1 and 15, 1856*]

Dear Friend

First, thank you for pointing out the difference between your personal and your editorial attitudes concerning my book; I therefore now address not the poet Laurent-Pichat, but the *Revue,* an abstract personality whose interests you represent. This is my reply to the *Revue de Paris*:

1. You kept the manuscript of *Madame Bovary* for three months, and thus you had every opportunity, before beginning to print the work, to know your own mind regarding it. The alternatives were to take it or leave it. You took it, and you must abide by the consequences.

2. Once the agreement was concluded, I consented to the elimination of a passage which I consider very important, because you claimed that to print it might involve you in difficulties. I complied gracefully, but I will not conceal from you (and now I am speaking to my friend Pichat) that I at once began to

regret bitterly ever having had the idea of publishing. Let us speak our minds fully or not at all.

3. I consider that I have already done a great deal, and you consider that I should do still more. *I will do nothing;* I will not make a correction, not a cut; I will not suppress a comma; nothing, nothing! But if you consider that I am embarrassing you, if you are afraid, the simple thing to do is to stop publication of *Madame Bovary*. This would not disturb me in the slightest.

Now that I have finished addressing the *Revue,* let me point out one thing to my friend:

By eliminating the passage about the cab you have not made the story a whit less shocking; and you will accomplish no more by the cuts you ask for in the sixth installment.

You are objecting to details, whereas actually you should object to the whole. The brutal element is basic, not incidental. Negroes cannot be made white, and you cannot change a book's blood. All you can do is to weaken it.

I need scarcely say that if I break with the *Revue de Paris* I shall nevertheless retain friendly feelings for its editors.

I know how to distinguish between literature and literary business.

To his brother ACHILLE

[*Paris,*] *January 1, 1857, 10 P.M.*

Thank you for your letter. This is how things stand:

We have moved heaven and earth, or, more accurately, we have stirred up the most exalted filth in Paris; I have collected some pretty character studies.

My case is a *political issue,* because the authorities want at all costs to destroy the *Revue de Paris,* which is a thorn in the government's side; the magazine has already had two official warnings, and it is a very clever move to suppress it, for its third offense, on anti-religious grounds—for the main charge against me is a description of Extreme Unction copied from the *Rituel de Paris*. But these good judges are so asinine that they are completely ignorant of the religion whose defenders they are; my investigating magistrate, Treilhard, is a *Jew,* and it is he who is prosecuting me. It is all sublimely ludicrous.

As for Treilhard, I beg you and if necessary *forbid* you to write him; that would compromise me; please be warned.

So far, I have behaved very well; let us not do anything to lower ourselves.

The proceedings against me will probably be stopped tonight by a telegram from somewhere outside Paris; it will take these gentlemen by surprise, and they are all quite capable of leaving their calling-cards at my door tomorrow afternoon.

I'm going to be the lion of the week; all the high-class whores are fighting for copies of *Bovary,* hoping to find obscenities that aren't there. Tomorrow I shall visit Rouland[26] and the chief of police. In the midst of all this the *Moniteur* is making me some very nice offers. What do you make of it?

My case is a very complicated one, and neither I nor my book is connected in any way with the persecution I am being subjected to. I am a mere pretext. My role is to save (this time) the *Revue de Paris*—unless the *Revue* goes down and carries me with it.

Blanche, Florimont, etc., etc., are working for me; everyone is being extremely kind.

By the time you receive this, my case will probably have been dropped; but since it may drag on, ask some people in Rouen who you think might be effective to write to Paris, but don't write anything yourself.

26 Minister of education.

To his brother ACHILLE

Saturday, 10 A.M., [Paris, January 3, 1857]

First, thank you for your offer, but there is absolutely no reason for you to come. And then forgive my incoherent letters; I am so rushed, harassed, fatigued, that I probably say a lot of stupid things. I have been on the go for three days; I don't return for dinner in the evening until nine, and I spend twenty francs a day on cabs.

Everything you have done is good. The main thing was and still is to have Rouen put pressure on Paris. The reports concerning the influential position that father had and that you have in Rouen are most useful. They thought they were attacking some nonentity, and the first thing that gave them pause was the discovery that I had private means. The ministry of the interior must be made to realize that we are, at Rouen, what is called "a family"—that is to say that we have deep roots in the community, and that by attacking me, especially for immorality, they will alienate many people. I expect excellent results from the prefect's letter to the minister of the interior.

I repeat: it is a political affair.

There was a double objective: to ruin me completely, and to buy me off; I tell you this in the strictest confidence. The offers made me by the *Moniteur* followed so closely after my persecution that there is obviously some scheme behind them.

It was a very shrewd move to try to suppress a political journal for offense against public decency and religion. The authorities seized on the first pretext, and they thought that the man they were attacking had no backing. Now these gentlemen of the judiciary are being so importuned by the *grandes dames* whom we have turned loose on them that they are completely at a loss; B——'s testimonials concerning my character will come on top of all this. The director of fine arts, in full uniform and covered with decorations, came up to me yesterday in front of two hundred people at the ministry of state to congratulate me on *Bovary;* he mentioned the scene of the agricultural show, with Tuvache and Lieuvain, etc. etc. I assure you that I am now looked upon as a person of consequence, in any case. If I come through (which seems to me very probable), my book will sell extremely well!

It will probably be decided tonight whether or not I shall have to appear in court. No matter! Keep after the prefect and don't stop until I tell you. . . .

Try to get someone to indicate in a clever way that it would be dangerous to attack me, to attack *us,* because of the coming elections.

To MADAME MAURICE SCHLESINGER

Paris, January 14, 1857

How touched I was by your kind letter, dear Madame! I can give you full answers to the questions you ask concerning the author and the book. Here is the whole story:

The *Revue de Paris,* in which I published my novel (in installments from October 1 to December 15), had previously received two warnings—being an anti-government organ. The authorities thought that it would be a clever move to suppress it entirely, on the grounds of immorality and atheism; and quite at random they picked out some passages from my book which they called licentious and blasphemous. I was summoned before the investigating magistrate and the proceedings began. But friends made strenuous efforts on my behalf, sloshing about for me in the most exalted filth of the capital. Now I am assured that everything has been stopped, though I have heard nothing official. I have no doubts of my success; the whole thing has been too stupid. Consequently, I shall be able to publish my novel in book form. You will receive it in about six weeks, I think, and for your amusement I will mark the incriminated passages.

One of them, a description of Extreme Unction, is nothing but a page from the *Rituel de Paris,* put into decent French; but the noble guardians of our religion are not very well versed in catechism.

Still, I might very well have been convicted and despite everything sentenced to a year of imprisonment, not to mention a fine of a thousand francs. In addition, each new volume by your friend would have been severely scrutinized by the gentlemen of the police, and a second offense would have put me in a dungeon for five years: in short, I'd have been unable to print a line. Thus, I have learned: (1) that it is extremely unpleasant to be involved in a political affair; (2) that social hypocrisy is a serious matter. But this time it was so stupid that it grew ashamed of itself, loosened its grip, and crawled back into its hole.

As for the book itself, which is moral, ultra-moral, and which might well be awarded the Montyon prize[27] were it a little less frank (an honor which I covet but little), it has had as much success as a novel can have in a magazine.

The literary world has paid me some pretty compliments—whether sincere or not I do not know. I am even told that Monsieur de Lamartine is loudly singing my praises—which surprises me very much, for everything in my book must annoy him! The *Presse* and the *Moniteur* have made me some very substantial offers. I have been asked to write a comic (!) opera and my *Bovary* has been discussed in various publications large and small. And that, dear Madame, with no modesty whatever, is the balance sheet of my fame. Have no worry about the critics—they will treat me kindly, for they well know that I have no desire to compete with them in any way; on the contrary, they will be charming—it is so pleasant to have new idols with which to overturn the old.

27 See note on page 17.

So I shall resume my dull life, so calm and flat, in which sentences are adventures and the only flowers I gather are metaphors. I shall write as in the past, solely for the pleasure of writing, for myself alone, with no thought of money or publicity. Apollo will doubtless set this to my credit, and one day perhaps I shall succeed in producing something good. For do not persistence and energy overcome all obstacles? Every dream finds its form in the end; there are waters for all thirsts, there is love for all hearts. And then there is no better way of getting through life than to be incessantly preoccupied by an idea—by an ideal, as the grisettes say. . . . Since all alternatives are absurd, let us choose the noblest. Since the sun is beyond our reach, let us stop by our windows and set the lights blazing in our room. . . .

Will you never return to Paris? Is your exile permanent? Have you a grudge against poor France? And what has become of Maurice? What is he doing? How alone you must feel since Maria left![28] I understood the happiness of which you wrote, and I understood also the unhappiness which you passed over in silence. When the days are too long or too empty, think a little of one who kisses your hands most affectionately.

To his brother ACHILLE

[*Paris, probably January 16, 1857*]

I had stopped writing because I thought the case against me had been dropped. Prince Napoleon[29] had said so on three occasions to three different people; M. Rouland had been told so in person at the ministry of the interior, etc., etc.; Edouard Delessert had been asked by the empress (with whom he dined last Tuesday) to tell his mother that the matter was shelved.

28 The Schlesingers' daughter, Maria, had recently married.
29 An anti-clerical senator, cousin of the emperor.

To his brother ACHILLE [*1857*]

Yesterday morning I learned from Sénard[30] that I should have to appear in Police Court; Treilhard had told him so the previous afternoon at the Palais de Justice. I immediately sent word to the Prince, who replied that it was not true; but he is mistaken.

That is all I know; I am caught in a whirlpool of lies and infamies; underneath it all there is *something,* someone invisible and relentless; at first I was only a pretext, and now I think that the *Revue de Paris* itself is only a pretext. Perhaps someone has something against one of my sponsors? They have been even more impressive for their *quality* than for their quantity.

Everyone denies all responsibility and puts the blame on someone else.

What is certain is that proceedings were dropped, then resumed. Why this about-face? Everything started from the ministry of the interior; the judiciary obeyed—it was free, entirely free, but . . . I expect no justice whatever. I will serve my prison term. And of course I will ask no clemency—that would dishonor me.

If you can succeed in learning anything, in understanding the situation, let me know.

I assure you that I am not a bit disturbed; the whole thing is too stupid, too stupid!

And I have no intention of being gagged—far from it. I shall continue to work as before, that is, just as honestly and independently. I have more novels up my sleeves for them—good ones, that will tell the truth. I have made plenty of notes; only I shall wait to publish until better days break over Parnassus.

In the midst of it all, the success of *Bovary* continues; the book has really caught hold; everyone has read it, or is reading it, or wants to read it. The persecution brings me everyone's sympathy. If my book is bad, it will serve to make it seem better;

30 See biographical note on Frédéric Baudry.

if on the contrary the book is destined to endure, this will be its pedestal.

Voilà!

Any moment now I am expecting the summons which will tell me on what day I shall have to take my place (for the crime of having written in French) on the bench reserved for pickpockets and pederasts.

To his brother ACHILLE

[*Paris, January 18, 1857*]

The case is definitely scheduled for next Thursday; I stand a good chance of winning and a good chance of losing; the literary world is talking about nothing else.

Today I spent an hour or more alone with Lamartine, who showered me with compliments. Modesty prevents me from repeating the ultra-flattering things he said to me. One thing is sure—he knows my book by heart, fully understands what I intend by it, and fully understands *me.* He is going to give me a laudatory letter to submit to the court. I shall also ask other prominent writers to give me testimonials as to the morality of my book; this is important, Sénard says.

My stock is going up: I have been asked to write for the *Moniteur* at ten sous a line—which would make, for a novel like *Bovary,* about ten thousand francs. That is what entanglement with the law does for me. My reputation is made whether I am convicted or not.

It was Lamartine who made the overtures. I am considerably surprised; I should never have expected the creator of Elvire to fall in love with Homais! . . .

To his brother ACHILLE

[*January 31, 1857*]

This morning you must have received a telegram sent you in

my name by one of my friends, telling you that the verdict will be announced a week from tomorrow: justice still hesitates. . . .

Sénard's speech for the defense was splendid. He annihilated the public prosecutor, who writhed in his seat and declined to answer. We buried him under a shower of quotations from Bossuet and Massillon, licentious passages from Montesquieu, etc. The courtroom was jammed. Everything went very well and I was in excellent form. On one occasion I permitted myself to contradict the public prosecutor, who was immediately shown up as dishonest and who retracted. You will be able to read the full text of the proceedings, for I hired a stenographer (at sixty francs an hour) who took down everything.[31] Sénard spoke for four hours. It was a triumph for him and for me.

He began by speaking about father, then about you, then about me; after which he gave a complete analysis of the novel, refuted the charges, and defended the incriminated passages. On this point he was splendid; the public prosecutor must certainly have been given an official drubbing that evening. Best of all was the passage about Extreme Unction. The public prosecutor was covered with confusion when Sénard took a *Rituel de Paris* out of his desk and read it; the passage in my novel is merely a toned-down reproduction of the text of the *Rituel;* we gave them a good lesson in literature.

All during his speech Sénard represented me as a great man and spoke of my book as a masterpiece. About a third of it was read aloud. He made good use of Lamartine's approval. "You owe this man not only an acquittal," he said, "but apologies!" And: "So you presume to attack the younger son of Monsieur Flaubert! . . . No one, sir, not even you, could give *him* lessons in morality!"

31 The text of the proceedings of Flaubert's trial, an interesting document, is sometimes printed as an appendix to French editions of *Madame Bovary,* but it is included in no current English or American edition.

To MAURICE SCHLESINGER

[*February, 1857*]

My dear Maurice

Thank you for your letter. I shall answer briefly, for the whole thing has left me so exhausted in body and mind that I haven't the strength to walk a step or hold a pen. It was a struggle to win my case, but I succeeded.

I have received very flattering compliments from all my fellow-writers, and my book is going to sell unusually well for a first novel. But my ultimate feeling about the trial is one of displeasure. It has caused the book's success to be of a distorted kind, and I do not enjoy having Art mixed up with this sort of thing. I feel this very strongly, and the uproar has disgusted me so profoundly that I am hesitant about publishing my novel in book form. I should like to return, once and for all, to the solitude and the silence from which I emerged; I should like to publish nothing, and never again have myself talked about. Social hypocrisy is so rampant that it seems to me impossible, nowadays, to say anything.

Men of the world, even those most kindly disposed toward me, consider me immoral and impious! They advise me to avoid saying this or that in the future, to be careful, etc., etc. How distasteful it all is!

People no longer want to be portrayed; the daguerreotype is an insult, history is satire! Such is the point we have reached. When I rummage in my poor brain I find nothing that is not reprehensible. What I had planned to publish after my novel, namely a book on which I have spent several years of research and arid study,[32] would land me in prison. And all my other plans have similar drawbacks. But now you will begin to realize in what a merry frame of mind I am.

32 Flaubert feared that *La Tentation de Saint Antoine* would be condemned on religious grounds.

To MAURICE SCHLESINGER [*1857*]

I have spent the last four days lying on my sofa reflecting on my situation; it is anything but gay, even though I am beginning to receive a few laurels—mingled, it is true, with thistles.

I answer all your questions: if the book does not appear, I will send you the issues of the *Revue* in which it was printed. This will be decided within a few days. M. de Lamartine has not written to the *Revue de Paris;* he goes about praising the literary merit of my novel, and at the same time tells everyone that it is cynical. He compares me to Lord Byron, etc.! This is all very fine, but I should prefer a little less exaggeration along with a little less reticence. He spontaneously sent me congratulations, then dropped me at the crucial moment. In short, he did not behave toward me like a gentleman, and he even broke a promise. Nevertheless we remain on good terms.

III

SAINT POLYCARP

1857-1880

DURING the composition of *Madame Bovary* Flaubert had written to Louise Colet: "Saint Polycarp used to stuff up his ears, flee from wherever he was, and cry: 'In what times, O Lord, hast thou caused me to be born!' I am becoming like Saint Polycarp." In his later years Flaubert used to pretend to be Saint Polycarp's reincarnation, and his friends gave parties for him on the saint's feast day.

Along with his ever-mounting disgust for contemporary society, however, the rumblings of which are continuously heard in the correspondence, the years after the completion of *Madame Bovary* witnessed the flowering of his art. He continued to live a laborious and celibate life at Croisset, varied chiefly by regular brief stays in Paris; hardships imposed by the Franco-Prussian war and by the business failure of his niece's husband caused only brief interruptions in his work. Indeed, external misfortunes—which included the deaths of many of his friends—served only to enhance his faith in art as supreme escape and refuge.

Immediately after finishing *Madame Bovary* Flaubert returned to *Saint Antoine*. He did considerable cutting and revising, and several excerpts were published in Théophile Gautier's magazine, *L'Artiste*. But once again the author put his manuscript aside, and quite rapidly he decided to write his next book about ancient Carthage—it would be a kind of revenge against the Norman drabnesses of *Bovary* but no less exact and objective in treatment. For purposes of documentation he read, between March and July of 1857, about a hundred volumes on Carthage, and he visited the city's ruins early the next year. He worked steadily on the book until shortly before its publication in November, 1862. *Salammbô* sold well, to Flaubert's own surprise and despite a rather unfavorable press: Sainte-Beuve complained that the book was bloody, sadistic, and operatic—perhaps thus stating the elements of its popular appeal. The modern reader is less apt to be impressed by the novel's gorgeous trappings than by the fact that its priestess-heroine is another victim, like Emma Bovary, of the insoluble, always fascinating conflict between dream and reality, one of Flaubert's fundamental themes.

This theme received its most masterly treatment in Flaubert's next novel, *L'Education sentimentale.* The title was taken from one of his own youthful novels, and the hero's passion for Madame Arnoux depicts the author's infatuation for Elisa Schlesinger. Flaubert intended the book as a portrait of his own generation, which came to manhood between 1840 and the revolution of 1848, and whose failure (for he considered it a distinctly "lost" generation) he attributes to the destructive effects of romanticism. A famous scene late in the novel depicts the hero, who, after wasting his life in pursuit of an unattainable woman, finds her at last in his arms; but she is now a white-haired wraith, no longer the desirable creature she was. It was no doubt this theme of frustration and of the savorlessness of life that led Flaubert to wish that he had entitled the novel *Les Fruits secs.* But the value of the book goes far beyond the striking presentation of an idea. It is the finest example of Flaubert's realism, of his genius for constructing an absorbing narrative out of almost imponderable elements, without recourse to any of the more obvious devices of plot or language intended to create suspense. He performed his usual feats of documentation, studying the origins of socialism, reading the back files of newspapers, and visiting porcelain factories, hospitals, race courses, and countless other establishments.

One of the persons to whom he turned in search of details about the revolution of 1848 (in which he had taken little interest at the time) was George Sand. Between the champion of "art for art's sake," whose contempt for politics was limitless, and the socially conscious "leftist" author of romantic novels, there developed a great and tender friendship. Flaubert's correspondence with her stands next in importance only to that with Louise Colet, of which it is, in a sense, a calmer and more mature sequel, undisturbed by storms of physical passion. Especially after the death of Louis Bouilhet, in 1869, George Sand became the principal recipient of his confidences—a role still later filled by Turgenev.

The first public reaction to *L'Education sentimentale* was unfavorable, and Flaubert lamented its failure: only rare spirits, such as Zola, realized its significance, and its acceptance as a classic has come slowly. Nevertheless, Flaubert's prestige among his fellow-writers had by now become solidly established, and partly as a result of being invited to the Magny dinners he could count among his friends many of the other eminent men of his time. He frequented the salon of Princess Mathilde Bonaparte and was invited by the emperor and the empress to the Tuileries and to Compiègne.

After the nightmare of the Franco-Prussian war and the Commune he once again took up *Saint Antoine,* and it was finally published, in a version a fraction the length of the original, in 1874. Even before that he had begun wide reading for *Bouvard et Pécuchet,* the most devastating of his books in conception and the most grindingly difficult in execution: a burlesque panorama of the bourgeoisie groping stupidly and helplessly in the jungle of modern knowledge. The demands of this project, added to various personal hardships, brought on acute depression; and in 1875-76 he sought relief in the creation of the charming, masterly *Trois contes: Saint Julien, Un Cœur simple,* and *Hérodias.* Then he returned doggedly to his "monstrous" book, but it was not quite completed when he was stricken with apoplexy. Among the pleasures of his last years had been the fostering of the talent of Alfred Le Poittevin's nephew, Guy de Maupassant; and it was this young "disciple" who had the task of describing his master's death to the fellow-artist whom Flaubert had lately come to call his only remaining friend: Ivan Turgenev, who was absent in Russia.

To MADEMOISELLE LEROYER DE CHANTEPIE

Paris, March 18, [*1857*]

I hasten to thank you; I have received everything you sent. Thank you for the letter, the books, and above all for the portrait. I am touched by this delicate attention.

I am going to read your three volumes slowly and attentively —that is (I am sure in advance), as they deserve.

But I am prevented from doing so for the moment, since before returning to the country I have to do some archaeological work in one of the least-known periods of antiquity—a task which is preparation for another task. I am going to write a novel[1] whose action will take place three centuries before Christ. I feel the need of taking leave of the modern world: my pen has been steeped in it too long, and I am as weary of portraying it as I am disgusted by the sight of it.

With a reader such as you, Madame, one who is so understanding, frankness is a duty. I therefore answer your questions: *Madame Bovary* is based on no actual occurrence. It is a *totally fictitious* story; it contains none of my feelings and no details from my own life. The illusion of truth (if there is one) comes, on the contrary, from the book's impersonality. It is one of my principles that a writer should not be his own theme. An artist must be in his work like God in creation, invisible and all-powerful; he should be everywhere felt, but nowhere seen.

Furthermore, Art must rise above personal emotions and nervous susceptibilities. It is time to endow it with pitiless method, with the exactness of the physical sciences. Still, for me the capital difficulty remains style, form, that indefinable Beauty implicit in the conception and representing, as Plato said, the splendor of Truth.

For a long time, Madame, I led a life like yours. I too spent several years completely alone in the country, hearing in winter

1 *Salammbô.*

no sound but the rustle of the wind in the trees and the cracking of the drift-ice on the Seine under my window. If I have arrived at some understanding of life, it is because I have lived little in the ordinary sense of the word; I have eaten meagerly, but ruminated much; I have seen all kinds of people, and visited various countries. I have traveled on foot and on camel-back. I am acquainted with Parisian speculators and Damascus Jews, with Italian ruffians and Negro mountebanks. I made a pilgrimage to the Holy Land and was lost in the snows of Parnassus—which may be taken symbolically.

Do not complain; I have been here and there in the world and have a thorough knowledge of that Paris you dream of; there is nothing to equal a good book at your fireside, the reading of *Hamlet* or *Faust* on a day when your responses are keen. My own dream is to buy a little palace in Venice, on the Grand Canal.

So there, Madame—part of your curiosity is gratified. To complete my portrait and biography, add only this: I am thirty-five, five feet eight, with the shoulders of a stevedore and the nervous irritability of a young lady of fashion. I am a bachelor and a recluse.

In closing, let me thank you again for sending me the picture. It will be framed and hung between those of loved ones. I suppress a compliment which is at the tip of my pen, and beg you to believe me your affectionate colleague.

To CHARLES BAUDELAIRE

Croisset, July 13, [*1857*]

Dear Friend

I began by devouring your volume[2] from end to end, like a kitchenmaid pouncing on a serial, and now for the past week I have been rereading it line by line, word by word, and I must

2 *Les Fleurs du mal.*

tell you that it delights and enchants me. You have managed to give romanticism a new lease on life. You resemble no one—the highest of all virtues. The originality of your style springs from the conception; each sentence is crammed to the bursting-point with thought. I love your sharpness, with the refinements of language which set it off, like the ornaments on a Damascus blade.

These are the pieces which most struck me: Sonnet XVIII, *La Beauté,* for me a work of the loftiest quality; and then *L'Idéal, La Géante* (which I already knew), Piece XXV *"Avec ses vêtements ondoyants et nacrés," Une charogne, Le Chat, Le Beau navire, A une dame créole* and *Le Spleen,* which went straight to my heart, its tone is so right. Ah! how well you understand the wretchedness of existence! Of this you may boast without fear of falling into the sin of pride. I shall add no more to my list—I should give the impression of copying the table of contents. But I must tell you that I am utterly enchanted by Piece LXXV, *Tristesses de la lune*:

> *. . . Qui d'une main distraite et légère caresse*
> *Avant de s'endormir, le contour de ses seins. . . .*

and I greatly admire the *Voyage à Cythère,* etc., etc.

As for criticisms, I make none, because I am not sure that I should agree with them myself a quarter of an hour from now. In short, I am afraid of saying something inept that I should immediately regret. When I see you this winter in Paris, I shall merely ask you a few questions, modestly and tentatively.

To sum up, what I love above all in your book is that in it Art occupies first place. Furthermore, you write of the flesh without loving it, in a melancholy, detached manner that I find sympathetic. You are as unyielding as marble and as penetrating as an English fog.

Once again, a thousand thanks for your present; I shake your hand warmly.

To CHARLES BAUDELAIRE

Friday, August 14, [*1857*]

I have just learned that you are being prosecuted because of your book. Apparently I am rather late in hearing about this. I am in ignorance of everything, for I live here as though I were a hundred thousand leagues from Paris.

Why? Against what have you committed an "offense"? Religion? "Public decency?" Has your trial taken place? When will it be? Etc.

This is something new, to prosecute a book of verse—up to now the bench has left poetry severely alone.

I am deeply indignant. Be good enough to give me details, and accept a thousand very cordial handshakes.

To CHARLES BAUDELAIRE

[*Croisset,*] *August 23, 1857*

Dear Friend

The articles about your book have come, and I have greatly enjoyed the one by Asselineau. He is very kind to me, incidentally; please give him my thanks. If you can do so without too much trouble, keep me informed about your case; I am as interested in it as though it were my own. This prosecution is senseless, and revolts me.

And official honors have just been paid Béranger—that wretched bourgeois, immortalizer of easy conquests and old clothes. Considering the present wave of enthusiasm for this peerless character, I should think that a few excerpts from his songs (which are not songs, but odes to Philistinism) might be read in court with excellent effect. I recommend *Ma Jeanneton, La Bacchante, La Grand'mère,* etc. These are just about as moral as they are poetic. And since you are probably charged with offense against public decency and religion, it might not be a bad move to draw a comparison between you and him. Pass on this idea to your lawyer for what it is worth.

That is all I have to tell you, and I shake your hand.

To ERNEST FEYDEAU

Croisset, Sunday, [*December 19, 1858*]

. . . You ask what I am doing. Here is your answer: I get up at noon and go to bed between three and four in the morning. I take a nap about five. I scarcely ever see the daylight—a horrible way to live in winter—and am thus totally unable to distinguish the days of the week or day from night. My existence is extravagantly unsociable; I love its uneventfulness, its quiet. It is complete, objective nothingness. And I am not working too badly, at least for me. In eighteen days I have written ten pages, read *Anabasis* in its entirety, and analyzed six treatises by Plutarch, the great hymn to Ceres (in the *Poésies homériques,* in Greek), and Erasmus' *Encomium moriae;* plus Tabarin at night, or rather in the morning, in bed for diversion. So there you are. And in two days I shall begin Chapter III. This will be Chapter IV if I retain the preface; but no—no preface, no explanation. Chapter I took me two months last summer. Nevertheless, I shan't hesitate to scrap it even though in itself I'm very fond of it.

I'm in a funk because in Chapter III I am going to use an effect already used in Chapter II. Clever writers would think up tricks to get out of the difficulty, but I'm going to plunge straight into it, like an ox. Such is my system. But how I'll sweat! And how I'll despair while constructing said passage!

Seriously, I think that no one has *ever* undertaken a subject so difficult as regards style. At every line, every word, language fails me, and the insufficiency of vocabulary is such that I'm often forced to change details. It will kill me, my friend, it will kill me. No matter; it begins to be fun.

In short, I have finally achieved an erection by dint of whipping and manipulation. Let's hope there's joy to come.

To ERNEST FEYDEAU

Croisset, Tuesday evening, [*January 11, 1859*]

. . . No, my friend! I do not admit that women are competent to judge the human heart. Their understanding of it is always personal and relative. They are the hardest, the cruelest of creatures. "Woman is the desolation of the righteous," said Proudhon. I have little admiration for that gentleman, but his aphorism is nothing less than a stroke of genius.

As far as literature goes, women are capable only of a certain delicacy and sensitivity. What is truly lofty, truly great, escapes them. Our indulgence toward them is one of the reasons for our moral debasement. All of us display an inconceivable cowardice toward our mothers, our sisters, our daughters, our wives, and our mistresses. In no other age have women's breasts been the cause of more vile actions! And the Church (Catholic, Apostolic, and Roman) has given proof of the greatest good sense in promulgating the dogma of the Immaculate Conception—it sums up the emotional life of the nineteenth century. Poor, scrofulous, fainting century, with its horror of anything strong, of solid food, its fondness for lying in its mother's lap like a sick child!

"Woman, what have I to do with thee?"[3] is a saying that I find finer than all the vaunted words of history. It is the cry of pure

[3] John, 2:4.

reason, the protest of the brain against the womb. And it has the virtue of having always aroused the indignation of idiots.

Our "cult of the mother" is one of the things that will arouse the laughter of future generations. So too our respect for "love": this will be thrown on the same refuse-heap with the "sensibility" and "nature" of a hundred years ago.

Only one poet, in my opinion, understood those charming animals—namely, the master of masters, Shakespeare the omniscient. In his works women are worse or better than men. He portrays them as extra-exalted beings, never as reasonable ones. That is why his feminine characters are at once so ideal and so true.

In short, never place any faith in their opinion of a book. For them, temperament is everything; they are only for the occasion, the place, the author. As for knowing whether a detail (exquisite or even sublime in itself) strikes a false note in relation to the whole—no! A thousand times no!

I note with pleasure that printers' ink is beginning to stink in your nostrils. In my opinion it is one of the filthiest inventions of mankind. I resisted it until I was thirty-five, even though I began scribbling at eleven. A book is something essentially organic, a part of ourselves. We tear out a length of gut from our bellies and serve it up to the bourgeois. Drops of our hearts' blood are visible in every letter we trace. But once our work is printed—farewell! It belongs to everyone. The crowd tramples on us. It is the height of prostitution, and the vilest kind. But the convention is that it's all very noble, whereas to rent out one's ass for ten francs is an infamy. So be it! . . .

To ERNEST FEYDEAU

[*Croisset, first half of October, 1859*]

Your letter went to my heart, my poor friend! What can I say? What banality can I offer? I am thinking of you, and can do no more. Is all hope gone? Poor woman![4] It is frightful. You are having and you are going to have "important" experiences, and you are going to be able to turn them into "important" writings. It's a high price to pay. The bourgeois little suspect that we give them our hearts to eat. The race of gladiators is not dead; every artist is one. He amuses the public with his agonies. You must be exhausted, crushed, broken. The only way not to suffer too much at these dreadful moments is to study one's self endlessly; this is possible, for at such times one's mind is extraordinarily keen.

My mother asks me to tell you how sorry she is for you; she well knows what you are going through. Adieu, my friend, be brave.

To EDMOND and JULES DE GONCOURT

Croisset, July 3, [*1860*]

Since you ask about Carthage, I answer as follows:

I think that my eyes were bigger than my stomach. So-called realism is almost impossible with such a subject. There is always the poetic style to fall back on, but this means a relapse into a whole series of old chestnuts, from *Télémaque* to *Les Martyres.* I shan't mention the archaeological research, all trace of which must be hidden, or the language necessitated by the next-to-impossible form. To produce the effect of truth I should have to be obscure, talk gibberish, and stuff the book with footnotes; whereas if I stick to the usual literary tone everything becomes banal. *"Problème!"* as Père Hugo would say.

Despite all this, I keep on, but I am eaten with doubts and worries. I console myself with the thought that I'm attempting something worth while.

The standard of the Doctrine[5] will be boldly unfurled this

[4] Madame Feydeau, who died October 18.
[5] Of art for art's sake—*l'art pour l'art.*

time, you may be sure. For this book proves nothing, says nothing, is neither historical, nor satirical, nor humorous. On the other hand, it may be stupid.

I am now beginning Chapter VIII, after which there will be seven more to do; I shan't be finished for another eighteen months.

It was not out of mere politeness that I congratulated you on your last book and on the kind of work you are doing. I love history madly. The dead are more to my taste than the living. Whence comes this seductiveness of the past? Why have you made me infatuated with the mistresses of Louis XV? Incidentally, a love of this kind is something entirely new. The historical sense dates from only yesterday, and it may well be the best thing the nineteenth century has to offer.

What will you do next? As for me, I am giving myself over to the Cabala, to the Mishna, to the military art of the ancients, etc.—a mass of reading that does me no good but that I undertake because I am over-conscientious and also, a little, because I like it. Beyond that, I'm distressed by the assonances I find in my prose. My life is as flat as my writing-table. Day follows day, and—outwardly at least—each is like the other. In my fits of despair I dream of travel: a poor remedy.

You both seem to be virtuously bored in the bosom of your family, amid rustic enchantments. I well understand this state of mind—an understanding that comes of experience.

To MADAME ROGER DES GENETTES

[*Croisset, July, 1862*]

To you I can say everything. Well then, our god is on the downgrade. *Les Misérables* exasperates me, and it is impossible to criticize it without being taken for a police spy. The author's position is impregnable, unassailable. I, who have spent my life worshipping him, find myself full of indignation; I have to explode.

I find neither truth nor greatness in this book. As for the style, it seems to me deliberately incorrect and low. It is a device for flattering the populace. Hugo takes pains to be nice to everyone; Saint-Simonians, Philippistes, and even innkeepers—he kowtows to them all. And the characters—cut out of whole cloth, as in French tragedy! Where will you find prostitutes like Fantine, convicts like Valjean, and politicians like the stupid idiots of the ABC?[6] Not one of them is ever portrayed as truly suffering; they are puppets, candy figures, from Monseigneur Bienvenu right through the list. In his socialist rage, Hugo slanders the Church just as he slanders the poor. Where will you find a bishop who asks a revolutionary for his blessing? Where will you find a factory that will discharge a girl for having a baby? And the digressions—there are so many of them! The passage about fertilizers must have delighted Pelletan. This book is just the thing for the Catholic-socialist rabble, for all the philosophical-evangelical vermin. What a charming character is Monsieur Marius, living three days on a cutlet; and Monsieur Enjolras, who has given only two kisses in his life, poor boy! As for their speeches, they talk very well, but all alike. The drivel of Gillenormant, the last ravings of Valjean, the humor of Cholomiès and Gantaise—it's all from the same mold. Always quips and jokes, artificial high spirits, and never anything comic. Lengthy explanations of irrelevant matters, and none whatever when it comes to anything important. But plenty of sermons to show that universal suffrage is a very fine thing, that the masses should be educated; this is repeated ad nauseam. Despite its occasional good bits this book is decidedly childish. Observation is a secondary quality in literature, but a contemporary of Balzac and Dickens has no right to depict society so

6 *Les Misérables*, Book IV.

falsely. The subject is a very good one, but it called for unemotional, highly scientific handling. It is true that Père Hugo despises science—and here he proves it. . . .

Posterity will not forgive him for trying to be a thinker—a role contrary to his nature. See where his mania for philosophical prose has led him! And what philosophy! That of the pompous Philistine, of Poor Richard, of Béranger. He is no more a thinker than Racine or La Fontaine, of whom he has a low opinion: like them he represents the drift and the body of the banal ideas of his time, and he does it so completely that he neglects his own art. That is my opinion; I keep it to myself, needless to say. Everyone who touches a pen owes too much to Hugo to wish to venture a criticism; but I see that the gods are growing old, at least on the face of it.

I await your answer and your anger.

To LAURE DE MAUPASSANT

Paris, [January, 1863]

. . . Since you mention *Salammbô,* you will be glad to hear that my little Carthaginian is making her way in the world. My publisher announces the second edition for Friday. Big and little newspapers are speaking about me; I'm the occasion for large quantities of stupid talk. Some critics are vilifying me, some exalting me. I have been called a "drunken helot," charged with "poisoning the air" around me, compared to Chateaubriand and Marmontel, accused of trying to get myself elected to the Institute; and one lady who had read my book asked a friend of mine whether Tanit weren't a devil. *Voilà!* Such is literary fame. Gradually the mentions come at longer and longer intervals, then you're forgotten and it's over.

No matter; I wrote a book for a very limited number of readers and it turns out that the public is snatching at the bait.

Blest be the god of the book trade! I was very glad to know that you liked it, for you know how I value your intelligence, my dear Laure. You and I are not only friends from childhood, but almost classmates. Do you remember our reading the *Feuilles d'automne* together at Fécamp, in the little upstairs room? . . .

To IVAN TURGENEV

Croisset, near Rouen, March 16, [*1863*]

Dear Monsieur Turgenev

How grateful I am for your present! I have just finished your two volumes, and cannot resist telling you that they enchant me.

I have long looked on you as a master, but the more I read you the more spellbound I am by your talent. I admire your manner, at once vehement and restrained; and your sympathy, which extends to the most insignificant beings and makes the very landscapes articulate. We see them, and they set us dreaming.

Whenever I read *Don Quixote* I long to ride my horse down a white and dusty road and to eat olives and raw onions in the shadow of a rock; and similarly your stories of Russian life make me want to be jolted across snow-covered fields in a telega, with the howling of wolves in the distance. Your books give off a bitter-sweet perfume, a charming sadness, which penetrates to the very depths of my soul.

What art you have! What a mixture of compassion, irony, observation, and color! How you combine all those elements! How you manage your effects! What sureness of hand!

You are always concrete, yet always universal. How many things which I myself have felt and experienced I have rediscovered in your pages! In *Three Meetings,* in *Yakov Pasynkov,* in the *Diary of a Superfluous Man*—everywhere.

But what has not been sufficiently praised in you is your heart—that is, the *feeling* that is always present, some deep and hidden sensitivity.

I was very happy, a fortnight ago, to make your acquaintance and shake your hand. Let me shake it again, more strongly than before.

To his niece CAROLINE

Paris, Wednesday, 3 o'clock, [*end of December, 1863*]

Mon Bibi:

. . . Now let's talk about the big thing.

So, poor Caro, you are still in the same uncertainty, and perhaps even now, after a third meeting, you've advanced no further. It is such a serious decision to make that I should be in exactly the same state of mind were I in your pretty skin. Look, think, explore yourself heart and soul; try to discover whether you have any chances of happiness with this gentleman. Human life feeds on other things than ideals[7] and exalted sentiments; but on the other hand if a bourgeois existence makes you die of boredom, how can you make up your mind? Your poor grandmother wants you to marry, fearing to leave you alone, and I too, dear Caro, should like to see you united to a decent boy who would make you as happy as possible. The other night when I saw you crying so bitterly your unhappiness touched my heart. Your two old companions love you dearly, my darling, and the day of your marriage will not be a merry one for us. I am not jealous by nature, but I shall begin by having no liking for whoever becomes your husband. However, that's not the question. I will learn to forgive him, and will love and cherish him if he makes you happy.

7 "*Idées pratiques*" in the Conard edition. Unless *pratiques* is a misprint for *poétiques,* the context indicates that Flaubert was perhaps influenced by Kantian terminology, according to which the realm of the practical is identical with the realm of ethics.

So you see I can't even pretend to advise you. What speaks well for Monsieur Commanville is the way he has gone about things; moreover, we know his character, his background, and his connections, about all of which it would be next to impossible to learn anything in a Parisian milieu. Here in Paris you might perhaps find young men who are more brilliant; but wit and charm belong almost exclusively to bohemians. Now the idea of my dear niece being married to a poor man is so unbearable that I won't consider it for a moment. Yes, my darling, I declare that I should rather see you marry a rich Philistine than a great man without means. For the great man wouldn't be only poor; he would be brutal and tyrannical, and make you suffer to the point of madness or idiocy. The unpleasantness of living in Rouen has to be considered, I know; but it is better to live in Rouen with money than to be penniless in Paris; and for that matter why shouldn't you move to Paris later if the business goes well?

I am like you, you see; I don't know what to think; I keep saying yes and no. I'm too interested in the question to be able to see clearly. It will be hard for you to find a husband who is your superior in intelligence and education—if I knew one who had those qualifications and met all other requirements I'd set out and secure him for you at once—so you must think of choosing some good boy who is your inferior. But will you be able to love a man you look down on? Will you be happy with him? That's the whole question. You'll doubtless be badgered to give a quick answer. Don't do anything in a hurry; and whatever happens, sweetheart, you know you can depend on the affection of your old uncle, who sends you a kiss.

Write me long letters with many details.

To MADAME ROGER DES GENETTES

[*Summer, 1864*]

. . . Before long I'll be able to give a course in socialism; at least I know its spirit and its meaning. I have just swallowed Lamennais, Saint-Simon, and Fourier, and am now going over all of Proudhon.[8] If you want to know *nothing* about these people, then read the criticisms and résumés written about them; they have always been refuted or praised to the skies, never expounded. One salient feature is common to them all: hatred of freedom, hatred of the French Revolution and of philosophy. All these people are of the Middle Ages; their minds are caught in the past. And what schoolmasters! What pedants! Seminarians on a spree, bookkeepers in delirium! The reason for their failure in '48 was that they stood outside the mainstream of tradition. Socialism is an aspect of the past, like Jesuitism. Saint-Simon's great teacher was Monsieur de Maistre, and how much Proudhon and Louis Blanc owe to Lamennais has never been sufficiently gone into. The Lyons school, the most active, is entirely mystic, like the Lollards. The bourgeois understood nothing of all this. They instinctively sensed what stands at the core of all social utopias: tyranny, negation of nature, the death of the soul. . . .

To GEORGE SAND

[*Croisset, early November, 1866*]

I arrived here Saturday night; all my errands are done, and this afternoon I'll get back to work.

Sainte-Beuve seems to me very ill; I fear he may not last long.

Yesterday and the day before I dined with Turgenev. That man's imagery is so powerful, even in conversation, that he *showed* me G. Sand leaning on her elbow on the balcony of

8 Flaubert is documenting himself for *L'Education sentimentale.*

Madame Viardot's château at Rosay. There was a moat under the turret, in the moat a boat, and, sitting in this boat, Turgenev, looking up at you; the light of the setting sun was shining on your black hair.

To ERNEST FEYDEAU

Croisset, [*late 1866 or early 1867*]

Dear Ernest

I don't know whether you are still in existence, but since I am writing to ask you a favor I hope that you will give a sign of life. This is what I should like to know—it concerns my book:

My hero Frédéric quite properly wants to have a little more money in his pocket, and he plays the market; he makes a little, then loses everything, fifty or sixty thousand francs. He is a young man of middle-class family, completely ignorant in such matters—even a three percent government bond is for him a mystery. This takes place in the summer of 1847.

So: from May to the end of August, what were the securities favored by speculators?

My story has three phases:

1. Frédéric goes to a broker with his money and follows the broker's advice. Is that how it's done?

2. He makes a profit. How? How much?

3. He loses everything. How? Why?

It would be very good of you to send me this information—the episode shouldn't take up more than six or seven lines in my book. But explain it all to me clearly and exactly.

Keep the date in mind—1847, the summer of the Praslin and Teste scandals.

And tell me something about yourself.

To GEORGE SAND

Friday morning, [Paris, May 10, 1867]

. . . Axiom: hatred of the Bourgeois is the beginning of virtue. But for me the term "bourgeois" includes the bourgeois in overalls as well as the bourgeois who wears a frock coat. It is we, and we alone—that is, the educated—who are the People, or, more accurately, the tradition of Humanity.

Yes, I am capable of disinterested anger; and I love you the more because you love me for this. Stupidity and injustice make me roar. And in my corner I grumble against many things that are "none of my business."

How sad that we live apart, *chère maître!* I admired you before I met you. And from the day I first saw your beautiful, kindly face, I have loved you. *Voilà.* . . .

To GEORGE SAND

[Croisset, about June 15, 1867]

Early this week I spent a day and a half in Paris to attend the ball at the Tuileries. I'm not joking when I say it was splendid. As a matter of fact, the whole trend in Paris is now toward the colossal. Everything is becoming wild and out of proportion. Perhaps we're returning to the ancient East. One keeps expecting idols to come out of the ground; there's the threat of a new Babylon. And why not? The individual has been so negated by democracy that he will be reduced to a state of complete impotence, as under the great theocratic despotisms.

I disliked the Czar of Russia; he seemed like a boor. Along with Floquet,[9] who, with no danger to himself, keeps crying "Long live Poland!" we have fashionable people signing the visitors' book at the Elysée. What a period!

[9] Following the czar's repression of the Polish uprising in 1863, French sympathy for Poland was exploited by those in opposition to the imperial regime. Charles Floquet was a leading republican.

To HIPPOLYTE TAINE [*1868?*]

My novel goes *piano*. As I advance, new difficulties turn up; it's like dragging a load of stones. And you complain of something that takes you six months! As for me, I still have two years, at least. How the devil do you handle transitions of ideas? That's what is holding me up. Moreover, this book requires tedious research. Monday, for example, I visited, one after the other, the Jockey Club, the Café Anglais, and a lawyer. . . .

A week ago I was enraptured by a camp of gypsies that stopped at Rouen. This is the third time I have seen them, each time with pleasure. The marvelous thing is that they aroused the *hatred* of the bourgeois, even though they were harmless as lambs. I earned the disapproval of the crowd by giving them a few sous, and I heard some delightfully Philistine remarks. This hatred stems from a deep and complex source; it's to be found in all champions of order. It's the hatred felt for the bedouin, the heretic, the philosopher, the recluse, the poet; and it contains an element of fear. I, who am always on the side of minorities, am driven wild by it. It is true that many things drive me wild. The day I stop being indignant I'll have nothing left to live for.

To HIPPOLYTE TAINE

[*1868?*]

. . . The characters I create "affect" me, pursue me, or rather I am in them. When I was describing the poisoning of Emma Bovary, I had such a taste of arsenic in my mouth, was poisoned so effectively myself, that I had two attacks of indigestion one after the other—two very real attacks, for I vomited my entire dinner. . . .

Do not liken the inner vision of the artist to that of a man suffering from actual hallucinations. I know these two states perfectly; there is a gulf between them. In genuine hallucination there is always fear; you feel that you are losing hold of your personality; you think you are about to die. In poetic vision, on the contrary, there is joy; something comes into you; nevertheless, here also you lose your bearings. . . . This vision often builds up slowly, piece by piece, like the various parts of a theatrical setting being put into place; but often, too, it is sudden, fleeting like hypnagogic hallucinations. Something passes before your eyes; you have to seize it avidly. . . .

To EDMOND and JULES DE GONCOURT

[*Croisset, May, 1868*]

. . . Last Sunday I returned to my apartment at eleven-thirty, went to bed hoping to sleep soundly, and blew out my candle. Three minutes later, trombones and drums! It was a wedding at Bonvalet's. Said restaurateur's windows were wide open, due to the hot night; I didn't miss a single quadrille, a single shout. The band (I have the honor to repeat) was enlivened by *two drums!*

At six in the morning, entry of masons. At seven, I betook myself to the Grand Hôtel. There, three-quarters of an hour on my feet before finding a room. Scarcely was I there (in the room) when hammering began in the adjoining apartment. Another promenade in the same hotel to find a refuge. At nine o'clock I gave up and went to the Hôtel du Helder, where I found a miserable closet, black as a tomb. But the peace of the grave was lacking: there were the shouts of guests, the rumbling of carriages in the street, the clanking of tin pails in the court. From one o'clock to three, I packed my bags and then left the Boulevard du Temple. From four to six, I tried to sleep at Du Camp's, rue du Rocher. But I had reckoned without another crew of masons, who were building a garden wall. At six, I transported myself to a public bath, rue Saint-Lazare. There, children playing in the yard, a piano. At eight, I returned to the rue du Helder, where my servant had laid out on my bed everything I needed for the Tuileries ball. But I had not yet dined, and thinking that hunger had perhaps weakened my nerves, I went to the Café de l'Opéra. I had scarcely entered, when a gentleman vomited beside me. At nine, return to the Hôtel du Helder. The thought of having to dress drained the strength from me like a fourfold bloodletting. I rebelled, and decided to return to the country as quickly as I could. My servant packed my trunk.

That's not all. Final episode: my trunk rolled off the top of the cab and crashed onto my shoulder. I still carry the bruises.

Voilà!

To GEORGE SAND

[*Croisset, late September, 1868*]

You are surprised,[10] *chère maître?* Not I! I told you so, but you wouldn't believe me. I am sorry for you. It is sad to see such a change in someone you love. The substitution of one soul for another, in a body which remains the same as before, is a heartbreaking sight. One feels betrayed. I have experienced this more than once.

Still, what is your conception of women, oh you who are of the third sex? Are they not, as Proudhon says, "the desolation of the righteous"? Have they ever been able to do without chimeras? After love, piety; it's natural. When the soubrette no longer has men in her life she turns to God, that's all.

Few are the human beings who have no need of the supernatural. Philosophy will always be the exclusive property of aristocrats. Fatten the human cattle, bed them with straw up to their bellies, even gild their stable—to no avail: they remain

10 An actress friend of George Sand's had just been converted to Catholicism.

brutish for all that. The only progress to be hoped for is that the beasts may be made a little less vicious. But as for elevating the ideas of the masses, giving them a broader and therefore less human conception of God, I am very dubious, very dubious.

I am now reading an honest little book (by a friend of mine, a judge) about the Revolution in the department of the Eure. It is full of documents written by bourgeois of the period, ordinary small-town citizens. I assure you there are few of that caliber nowadays. They were educated and courageous, full of good sense, ideas, and generosity.

Neo-Catholicism on the one hand and socialism on the other have brought France to stupidity. Between the Immaculate Conception and free lunches for workingmen, everything marches toward ruin.

I told you that I do not flatter the democrats in my book. The conservatives are not spared either, I assure you. I am now writing three pages on the abominations committed by the National Guard in June 1848, which will make me highly popular with the bourgeois! I am doing my best to rub their noses in their own turpitudes. . . .

To LOUIS BONENFANT

Croisset [*1868?*]

Dear Friend,

I have not thanked you enough. Your account is excellent in every way, and furnishes me with good details. You've done me a real service in sending it. I'm grateful to cousin Emilie, too, for her list of Nogent expressions; but I repay her kindness with the blackest ingratitude, because:

I cannot do as she would like, which is to change the name of the hero of my novel. You probably remember that four years ago I asked you whether there were still people named Moreau living in Nogent. You replied that there were none, and you supplied me with several local names that I could feel free to use. On the strength of the information you gave me I went blithely ahead. It is too late to change. A proper name is extremely important in a novel—crucial. It is no more possible to give a character a new name than a new skin; it's like wanting to turn a Negro white.

So much the worse for the Moreaus now living in Nogent! Not that they'll have any cause for complaint: my Monsieur Moreau is a very chic young gentleman.

To GEORGE SAND

Croisset, Tuesday, February 2, 1869

Ma chère Maître:

Your old troubadour is a weary man. I spent a week in Paris chasing data—a ghastly week—seven to nine hours of cab fare a day, a fine way to get rich with literature! Well—

I have just read over my outline—the amount I still have to write overwhelms me, or rather sickens me to the point of nausea. It's always so when I get back to work; it's then that I'm bored, bored, bored! But this time it's worse than ever. That's my reason for so dreading any interruption of the grind. I had no choice, however. I had myself carted to undertakers', to Père-Lachaise, to the valley of Montmorency, past stores selling religious articles, etc.

I still have four or five months' work ahead of me. What a sigh of relief I'll give when it's done, and I assure you it will be a long day before I tackle the bourgeois again. It's time I enjoyed myself.

I saw Sainte-Beuve and Princess Mathilde, and I know everything about their break, which seems to me irrevocable. Sainte-

Beuve quit Dalloz[11] in a rage and went over to *Le Temps.* The princess begged him not to. He wouldn't listen. That's the whole story. My opinion, if you care to have it, is this: the first offense was committed by the princess, who was sharp; but the second and more serious wrong lies at the door of Sainte-Beuve, who behaved anything but gallantly. When you have as your friend such a good-natured creature as the princess, and when this friend has given you an income of thirty thousand francs a year, you owe her a certain consideration. It seems to me that were I in Sainte-Beuve's place I should have said: "Since it displeases you, let's speak no more about it." His manners and his attitude were both at fault. What disgusted me a little, between you and me, was the eulogy he made of the emperor. To me! A eulogy of Badinguet![12]

The princess took the thing too seriously from the beginning. I wrote her so, justifying Sainte-Beuve, who, I am sure, found me cold. It was at that point, to vindicate himself in my eyes, that he protested his love for Isidore. This humiliated me a little; for it amounted to taking me for a downright fool.

I think his goal is to be given a national funeral, like Béranger, and that he is jealous of Hugo's popularity. Why should anyone write for the newspapers when he can write books and isn't dying of starvation? He is far from being a sage, that man; he is not like you!

Your strength charms and amazes me. I mean the strength of your entire personality, not only of your brain.

You spoke of criticism in your last letter, saying that it will soon disappear. I think the contrary, that its dawn has barely begun. It's simply that its trend is the reverse of what it once was. In the time of La Harpe critics were grammarians; in the

11 Owner and editor of the *Moniteur Universel,* to which Sainte-Beuve had contributed many of his famous *Lundis.* Sainte-Beuve is ill at this time; this is the last year of his life.

12 "Badinguet" and "Isidore" were popular nicknames for Napoleon III.

time of Sainte-Beuve and Taine they are historians. When will they be artists, nothing but artists, real artists? Where have you seen a criticism that is concerned, intensely concerned, with the work *in itself?* The milieu in which it was produced and the circumstances which occasioned it are very closely analyzed; but the unconscious poetics which are its source? Its composition? Its style? The author's point of view? Never!

Such criticism would require great imagination and great generosity, I mean an ever-ready faculty of enthusiasm, and then *taste,* a rare quality even among the best—rare to such a point that it is no longer even mentioned.

What infuriates me daily is to see masterpieces and turpitudes put on the same level. Insignificance is exalted and greatness disparaged; nothing could be more stupid or more immoral.

In Père-Lachaise I was overcome with a deep and painful disgust for humanity. You cannot imagine the fetishism of the tombs. The true Parisian is more idolatrous than a Negro. It made me want to lie down in one of the graves. . . .

To GEORGE SAND

Tuesday night, [*Croisset, March 2-3, 1869*]

What do I have to say about it, *chère maître?* Whether children's sensitivity should be fostered or discouraged? It seems to me that in this matter one shouldn't have preconceived ideas. It's according to whether they tend toward too much or too little. Moreover, you can't change essential character. There are affectionate natures and cold natures—there is no remedy for that. Furthermore, the same sight, the same lesson, may produce opposite effects. Nothing should have hardened me more than being brought up in a hospital and playing as a small child in a dissecting-room. And yet no one is more easily moved than I by the sight of physical suffering. It is true that I am the son of an extremely human man, sensitive in the good meaning of the word. The sight of a dog in pain brought tears to his eyes. And yet this in no way impaired his efficiency when performing operations, and he invented some terrible ones.

"Show children only the sweet and good side of life, up to the time when reason can help them accept or combat evil." Such is not my opinion. For then something terrible is bound to take place in their hearts, an infinite disillusionment. Besides, how can reason develop if it does not apply itself (or if it is not applied daily) to distinguishing right from wrong? Life must be incessant education; everything must be learned, from talking to dying.

You say some very true things about the *unknowingness* of children. He who could see clearly into their little brains would discover the roots of the human race, the origin of the gods, the sap that is the cause of later actions, etc. A Negro speaking to his idol, a child to its doll, seem to me very close.

The child and the barbarian (the primitive) do not distinguish reality from fantasy. I remember very clearly that at the age of five or six I wanted to "send my heart" to a little girl I was in love with (I mean my physical heart). I pictured it lying on a bed of straw, in an oyster basket!

But no one has gone as far as you in these analyses. Your *Histoire de ma vie* has pages on this subject that are extraordinarily profound. This is true, since minds very far removed from yours have found them amazing—as witness the Goncourts.

Our good Turgenev is expected in Paris by the end of March. It would be nice if the three of us could dine together.

I have been thinking more about Sainte-Beuve. To be sure, one can do without an income of 30,000 francs. But there is something still easier: having such an income, not to spout every week in the newspapers. Why doesn't he write books, since he's rich and talented?

I am rereading *Don Quixote.* What a giant of a book! Is there anything finer?

To GEORGE SAND

[*Croisset, late June or early July, 1869*]

What a sweet and charming letter! There is no one but you—I truly begin to believe it. A wind of stupidity and madness is blowing over the world, and there are few who stand strong and upright against it.

This is what I meant when I wrote you that politics is obsolete. In the eighteenth century, diplomacy was paramount. "Cabinet secrets" really existed. Peoples were still sufficiently meek to submit to divisions and unions. That order of things, it seems to me, took its last bow in 1815. Since then, the only quarrel has been about the external form suitable for that fantastic and odious being called the State.

Experience shows (it seems to me) that no form is intrinsically good; Orleanism, republic, empire, no longer mean anything, since the most contradictory ideas can be filed in each of those pigeonholes. All the flags have been so defiled with blood and shit that it is time we had none at all. Down with words! No more symbols! No more fetishes! The great moral of the present regime will be to prove that universal suffrage is as stupid as divine right, though a little less odious.

The problem shifts, therefore. It is no longer a question of striving for the best form of government, since one form is as good as another, but of making Science prevail. That is the most urgent. The rest will follow inevitably. Pure intellectuals have been of greater use to the human race than all the Saint Vincent de Pauls in the world! And politics will continue to be absurd until it becomes a province of Science. A country's government ought to be merely a section of the Institute—and the least important one of all.

Instead of concerning yourself with relief funds or even with agriculture, send a Robert Houdin[13] to perform miracles in every village in France. Isidore's greatest crime is the bottomless ignorance in which he allows our beautiful country to rot. *Dixi.*

To MAXIME DU CAMP

Croisset, July 23, 1869

Dear old Max, I feel the need of writing you a long letter; I don't know whether I'll have the strength, but I'll try. Since his return to Rouen our poor Bouilhet was convinced that he would never leave the place alive. Everybody, including myself, teased him about his pessimism. He was no longer the man you knew; he had changed completely, except for his literary intelligence, which remained the same. All in all, when I returned from Paris early in June, I found him in lamentable state. A trip which he made to Paris in connection with *Aïssé,* when Chilly asked him to make changes in the second act, took so much out of him that he could barely drag himself from the train to the Odéon. When I went to see him the last Sunday in June, I found Dr. Péan of Paris, another brute from Rouen named Leroy, Dr. Morel the alienist, and an excellent pharmacist he knew named Dupré. Bouilhet *didn't dare* consult Achille, suspecting that he was very ill and fearing to be told the truth. Péan sent him to Vichy, whence Willemin quickly sent him back to Rouen. On his arrival in Rouen, he finally called in Achille. But his case was hopeless, as indeed Willemin had written me.

During the past fortnight . . . I went to see Bouilhet every other day and *found him improving*. His appetite was excellent,

13 A celebrated magician of the time.

as were his spirits, and the swelling in his legs was subsiding. His sisters came from Cany to lecture him about religion and were so disgusting that they shocked a decent canon from the cathedral. Our poor friend was *superb*; he told them clearly what they could do. When I last left him, Saturday, he had a volume of La Mettrie on his bed-table; it reminded me of poor Alfred reading Spinoza. No priest was admitted to his house. As late as Saturday he was still sustained by his anger against his sisters, and I left for Paris hoping that he might still live a long time. At five o'clock on Sunday he became delirious and began to compose aloud the plot of a medieval drama on the Inquisition; he called me to show it to me and was enthusiastic about it. Then he was seized with trembling, stammered "Adieu! Adieu!," burying his head in Léonie's breast, and died very peacefully.

Monday at nine o'clock my janitor awoke me with a wire informing me of the event in telegraphic style. I was alone; I packed my suitcase and sent the news to you; I went to tell it to Duplan in his office; and, in the great heat, I tramped the streets in the neighborhood of the station. From Paris to Rouen the train was crowded, and I had opposite me a cocotte who smoked cigarettes, put her feet up on the seat, and kept singing. When I saw the towers of Mantes I thought I would lose my mind, and am sure that I came close to doing so.[14] Seeing that I was pale, the cocotte offered me eau de Cologne. That revived me, but I had a terrible thirst: ours in the desert of Kosseïr was nothing in comparison. Finally I reached the rue Bihorel: I spare you the details. I have never known anyone kinder than young Philippe; he and Léonie took *marvelous* care of Bouilhet. They did something that I consider admirable: to reassure him, persuade him that he was not dangerously ill, Léonie refused to marry him,

14 Memories of his meetings with Louise Colet in Mantes always made Flaubert emotional when his train between Paris and Rouen passed through that city.

and her son encouraged her in this attitude. Bouilhet had fully intended to marry her, and had even obtained all the necessary documents. On the part of the young man, especially, I find such conduct quite gentlemanly.[15]

D'Osmoy and I were the chief mourners; there was a large crowd at the cemetery, at least two thousand people. The prefect, the attorney-general, etc.—all the local notables. Will you believe that as I followed his coffin I relished very keenly the grotesqueness of the ceremony? I could hear him making remarks about it; within myself he was speaking to me; I felt that he was there beside me, and that together we were attending the funeral of somebody else. The heat was terrible; there was a storm in the offing. I was drenched with sweat, and the climb to the cemetery finished me. His friend Caudron (former clerk of Mayor Verdrel) had chosen a plot close to my father's, and I leaned on a railing to catch my breath. When the coffin was resting on poles over the grave and the speeches were about to begin (there were three) I gave up; Achille and a stranger took me away. The next day I went to fetch my mother at Serquigny. Yesterday I was in Rouen to get all his papers; today I have been reading the letters people have written me. Ah, it's a bitter blow!

By his will he leaves thirty thousand francs to Léonie and something more besides. All his books and papers go to Philippe, whom he directs to consult with four friends as to what should be done with the unpublished works: I, d'Osmoy, you, and Caudron; he leaves an excellent volume of poems, four plays in prose, and *Aïssé*. Chilly dislikes the second act; I don't know what he will do about it. This winter you will have to come here with d'Osmoy and we shall decide together what should be published. Thank le Mouton[16] for her kind words.

15 *"assez gentleman."*
16 Madame Husson, Du Camp's mistress.

I have too much of a headache. Adieu—besides, what more could I say? I embrace you warmly, and am all yours, my dear Max. Now there is only you, only you!

Gve Flaubert

All the letters I have received contain the phrase "Close up the ranks!" A gentleman *whom I do not know* sent me his card with these two words: *Sunt lacrymae!*

To GEORGE SAND

December 3, 1869

Chère bon maître,

Your old troubadour is being greatly berated in the press.[17] Read last Monday's *Constitutionnel* and this morning's *Gaulois* —they mince no words, and flatly call me a moron and a scoundrel. Barbey d'Aurevilly's piece in the *Constitutionnel* is a model of this genre, and the one by our friend Sarcey, though less violent, does not lag behind. These gentlemen protest in the name of morality and the Ideal! I have also been unfavorably noticed in the *Figaro* and in *Paris,* by Cesena and Duranty. I don't care in the least, though I am surprised by the hatred and dishonesty.

The *Tribune,* the *Pays,* and the *Opinion Nationale,* on the other hand, have praised me to the skies. As for my friends, people who received copies adorned with my signature, they are afraid of compromising themselves, and speak to me about other things. Instances of courage are rare. Nevertheless, the book is selling well despite the political situation, and Lévy seems to be satisfied.

I know that the bourgeois of Rouen are furious at me because of Old Roque and the Tuileries story.[18] They consider that the

17 For *L'Education sentimentale.*
18 *L'Education sentimentale,* end of Chapter One of Part III.

publication of such books should be forbidden (I quote verbatim), that I am hand in glove with the Reds, that I am quite capable of fanning revolutionary passions, etc. In short, I have gathered very few laurels so far, and am receiving no bouquets. . . .

All the papers adduce as proof of my baseness the episode of the Turk, which is garbled, of course; and Sarcey compares me to the Marquis de Sade, whom he admits he has not read.

None of this destroys my composure. But what, I wonder, is the use of publishing?

To GEORGE SAND

[*March 15, 1870*]

Chère Maître:

Last evening I received a telegram from Madame Cornu reading as follows: "Please come. Important." I therefore called on her today, and here is the story:

The Empress claims that you have made slighting allusions to her in the last number of the *Revue* [*des Deux Mondes*]. "How could she! With everyone attacking me now! I shouldn't have believed it! Why, I tried to have her elected to the Academy! What have I done to her? Etc." In brief, she is dismayed, and the Emperor too. He is not indignant, but "distressed" (*sic*).

Madame Cornu vainly insisted that she was mistaken, that you had made no allusion to her whatever, and tried to explain to her how novels are written.

"Well, then," said the Empress, "have her write to the newspapers that she had no intention of offending me."

"That is precisely what she will not do, I am sure."

"Then you write to her, and ask her to tell you so."

"I should not presume to take such a step."

"But I want to know the truth! Do you know someone who . . ."

(At this point Madame Cornu suggested me.)

"Oh, don't say that I spoke to you about this!"

Such is the dialogue that Madame Cornu reported to me. She would like you to address me a letter saying that the Empress was not your model. I am to send this letter to Madame Cornu, who will pass it on to the Empress. I find the whole thing stupid. These people are certainly sensitive: you and I have to put up with a good deal more than that! Now, my very dear colleague, in God's name do exactly as you please. The Empress has always been very kind to me and I have no objection to doing her a favor. I have read the passage in question and find nothing offensive in it. But a woman's brain is a peculiar thing!

I am very tired of my own (my brain, that is), or rather it's at a decidedly low ebb for the moment. Try as I may, I don't get ahead with my work. Everything annoys me and hurts me; and since I control myself in the presence of others I am occasionally seized by fits of weeping during which I feel that my end has come. It's the onset of old age: something quite new for me. The shadow engulfs me, as Victor Hugo would say.

Madame Cornu spoke to me enthusiastically about a letter you wrote her concerning a method of teaching.

To MADAME HORTENSE CORNU

Sunday Evening, [*March 20, 1870*]

In your devotion you took needless alarm, dear Madame; I was sure of it, and enclose the reply which came to me by return mail.

People in society, I tell you once again, see allusions where there are none. When I published *Madame Bovary* I was several times asked: "Is it Madame So-and-so that you wrote about?" And I received letters from perfect strangers, among others one from a gentleman in Rheims congratulating me for having "avenged" him (his wife having been unfaithful).

To MADAME HORTENSE CORNU [*1870*]

All the pharmacists of the Seine-Inférieure recognized themselves in Homais, and wanted to call on me and box my ears; but best of all (I discovered this only five years later) there existed at that time in Africa an army surgeon's wife named Madame Bovaries who resembled Madame Bovary—the latter a name which I invented by garbling the name Bouvaret.

The first words of our friend Maury when he spoke to me about the *Education sentimentale* were these: "Did you know ——, an Italian, professor of mathematics? Your Sénécal is a portrait of him, physically and morally. Every detail is right—even his haircut!" Others claimed that in Arnoux I wanted to depict Bernard-Latte (the former publisher), whom I had never seen, etc.

All this is simply to say, dear Madame, that the public is mistaken in attributing to us intentions which we do not have.

I was quite sure that Madame Sand had not intended to portray anyone, because of (1) her high-mindedness, her taste, her respect for Art; and (2) her moral sense, her sense of fitness, and also her sense of justice.

I even think, between you and me, that this accusation somewhat offended her. Every day the newspapers drag *us* in the mud, and we never reply even though it is our profession to wield the pen; and yet people imagine that for the sake of "making an effect," for the sake of applause, we deliberately choose some man or woman as our target. Ah, no! We are not so humble! Our ambition aims higher; we are more honest. Our intellectual pride forbids us to use the methods required to please the rabble. You understand me, do you not?

But enough. I shall call on you some day soon. Meanwhile, in anticipation of that pleasure, dear Madame, I kiss your hands and am entirely yours.

To GEORGE SAND

[*March 20, 1870*]

Chère Maître:

I have just sent your letter (for which I thank you) to Madame Cornu, enclosing it in an epistle of mine in which I allow myself to express my mind rather sharply.

The two documents will be submitted to the Lady and will provide her with a little lesson in aesthetics. . . .

To GEORGE SAND

Croisset, Wednesday evening, [*July 20, 1870*]

What has become of you, *chère maître*—you and your dear ones?

As for me, I am nauseated, heartbroken at the stupidity of my fellow-countrymen.[19] The incorrigible barbarism of the human race fills me with deep gloom. This war enthusiasm, unmotivated by any idea, makes me long to die so that I need no longer witness it.

The good Frenchman is ready to fight, because: (1) he considers himself provoked by Prussia; (2) man's natural condition is savagery; (3) there is inherent in war a mystical element that enraptures the crowd.

Have we returned to the wars of the races? I fear so. The frightful butchery that is to come lacks even a pretext. It is the craving to fight for the mere sake of fighting.

I lament the destruction of bridges and tunnels, the waste of so much human work, the utter negation.

The peace conference[20] is wrong for the moment. Civilization seems to me a far-distant thing. Hobbes was right: *Homo homini lupus.*

19 France had declared war on Prussia the day before.

20 Conferences had been held by the Ligue Internationale Permanente pour la Paix in 1868 and 1869.

To GEORGE SAND [*1870*]

I have begun *Saint Antoine,* and it might go well if I didn't think of the war. And you?

The bourgeois here are at the end of their endurance. They consider that Prussia was too insolent, and want to "avenge themselves." Did you see that a gentleman in the Chamber of Deputies has proposed the sacking of the Duchy of Baden? Ah! Why can't I go live with the Bedouins?

To GEORGE SAND

Saturday, [*Croisset, September 10, 1870*]

Chère Maître,

Here we are at the bottom of the abyss![21] Even a shameful peace will perhaps not be accepted. The Prussians want to destroy Paris—such is their dream. I do not believe that the siege of Paris is imminent. But to force its surrender they will (1) intimidate it by a display of cannon, and (2) ravage the surrounding countryside. At Rouen, we are expecting a visit from these gentlemen. Since Sunday I have been lieutenant of my company,[22] and I drill my men and go to Rouen to take lessons in military art. The deplorable thing is that opinion is divided; some are for defense to the death and others for peace at any price.

I am dying of grief. What a house this is! Fourteen people,[23] all groaning, all driving me crazy. I curse women: they are the cause of all our misfortunes.

I expect Paris to suffer the fate of Warsaw, and you distress me with your enthusiasm for the Republic. At this moment, when we are being defeated by positivism at its purest, how can you still believe in phantoms? Whatever happens, those now in power will be sacrificed, and the Republic will suffer the same

21 The disaster of Sedan had taken place September 1.
22 Of local militia.
23 Refugee relations from the war zone are swelling the household.

fate. Note that I am fighting for our pathetic Republic, but I don't believe in it.

That is all I have to tell you now. I have many other thoughts, but cannot collect them—I feel as though I were submerged in cataracts, rivers, oceans of sadness. It is impossible to suffer more than this: at times I fear I am going insane. The very sight of my mother's face drains me of all energy.

This is where our maniacal refusal to recognize the Truth has led us, our passion for everything meretricious and humbug. We'll become another Poland, then another Spain. Then it will be Prussia's turn—she will be devoured by Russia.

As for me, I consider myself finished. My brain will never function again. It is impossible to write when self-respect is gone. All I ask is to die, so that I can be calm.

To GEORGE SAND

Wednesday, [*Croisset, mid-September, 1870*]

I am sad no longer. Yesterday I took up my *Saint Antoine*—I had to. We must resign ourselves; we must become accustomed to man's natural condition—that is, to evil.

The Greeks in the time of Pericles devoted themselves to Art without knowing where their next day's bread would come from. Let us be Greek! I confess, however, *chère maître,* that I feel more like a savage. Scholar though I am, the blood of my forefathers, the Natchez[24] or the Hurons, is seething in my veins; and I have a grim, stupid, animal desire to fight. Explain that if you can! The idea of signing a peace now exasperates me, and I should rather see Paris burned (like Moscow) than occupied by the Prussians. But we have not yet reached that point, and I think the tide is turning. I have read several letters from sol-

24 Flaubert pretended to believe a family legend that one of his ancestors had married a North American Indian girl.

diers. They are exemplary: a country in which such things are written can't be swallowed up. France is not through yet; one day she will show her teeth.

Whatever happens, another world is in the making, and I feel too old to adjust myself to new ways. How I miss you, how I long to see you!

Here we are resolved to march on Paris should Hegel's fellow-countrymen besiege it. Try to put some guts into your neighbors in Berry. Tell them to help you prevent the enemy from eating and drinking in a country that doesn't belong to him.

The war (I trust) will deal a heavy blow to the "authorities." Will the individual, negated and trampled by the modern world, come into his rights again? Let us hope so.

To MAXIME DU CAMP

Croisset, September 29, 1870

In answer to your letter of the nineteenth, received this morning, let us proceed in order. First of all I embrace you and pity you from the bottom of my heart; now let's talk. Since last Sunday there has been a general change; we know that it is a duel to the death. All hope of peace is gone; the greatest cowards are showing courage. Here is proof: the first battalion of the Rouen National Guard left yesterday, the second will go tomorrow. The municipal council has appropriated a million for the purchase of chassepots and cannon. The peasants are raging. I guarantee that within a fortnight all France will rise. Near Mantes a peasant has strangled a Prussian and torn him apart with his teeth. In short, there is now a genuine will to fight. Paris can and will hold out. Whatever the English press may say, there is general good feeling. There will be no civil war. The bourgeois have become sincerely republican: (1) because they are in a funk, and (2) because they can't do otherwise. There is no time for quarreling; I think the socialist commonwealth has been postponed indefinitely. We get our news by balloon and carrier-pigeon. The few private letters that have reached Rouen are unanimous in saying that during the past ten days we have had the upper hand in all the engagements fought around Paris; that of the 23rd was serious. The [London] *Times* is lying shamelessly. The armies of the Loire and Lyons are not myths. During the last twelve days 55,000 men have passed through Rouen. Cannon are being turned out in large numbers at Bourges and in central France. If we can relieve Bazaine and cut communication lines with Germany, we are saved. Our military resources amount to little in the open field, but our mitrailleurs are a considerable nuisance to the Prussians; they think our way of fighting beastly—at least they said so at Mantes. Our greatest shortage is in generals and officers. No matter; there is hope. As for me, I came close to madness and suicide, but have now completely recovered. I have bought a knapsack and am ready for everything.

I assure you things are beginning to be interesting. Tonight 400 militia arrived in Croisset from the Pyrenees. Two are quartered with me here—in addition to the two I have in Paris—my mother has two in Rouen, Commanville five in Paris and two in Dieppe. I spend my time drilling my men and doing night patrol. Since Sunday I have been working again, and am no longer depressed. Amid all this there are, or there have been, some exquisitely grotesque scenes; Humanity is seen in the raw at such moments. What distresses me is the immense stupidity we'll all drown in later.

All *gentillesse,* as Montaigne would say, is gone for a long time to come. A new kind of world will arise: children will be brought up to hate the Prussians. From now on we are doomed to the most abject militarism and positivism, unless the air is cleared by the powder and we emerge from the ordeal stronger and healthier. I think we shall soon be avenged by a general upheaval. When Prussia has the Dutch ports, Kourland, and Trieste, England, Austria, and Russia may repent. Wilhelm was wrong not to make peace after Sedan: our shame would have been complete. Now we'll begin to be interesting. As to our immediate success, who can tell? The Prussian army is a marvelous precision mechanism, but all mechanisms are disrupted by the unexpected; a straw can break a spring. Our enemy has science on his side; but sentiment, inspiration, despair are elements to be reckoned with. Justice must win; and this time justice is with us. Yes, you are right; we are paying for having lied to ourselves all these years. Everything was pseudo: pseudo-army, pseudo-politics, pseudo-literature, pseudo-prosperity, and even pseudo-courtesans. It was immoral to speak the truth. All last winter Persigny reproached me for "lacking ideals"! and he was quite possibly sincere. All kinds of things are going to come to light; it will be a nice chapter in history. It humiliates me to have become a savage; my heart is as dry as a stick.

Now that I have written this I'll don my uniform and take a military stroll in the Bois de Canteleu. Have you thought of the quantities of paupers we'll have? All the factories are closed, the workmen without jobs or bread: it will be nice this winter. Despite all this—perhaps I'm crazy—something tells me that we'll come out all right. My respects to the general, and all my affection to you.

To GEORGE SAND

Sunday evening, [*Croisset, October 30, 1870*]

I am still alive, *chère maître,* but not better for being so, such is my sadness. My reason for not writing earlier is that I was awaiting your news. I didn't know your whereabouts.

For six weeks we have been expecting the arrival of the Prussians from one day to the next. We keep listening, thinking we hear the sound of cannon in the distance. They are converging on the Seine-Inférieure; at present they are fourteen to twenty leagues away—even closer, for they occupy the Vexin, and have completely devastated it. What horrors! It makes one blush to be a human being.

If we have a victory on the Loire, their coming will be retarded. But shall we have this victory? When I feel hope I try to suppress it, and yet deep within me, despite everything, I cannot help keeping a little, just a little.

I think I am the saddest man in France. (Everything depends on a person's sensitivity.) I am dying of grief; that is the truth, and anything said in consolation irritates me. What breaks my heart is (1) human ferocity; (2) the conviction that we are about to enter an era of stupidity. We'll be utilitarian, militaristic, American, and Catholic, very Catholic! You'll see! This war with Prussia concludes and destroys the French Revolution.

"But what if we should be victorious?" you ask. This hypothesis goes against all historical precedents. Where have you ever seen the South defeat the North, Catholics prevail over Protestants? The Latin race is in its death throes. France will follow Spain and Italy; the era of the cad is upon us.

What a collapse! What a fall! What wretchedness! What abominations! Is it possible to believe in progress and civilization in the face of everything now taking place? What good is science? Prussia, full of scientists, is committing abominations worthy of the Huns—worse, because they are systematic, cold-blooded, deliberate, without the excuse of passion or hunger.

Why do they so execrate us? Don't you feel crushed by the hate of forty million people? The thought of such an immense, hellish abyss makes my senses reel.

There is no lack of ready-made slogans. "France will arise! Do not despair! Our punishment will benefit us! We were really too immoral!, etc." Oh, eternal nonsense! No! One does not recover from such a blow. I feel myself stricken to the core.

Were I twenty years younger, I might not think all this; were I twenty years older, I could resign myself to it.

Poor Paris! The city is heroic. But if it survives it will no longer be our Paris. All the friends I had there are dead or gone. I no longer have anything to hold on to. Literature seems to me vain and useless. Will I ever be capable of writing again?

Oh! To escape to a country without the sight of uniforms and the sound of drums, without talk of massacres and civic duty! But the earth is no longer habitable for us poor mandarins!

To his niece CAROLINE

Rouen, Sunday, December 18, 1870

Dear Carolo,

How you must be worrying about us! Be reassured—we are all alive; we have passed through a time of terrible emotion, and we are still plunged in indescribable difficulties. God be thanked that you have been away from it. At times I thought I should go mad. The night before we left Croisset was horrible. Your grandmother slept at the hospital all of one week; I spent a night there. At present we are in our apartment, with two soldiers quartered on us. At Croisset there are seven, plus three officers and six horses. So far we have no reason to complain of these gentlemen. But what humiliation, poor Caro! What ruin! What sadness! What wretchedness! Don't expect me to write you an account: it would be too long, and besides I shouldn't be up to it. For a fortnight it has been impossible for us to receive a letter from anywhere, or a newspaper, or to communicate with the outside; from the English papers you must know more about everything than we do. We have been unable to send a letter to your husband, and he has been unable to write to us. Let us hope that when the Prussians are completely entrenched in Normandy they will let us move about. The English consul in Rouen tells me that the Newhaven boat is out of service. As soon as it resumes, as soon as the road from Dieppe to Rouen is clear, come back to us, dear Caro! Your grandmother is growing so old! She longs for you so, needs you so! Such months as I have spent with her since your departure! My sufferings have been so atrocious that I wish them on no one, not even on those who caused them. When we are not doing errands for the Prussians (yesterday I was on my feet three hours getting them hay and straw) we are asking each other for news or sit weeping in a corner. I was not born yesterday, and during my life I have suffered many blows; but all was as nothing, compared with what I am enduring now. Nothing, nothing! How can we stand it? I marvel that it is possible.

And we don't know when it will end. Poor Paris still holds out! But eventually it will give in. And in the meantime France will be completely sacked, ruined. And what will happen then? What a future lies ahead! There will be no lack of sophists to prove that we'll be the better for it, and that "misfortune purifies." No! Misfortune makes us selfish and vicious and stupid. This disaster was inevitable; it is in accordance with the laws of history. But what a mockery are the words "humanity," "progress," "civilization." Oh, poor child, if you could know what it means to hear them drag their swords on the sidewalk, to have their horses whinny in your face! What a disgrace! What a disgrace!

My poor head is aching so that I have to make a great effort to write. How will this letter reach you? I have no idea. I was given hope this evening that I could send it to you by a roundabout way. Your uncle Achille Flaubert has had and is still having great difficulty in the municipal council—it held a session while workingmen were firing rifles outside the windows. I am constantly on the verge of vomiting; your grandmother never leaves the house, and when she walks in her room she has to support herself against the furniture and the wall. When you can return safely, do. I think it your *duty* to be near her. Your poor husband is sad because of your long absence, and he must feel worse now that another fortnight has passed. The Prussians are said to have been in Dieppe twice, but not to have stayed (the first time it was to get tobacco; people who have it hide it, and it gets steadily scarcer). But we know nothing definite about anything, for we are cut off as in a besieged city. This uncertainty comes on top of all our other anguish. When I think of the past it seems to me a dream. The Boulevard du Temple—what a paradise! Do you realize that at Croisset they are occupying *all* the rooms? There would be no place for us if we wanted to return. It is eleven at night, the wind is blowing, the rain is lashing the windows. I am writing you in your old bedroom, and can hear the snores of the two soldiers sleeping in your dressing-room. I toss and plunge in my sorrow like a boat foundering at sea. I never thought my heart could hold so much suffering and remain alive.

I embrace you with all my strength. When shall I see you?

Your old uncle, who can stand no more.

To GEORGE SAND

[*Croisset, April 29, 1871*]

This is an immediate answer to your questions about me. No, the Prussians did not loot my house. They took a few trifles—a dressing-case, a box, some pipes; but on the whole they did no damage. My study they respected. I had buried a large box full of letters and hidden my mass of notes on *Saint Antoine,* and I found it all intact.

The worst effect of the invasion for me is that it has aged my poor old mother by ten years. What a change! She can no longer walk unaided, and her weakness is heartbreaking. How sad it is to watch the slow deterioration of those you love!

To escape the thought of public disasters and my own, I have once more plunged furiously into *Saint Antoine,* and if I can continue at this pace without interruption it will be finished next winter. I should dearly love to read you the sixty pages that are done. When railway journeys become possible again, come and see me. Your old troubadour has been waiting a long time for you! Your letter of this morning touched me. What a fine fellow you are, and what a great heart you have!

I hear much lamentation about the war in Paris, but I don't lament; I find it easier to bear than the invasion. No further despair is possible—another proof of the depths to which we have fallen. "Ah, thank God! The Prussians are there!" is the universal cry of the bourgeois. I use the word "bourgeois" to include Their Honors the workingmen, and I'd like to throw the whole lot of them into the river. That's where they're headed, anyway. Then things will be quiet again. Our country is going to become dreary and industrial—a big Belgium. The disappearance of Paris (as seat of the government) will make France dull and stagnant. She will have no center, no heart, no mind.

As for the Commune, which is in its death throes, it is the latest manifestation of the Middle Ages. Will it be the last? Let us hope so.

I hate democracy (at least as it is understood in France): the glorification of grace at the expense of justice, the negation of right—the very opposite, that is, of a genuine community.

The Commune is rehabilitating assassins, just as Jesus forgave thieves; and we are looting the homes of the rich because we know we must curse Lazarus—not because he was a *bad* rich man, but simply because he was rich. The slogan that the Republic is above all argument is on a par with the dogma that the Pope is infallible. Always formulas! Always Gods!

Yesterday's God—universal suffrage—has just played a terrible joke on his faithful by electing "the assassins of Versailles."[25] What are we to believe in, then? Nothing! Such is the beginning of wisdom. Long ago we should have rid ourselves of so-called principles and espoused Science, critical inquiry. The only thing that makes sense (I always come back to it) is a government of mandarins, provided the mandarins know something—in fact, a great many things. The people never comes of age, and it will always be at the bottom rung of the social scale because it represents numbers, the mass, the inchoate. It is of little importance that many peasants should be able to read and no longer heed their priests; but it is infinitely important that many men like Renan and Littré should be able to live and be listened to. Our salvation now lies in a legitimate aristocracy, by which I mean a majority composed of something more than mere numbers.

Had we been more enlightened, had there existed in Paris more people who knew their history, we should not have been afflicted with Gambetta, Prussia, or the Commune. How did Catholics use to exorcise a great peril? They made the sign of the cross, commending themselves to God and the saints. We, who are advanced, shouted "Long live the Republic!," invoking the memory of '92; and mind you we had no doubt of success. The Prussians no longer counted, we kissed one another for joy and could barely restrain ourselves from rushing to the mountain passes of the Argonne.[26] Of course these passes mean nothing today, but still we must follow the tradition. I have a friend

25 The National Assembly, so dubbed by French radicals.

26 The battle of Valmy, in the Argonne (1792), was the first victory of revolutionary France over an invading army of Prussians and Austrians commanded by the Duke of Brunswick. The French army, under Dumouriez, was composed largely of fresh recruits.

in Rouen who proposed, in his club, the manufacture of pikes as a weapon against chassepots!

How much more practical it would have been to keep Badinguet and put him at forced labor after the signing of the peace! Austria did not stage a revolution after Sadowa, nor Italy after Novara, nor Russia after Sebastopol. But our dear Frenchmen rush to tear their house down as soon as their chimney takes fire. . . .

To LAURE DE MAUPASSANT

[*Croisset,*] *April 7, 1872*

My dear Laure,

My mother died yesterday morning!

We shall bury her tomorrow.

I am exhausted and grief-stricken.

I embrace you affectionately.

To GEORGE SAND

[*Croisset,*] *Tuesday, April 16, 1872*

Chère bon Maître,

I should have answered your first affectionate letter at once, but I was too sad; I lacked the physical strength. Today I am finally beginning to listen to the birds again and watch the new green leaves. The sunlight no longer bothers me—a good sign. If I could bear to resume work it would be my salvation.

Your second letter (that of yesterday) touched me to the point of tears. How kind you are! What an excellent human being! I do not need money at the moment, thank you; but if I did you are certainly the person I should ask for it.

My mother left Croisset to Caroline, with the stipulation that I retain my residence. So until the estate is completely settled I shall remain here. Before planning for the future I must find out how much I shall have to live on; then we'll see.

Will I have the strength to live absolutely and completely alone, away from everyone? I doubt it; I am growing old. Caroline cannot live here now; she has two homes already, and the house at Croisset is expensive to keep up. I think I shall give up my Paris quarters. I no longer feel any urge to go to Paris. All my friends are dead except poor Théo, and he won't last long, I fear. Ah, it's hard to grow a new skin at fifty!

I have realized during the past fortnight that my poor dear mother was the human being I loved the most. It's as though a part of my entrails were torn away.

To GEORGE SAND

[*Croisset,*] *Monday night, October 28, 1872*

. . . Even though I saw it coming, poor Théo's death[27] has left me heartbroken. He is the last of my close friends to go. With him, the list is closed. Whom shall I see now, when I go to Paris? Whom shall I talk with about the things that interest me? I am acquainted with thinkers (or at least people who are referred to as such) ; but where is there an artist?

I am convinced that he died of what he used to call the swinishness of the present age; he told me several times last winter that his life had been shortened by the Commune, etc.

The 4th of September[28] inaugurated an order in which people of his kind serve no function. You can't expect orange trees to produce apples. Craftsmen de luxe are useless in a society dominated by the plebs. How I mourn him! I miss him and Bouilhet horribly, and nothing can take their place. He was so good, and —whatever others may say—so simple! Some day (if literature

27 Théophile Gautier had died October 23.

28 The Third Republic was proclaimed September 4, 1870.

ever comes into its own again) he will be recognized as a great poet. Meanwhile he is a completely unknown writer. But then, so is Pierre Corneille!

He had two hates: hate of the Philistine in his youth—that fertilized his talent; and hate of the hooligan in his maturity—this killed him. He died of suppressed anger, of rage at being unable to say what he thought. He was stifled by Girardin, by Fould, by Dalloz, and by the Third Republic. I tell you this because I personally witnessed some abominable things; I am the only man, perhaps, to whom he completely opened his heart. He lacked that thing which in life is the most important both for one's self and for others: character. His rejection by the Academy was a terrible blow to him. What weakness, what lack of self-respect it implies! The seeking of any honor seems to me an act of incomprehensible modesty.

I did not attend his funeral, through the fault of Catulle Mendès, who telegraphed me too late. There was a crowd. A lot of riffraff came to attract attention to themselves, as usual; and today, Monday, the day the theatrical columns appear in the papers, there must be articles about him—he makes "good copy." All in all I don't pity him; I envy him; for indeed life is no gay affair.

No, I do not believe that happiness is possible; but tranquillity is. That is why I avoid everything that irritates me. A trip to Paris has now become a serious undertaking. Once I disturb the bottom, dregs rise to the surface and cloud everything. The slightest conversation with anyone at all exasperates me, for I find everyone idiotic. My sense of justice is continually offended. No one speaks of anything but politics—and what politics! Where do you find the shadow of an idea? What straw is there left to clutch at? Where is there a cause that arouses anyone's passions?

And yet I do not consider myself a monster of selfishness. My *self* is so dissipated in books that I spend whole days without being aware of its existence. I have my bad moments, it is true, but then I remind myself that I have no one to bother me and I get on my feet again. All in all, I feel that I follow my natural path: I live, that is, a life that is right for me.

As for sharing my life with a woman—marrying, as you advise—I find the prospect fantastic. Why? I do not know, but it is so. *You* solve that problem. Woman has never fitted into my existence; and then I'm not rich enough, and too old, and too decent to inflict myself on another forever. There is a core of monasticism in me that no one suspects. But we can talk about all this better than I can write it. . . .

Whenever I have let myself be drawn into worldly activity I have paid heavily for it. Therefore, no more! "Hide your life," as Epictetus says. My entire ambition now is to avoid trouble, and in this way I am sure of not troubling others—which is something. I am working madly, reading medicine, metaphysics, politics, everything. For I have undertaken a book that is immensely ambitious and will occupy me for a long time to come—a prospect that pleases me.[29]

To IVAN TURGENEV

Croisset, Wednesday, [*November*] *13,* [*1872*]

Your last letter touched me, dear Turgenev. Thank you for your exhortations. But alas! my sickness is incurable, I fear. Aside from my personal sorrows (within the past three years almost everyone I loved has died) I am crushed by the condition of society. Yes, it is so. It may be stupid, but it is a fact. I am drowning in the general stupidity. Since 1870, I have become a patriot. As I watch my country die, I realize that I have loved it. Prussia can lay down her arms: we shall perish without any help from her.

[29] He is beginning his reading for *Bouvard et Pécuchet.*

The bourgeoisie is so hopelessly confused that it no longer has even the instinct of self-preservation; and its successors will be worse. My sadness is like that of the Roman patricians of the fourth century. I feel an invincible flood of barbarism rising out of the depths. I hope to be dead before it sweeps everything away, but the period of waiting is not very agreeable. Never have things of the mind counted for less. Never have hatred of all greatness, scorn of Beauty, and execration of literature been so outspoken.

I have always tried to live in an ivory tower; but its walls are being battered by a tidal wave of filth that threatens to topple it. It is not a question of politics, but of the mental state of France. Have you read Simon's[30] circular letter, presenting a plan for the reform of public education? The section dealing with physical training is longer than that devoted to French literature—a significant little symptom!

If you were not living in Paris I should immediately turn over my apartment to my landlord. The hope of seeing you there occasionally is the only consideration that makes me keep it.

I can no longer talk with anyone without growing angry; and whenever I read anything by one of my contemporaries I rage. A fine state to be in! However, I am preparing a book in which I hope to spit out my bile, and which I'd enjoy talking over with you. As you see, I keep fighting: if I didn't work, there would be nothing left for me to do but jump in the river with a stone around my neck. As a consequence of 1870 many people became insane or stupid or rabid: I am in the third category—quite seriously. . . .

30 Jules Simon, minister of education.

To LAURE DE MAUPASSANT

Paris, February 23, 1873

You have got ahead of me, my dear Laure. For the last month I have been wanting to write you, to send you a declaration of affection regarding your son. I cannot tell you how charming I find him, how intelligent, good-natured, sensible, and witty—in short, to use a stylish word, *sympathique*. Despite the difference in our ages, I consider him a friend, and then he so reminds me of poor Alfred. Sometimes I am really startled by the likeness, especially when he bends his head as he has a way of doing when he reads poetry. What a man he was! In my memory he remains incomparable. There is not a day when I do not think of him. But then I am obsessed by the past, by the dead (*my* dead). Is this a sign of old age? I think so.

When shall we meet again? . . . Wouldn't you come with your two sons and spend a few days at Croisset? I have all the room in the world to offer you, and I envy you the serenity you seem to enjoy, my dear Laure, for I grow very gloomy. The world of today and existence in general weigh heavily and horribly on my shoulders. I am so disgusted with everything, and particularly with militant literature, that I have renounced all idea of publishing. Life is no longer a joy for people of taste.

Despite all this we must encourage him in this taste for poetry that he has. It is a noble passion, and literature compensates for many misfortunes; besides, he may even have some talent—who knows? So far he has not produced enough to make it possible for me to cast his poetic horoscope, and anyway, where is the man who can decide another's future?

I think our young friend something of an idler, not too fond of work. I should like to see him undertake something long and exacting, execrable though it might turn out to be. What he has shown me is certainly as good as anything published by the Parnassians. With time he will acquire an originality, an individual manner of seeing and feeling (which is everything). As to the result, as to his possible "success," what difference does it make? The principal thing in this world is to keep one's soul aloft, high above the bourgeois and democratic sloughs. The worship of art gives one pride: no one can have enough of it. Such is my morality. . . .

To IVAN TURGENEV

Thursday, July 2, 1874
Kaltbad, Rigi, Switzerland

I too am hot, and my state is superior, or inferior, to yours in that I am also colossally bored. I came here out of obedience, having been told that the pure mountain air would unredden my face and calm my nerves. So be it. But so far I am conscious only of immense boredom, due to solitude and idleness; besides, I am no man of Nature—her "wonders" move me less than those of Art. She overwhelms me, without inspiring me with any "great idea." I feel like telling her: "All right, all right, I just left you, I'll be back with you in a few minutes; leave me alone, I need other kinds of amusement." Also, the Alps are out of proportion with our little selves. They are too big to help us in any way. This is the third time they have had a disagreeable effect on me; I hope it may be the last. And then my fellow-vacationists—the honorable foreigners living in this hotel! All Germans or English, equipped with walking-sticks and field glasses. Yesterday I was tempted to kiss three calves that I met in a meadow, out of sheer humanity and affection. My trip got off to a bad start—at Lucerne I had a tooth extracted by one of the local artists. A week before leaving for Switzerland I made a tour in the Orne and Calvados, where I finally found the place to settle my two characters.[31] I am impatient to get started on this book, which terrifies me atrociously in advance.

31 Bouvard and Pécuchet.

To IVAN TURGENEV [*1874*]

You mention *Saint Antoine,* saying that it hasn't found favor with the general public. I knew this in advance, but I expected to be more widely understood by the elite. Had it not been for Drumont and Pelletan, I shouldn't have had a single favorable review. As yet I haven't seen any from Germany. But we're in God's hands; what's done is done, and as long as *you* like the book I'm amply rewarded. Popular success has deserted me since *Salammbô.* What I cannot reconcile myself to is the failure of the *Education sentimentale*; the utter lack of understanding it met with astonishes me. . . .

To IVAN TURGENEV

Dieppe, Wednesday, July 25 [*really 29*] [*1874*]

My dear Turgenev

I shall be back at Croisset Friday afternoon, and on Saturday, August 1st, shall at last begin *Bouvard et Pécuchet*! Such terror! It is as though I were embarking on an immensely long voyage toward unknown shores, from which I should not return.

Despite the immense respect that I have for your critical judgment (for in your case the Judge is on the same level as the Producer—which is saying not a little), I am not at all of your opinion as to the proper approach to this subject.[32] If it were treated briefly, made concise and light, it would be a fantasy—more or less witty, but without weight or plausibility; whereas if I give it detail and development I will seem to be believing my own story, and it can be made into something serious and even frightening. The great danger is monotony and boredom. That is what frightens me—and yet, there will always be time to compress and cut. Besides, I can never write anything short.

32 Turgenev had written him on July 12: "The more I consider it, the more I think it is a subject to treat presto, like Swift or Voltaire. As you described it to me, your plot seemed charming and funny. But beware of overdoing it, of being too scholarly."

To EMILE ZOLA [*1875*]

I am unable to expound an idea without pursuing it to the end. . . .

Politics is becoming incomprehensible in its stupidity. I do not expect the dissolution of the Chamber. Speaking of politics, at Geneva I saw something curious: the restaurant run by old Gaillard, the shoemaker who was a general of the Commune. I will describe it when I see you. It is a world in itself, the world as it exists in the dreams of democrats, and as I shall never see it, thank God. The things that will hold the center of the stage during the next two or three hundred years are enough to make a man of taste vomit. It is time to disappear. . . .

To MONSIEUR X—

Croisset, near Rouen, March 17, 1875

I cannot possibly grant your request; on several previous occasions I have already refused to allow *Madame Bovary* to be turned into a play. I think the idea a poor one. *Madame Bovary* is not a subject for the stage.

With all my regrets, believe me

Cordially yours,

To EMILE ZOLA

Croisset, Friday, August 13, [*1875*]

Dear Friend

You sound very sad. But you will cease your complaining when you learn what has happened to me. My nephew is *completely ruined,* and I have suffered serious losses in consequence. Will the situation improve? I doubt it.[33] I am heartbroken about it because of my niece. It is hard to see someone you love exposed to such humiliation.

33 A justified doubt. From now on he will be in increasingly reduced circumstances, stripping himself gradually of his capital—to the extent, finally, of more than a million francs—to save the Commanvilles' "good name."

To GEORGE SAND [*1875*]

My existence has been turned upside down; I shall still have enough to live on, but very differently from before. As for writing, I am utterly incapable of work. For nearly four months we have been going through the torments of hell, and during that time I have written a total of fourteen pages—bad ones. My poor head will not stand up against such a blow as this: that much seems obvious to me.

I must get away from these painful surroundings—therefore, early in September I go to Concarneau to join Georges Pouchet, who is down there experimenting on fish. I'll stay as long as I can, and will write you my news: I hope that yours may be better than mine.

So, that's how things stand. Life is no gay affair, and I am beginning a dismal old age. I shake your hand warmly. You are no longer worried about Madame Zola, I trust?

To GEORGE SAND

[*Paris, after December 20, 1875*]

I have given a great deal of thought to your good letter of the 18th, so affectionate and motherly. I have read it at least ten times, and confess that I am not sure I understand it. Just what do you think I should do? Be more specific.

I constantly do all that I can to broaden my mind, and I write according to the dictates of my heart. The rest is beyond my control.

I assure you that I do not paint the world in "desolate colors" for my own pleasure; after all, I cannot change my eyes. As for my "lack of convictions," alas! I am only too full of convictions. I burst with suppressed anger and indignation. But my ideal of Art demands that the artist show none of this, and that he appear in his work no more than God in nature. The man is nothing, the work is everything! This discipline, which may be based on a false premise, is not easy to observe. And for me, at least, it is a kind of perpetual sacrifice that I burn on the altar of good taste. It would be very agreeable for me to say what I think, and relieve M. Gustave Flaubert's feelings by means of such utterances; but of what importance is the aforesaid gentleman?

I think as you do, *mon maître,* that Art is not merely criticism and satire; that is why I have never deliberately tried to write either one or the other. I have always endeavored to penetrate into the essence of things and to emphasize the most general truths; and I have purposely avoided the accidental and the dramatic. No monsters, no heroes!

You say: "I have no literary advice to give you, I do not pass judgment on writers, your friends, etc." But why not? I want your advice; I long to hear your opinions. Who should give advice and opinions if not you?

Speaking of my friends,[34] you call them my "school." But I am wrecking my health trying *not* to have a school. *A priori,* I reject all schools. Those writers whom I often see and whom you mention admire everything that I despise and worry but little about the things that torment me. Technical detail, factual data, historical truth, and accuracy of portrayal I look upon as very secondary. I aim at *beauty* above all else, whereas my companions give themselves little trouble about it. Where I am devastated by admiration or horror, they are unmoved; sentences that make me swoon seem very ordinary to them. Goncourt is very happy when he has picked up in the street some word that he can stick into a book; I am very satisfied when I have written a page without assonances or repetitions. I would willingly exchange all Gavarni's captions for a few such marvels as Victor Hugo's *"l'ombre était nuptiale, auguste et solennelle,"* or Montesquieu's *"Les vices d'Alexandre étaient extrêmes comme*

[34] The Goncourts, Zola, Daudet—the naturalists.

ses vertus. Il était terrible dans sa colère. Elle le rendait cruel."

I try to think well in order to write well. But my aim is to write well—I have never said it was anything else.

You say that I lack any "well-defined and comprehensive perspective on life." You will not lighten my darkness—mine or anyone else's—with metaphysics. The words "religion" or "Catholicism" on the one hand, "progress," "brotherhood," "democracy" on the other, no longer satisfy the spiritual demands of our time. The brand-new dogma of equality, preached by radicalism, is given the lie by experimental psychology and by history. I do not see how it is possible today to establish a new principle, or to respect the old ones. Hence I keep seeking—without ever finding—that idea which is supposed to be the foundation of everything.

Meanwhile I repeat to myself what Littré once said to me: "Ah, my friend, man is an unstable compound, and the earth a very inferior planet." Nothing comforts me more than the hope that I shall soon be leaving it and shall not be moving to another, which might be worse. "I should prefer not to die," Marat said. Ah, no! Enough of toil and trouble!

I am now writing a little something of no consequence[35] which will be eminently suitable for young girls. The whole thing will run to only thirty pages. It will take me another two months. Such is my lightning pace. I will send it to you as soon as it appears—not the pace, the story.

To GEORGE SAND

Monday night, [*Croisset, April 3, 1876*]

I received your volume this morning, *chère maître.* I have two or three others that I have had on loan a long time; I am

35 Flaubert has interrupted work on *Bouvard et Pécuchet* and has begun *La Légende de Saint Julien l'Hospitalier.*

going to finish them in a hurry and shall read yours at the end of the week, during a little two-day trip that I have to make to Pont-l'Evêque and Honfleur for my *Histoire d'un cœur simple,* a trifle at present "in the works," as the saying is.

I am glad you liked *Jack.* It's a charming book, don't you think? If you knew the author, you would like him even more than his work. I have told him to send you *Risler* and *Tartarin.* You will thank me after reading them, I am sure in advance.

I do not share Turgenev's severity concerning *Jack,* nor the immensity of his admiration for *Rougon.* One has charm and the other strength. But neither of the two is concerned *above all* with what is for me the goal of Art, namely Beauty. I remember how my heart throbbed, and what violent pleasure I experienced, when I looked at one of the walls of the Acropolis, a wall that is completely bare (the one to the left as you climb the Propylaea). Well, I wonder whether a book, quite apart from what it says, cannot produce the same effect. In a work whose parts fit precisely, which is composed of rare elements, whose surface is polished, and which is a harmonious whole, is there not an intrinsic virtue, a kind of divine force, something as eternal as a principle? (I speak as a Platonist.) If this were not so, why should the right word be necessarily the musical word? Or why should great compression of thought always result in a line of poetry? Feelings and images are thus governed by the law of numbers, and what seems to be outward form is actually essence. If I were to keep going very long on this track I should find myself in a hopeless predicament, for Art must also come from the heart. Or rather, Art has only those qualities that we can give it; and we are not free. Each of us follows his path, independent of his own will. . . .

How hard it is to reach any understanding! Here are two men whom I greatly like and whom I consider to be true artists, Turgenev and Zola. For all that, they have no admiration whatever for the prose of Chateaubriand and even less for that of Gautier. Sentences that enrapture me seem to them hollow. Who is wrong? And how is it possible to please the public when those who are closest to you are so far away? All this saddens me considerably. Don't laugh.

To IVAN TURGENEV

Croisset, Sunday evening, June 25, [*1876*]

. . . The death of poor George Sand[36] distressed me immensely. I wept like a child at her funeral—twice: the first time when I kissed her granddaughter Aurore (whose eyes, that day, were so like hers as to be a kind of resurrection) and the second when I saw her coffin being carried away before my eyes. There were some unsavory goings-on. Out of respect for "public opinion"—that omnipotent and execrable impersonal power—her body was taken to the church. I will give you the details of this disgraceful business when I see you. I felt a tightening around my heart, I can tell you, and I felt a positive desire to kill Monsieur Adrien Marx.[37] The very sight of him took away my appetite that evening at Châteauroux. You are right to mourn our friend, for she loved you dearly and always referred to you as *"le bon Turgenev."* But why pity her? She had everything life had to offer, and will remain a very great figure.

The good countrypeople wept copiously around the grave. We were up to our ankles in mud in the little village cemetery, and a gentle rain was falling. Her funeral was like a chapter in one of her books.

Forty-eight hours later I was back at Croisset, where I find myself in surprisingly good spirits. I am enjoying the verdure,

36 On June 8.

37 The reporter of *"Solennités et cérémonies officielles"* for the *Moniteur Universel.*

the trees, and the silence in a way that is quite new to me. I have resumed cold showers (I am giving myself a ferocious course of hydrotherapy) and I work like a madman.

My *Histoire d'un cœur simple* will probably be finished toward the end of August.[38] After which I shall begin *Hérodias.* But how hard it is! Good God, how hard it is! The further I go the more I realize it. It seems to me that French prose can achieve a beauty hitherto undreamed of. Don't you find that our friends are but little interested in Beauty? And yet in all the world that alone is important!

And you? Are you working? Are you getting ahead with *Saint Julien?* What I am going to say is stupid as can be, but I *long* to see it printed in Russian! Not to mention the fact that to be translated by you "flatters my pride, my heart's weakness"—my only resemblance to Agamemnon.[39] . . .

To IVAN TURGENEV

Thursday, December 14, [*Croisset, 1876*]

I didn't know what to think of your silence, my good friend, so I asked my niece (who has been in Paris for some time) to call and find out whether my Turgenev was still alive.

You sound languid and depressed. Why? Is it money? What about me, then? I keep working in spite of that, and even more than ever. If I keep on at this pace *Hérodias* will be done by the end of February. By New Year's I hope to be at the halfway mark. How will it turn out? I have no idea. It promises to be a loud-mouthed affair, at any rate, for it's nothing but ranting, bombast, hyperbole. Down with restraint!

38 "I had begun *Un cœur simple* exclusively for her, solely to please her," Flaubert later wrote George Sand's son Maurice. "She died when I was in the middle of my work. So it is with all our dreams."

39 Who says, in Racine's Iphigénie:

"Ces noms de Roi des Rois et de Chef de la Grèce
Chatouillaient de mon cœur l'orgueilleuse faiblesse."

To GUY DE MAUPASSANT [*1878*]

Like you, I have read some bits of *L'Assommoir*. I did not like them. Zola is becoming a *précieuse* in reverse. He thinks that certain words are energetic, just as Cathos and Madelon[40] thought that certain words were noble. He is being carried away by his own "system." He has Principles, and they narrow his vision. Read his Monday articles, and you will see how he imagines he discovered "Naturalism." As for poetry and style, the two elements that are eternal, he never mentions them! Or question our friend Goncourt. If he is frank, he will admit that French literature did not exist before Balzac. Such is the result of abusing one's intelligence and being afraid of clichés. . . .

To MAXIME DU CAMP

Saturday, 4 P.M., [*Paris, May 9 or 16, 1877*]

Ouf! I have finished my melancholy task.[41] Our entire youth has been passing before me. It has left me *broken.*

Here are the only letters that I am saving—(1) to reread them occasionally (I cannot bring myself to destroy them) and (2) to use them as documents.

How nice you were in those days! How nice, how nice! And how we loved each other!

There are nineteen letters in this parcel. I thought you might like to look them over. Several will make you laugh and a few will bring tears to your eyes.

Tibissimi

To GUY DE MAUPASSANT

Croisset, August 15, 1878

. . . You complain about *le cul des femmes* being "monotonous." There is a simple remedy—not to use it. "Events are not varied," you say. That is a stock complaint of the realists, and

40 Characters in Molière's *Les Précieuses ridicules.*
41 The sorting of old letters.

besides, what do you know about it? The whole thing is to examine events more closely. Have you ever believed in the existence of things? Isn't everything an illusion? The only truth is in *"rapports"*—that is, our ways of seeing. "The vices are paltry," you say; but everything is paltry! "There are not enough different ways to turn a phrase!" Seek and ye shall find.

Come now, my dear friend, you seem badly worried, and your worry distresses me, for you could use your time more agreeably. You *must*—do you hear me?—you *must* work more than you do. I've come to suspect you of being something of a loafer. Too many whores! Too much rowing! Too much exercise! Yes, sir: civilized man doesn't need as much locomotion as the doctors pretend. You were born to write poetry: write it! *All the rest is futile*—beginning with your pleasures and your health: get that into your head. Besides, your health will be the better for your following your calling. That remark is philosophically, or rather, hygienically, profound.

You are living in an *enfer de merde,* I know, and I pity you from the bottom of my heart. But from five in the evening to ten in the morning all your time can be consecrated to the muse, who is still the best bitch of all. Come, my dear fellow, chin up. What is the use of constantly going deeper into your melancholy? You must set yourself up as a strong man in your own eyes: that's the way to become one. A little more pride, by God! . . . What you lack are "principles." Say what you will, one has to have them; it is a question of knowing which ones. For an artist there is only one: sacrifice everything to Art. Life must be considered by the artist as a means, nothing more, and the first person he should not give a hang about is himself. . . .

Let me sum up, my dear Guy: beware of melancholy. It is a vice. You take pleasure in affliction, and then when affliction has passed you find yourself dazed and deadened, for you have used up precious strength. And then you have regrets, but it is too late. Have faith in the experience of a sheikh to whom no folly is unknown! *Je vous embrasse tendrement.*

To his niece CAROLINE

[*Croisset,*] *January 21, 1879*

Chérie,

. . . We cannot say anything or plan anything, even regarding the immediate future, until after the sale.[42] I long for it to be over. Then I shall have at least a few thousand francs, which will enable me to keep going until I finish *Bouvard et Pécuchet.*[43] I am more and more exasperated by my straitened circumstances, and this permanent state of uncertainty makes me despondent. Despite tremendous efforts of will, I feel myself giving way to depression. It's high time all this was over. My health would be good if I could sleep. My insomnia is now chronic; whether I go to bed early or late, I never drop off before five in the morning—no wonder I have headaches all afternoon. I am doing immense amounts of reading and note-taking. Last night I took a walk on the quay in the moonlight despite the extreme cold; the beauty of the night was irresistible; and a little while ago, after lunch, I went for a long stroll in the garden. But my own company depresses me; that of books is better.

Friday and Saturday my mental and nervous state frightened me. I keep mulling over the same recriminations, and constantly wallowing in grief. Then I go back to my books and try to write my chapter. My imagination is aroused; but instead of working on fictitious beings it sets to work on myself, and everything begins all over again.

There is no point in complaining! But there is even less in

42 Of a saw mill belonging to his niece's husband. It was sold very disadvantageously two months later, forcing Flaubert to accept a government pension.

43 Flaubert had resumed work on it after finishing *Hérodias* (the last completed of the *Trois contes*) in 1877.

living! What is my future, now? Who is there to talk to, even? I live alone like an outcast, and the end of my solitude does not seem very near; for I shall have to spend two months in Paris this year if I want to finish *Bouvard et Pécuchet,* and during that time you'll be here—so that perhaps I won't see my little girl till mid-May. As for all three of us living in the little flat in Paris, that is physically impossible—there isn't even a room for the cook. Here at least there is nothing to irritate me; this wouldn't be the case in Paris.

Today is your birthday, my poor Caro! You were born amid tears—that brought you bad luck. Adieu; I am growing too sentimental, but I am weary of trying, of straining, of forcing my will—and for what? To what avail? Who benefits from all this?

I kiss you tenderly.

To MADAME BRAINNE

[*Croisset, before January 25, 1879*]

. . . As for a job, a post, my dear friend, never! never! never! I refused one, offered me by my friend Bardoux.[44] It was the same with the officer's cross of the Légion d'Honneur, which he also wanted to bestow on me.

Should things come to the worst, it is possible to live in a hotel on 1,500 francs a year. That is what I shall do, rather than take one centime of the government's money.

Don't you know this maxim (composed by me): "Honor dishonors; titles degrade; positions kill the mind." Besides—am I capable of occupying a position of any kind? After one day I'd be kicked out for insolence and insubordination. Misfortune does not make me more compliant—quite the contrary! More than ever I am a frantic idealist, resolved to die of hunger and fury rather than make the slightest concession.

[44] Minister of education, 1877-79.

I was quite low for several days, but my spirits are improving and I am working. That's the important thing, after all.

I was touched by your kind thought of me, my dear; but forget it, I beg you. Nevertheless, I thank you for the idea, just as though it were a present.

To GEORGES CHARPENTIER

Croisset, Sunday, [*February 16, 1879*]

My dear Friend,

I am not "unjust," for I am not "angry" at you and have never been so. Only, I thought that you should have told me at once, straight out, that the proposition did not suit you. In that case I should have gone elsewhere. Let's not mention it again, and continue as before.

At the end of *Saint Julien* I wanted to put the stained-glass window from the Rouen cathedral. It was merely a matter of coloring the plate in Langlois's book.[45] And I should have liked this illustration *precisely because* it is not an illustration, but an historical document. Comparing the picture with the text, the reader would have been puzzled, and would have wondered how I derived the one from the other. I dislike all illustrations, especially where my own works are concerned, and as long as I am alive there shall be none. *Dixi.* I am just as stubborn about my photograph, and almost broke with Lemerre about it. I'm sorry, but I have principles. *Potius mori quam foedari.*

I am fed up with *Bovary.* The constant mention of this book gets on my nerves. It's as though everything I wrote after it

45 A scholarly treatise on stained glass by Eustache-Hyacinthe Langlois, containing a plate of the window of Saint Julien l'Hospitalier in the Rouen cathedral. Flaubert's story had been inspired by this window and by a statue of the saint which he had seen in his youth in the church at Caudebec. The "proposition" which did not suit Charpentier was a special edition of the story, illustrated with a reproduction of Langlois's plate.

didn't exist. I assure you that if I weren't in need of money I should take steps to see that it was never reprinted. But necessity compels me to do otherwise. So—print away! As for the money, there is no reason to send it here. Pay me when I come to Paris. One observation: you mention a thousand francs for two thousand copies, which means ten sous a copy. It seems to me that you used to give me twelve or even thirteen per copy, but I may be mistaken.

Now something else. Next August 10th my contract with Lévy will expire. The rights to *L'Education sentimentale* will revert to me. I'd very much like to get something out of it. . . .

To his niece CAROLINE

Saturday, 2 o'clock [*February 22, 1879*]

Mon Loulou,

Here is the real truth. I wanted to keep the story from you, to spare you pain and indignation. The upshot of it is that I was once again wrong in following the advice of others and mistrusting my own judgment. But I am incorrigible; I always trust the opinion of others, and then find myself in trouble. Here goes:

Early in January, Taine wrote to tell me that Monsieur de Sacy was at death's door and that Bardoux was ready to give me his post:[46] 3,000 francs and living-quarters. Although I was tempted by the apartment (which is splendid), I replied that this post did not suit me, because I should be poorer having to

[46] As administrator of the Bibliothèque Mazarine, one of the public libraries of Paris. To identify all the characters and references in this letter would be to drown the reader in footnotes, even though while going down he might swallow a course in early Third Republic political intrigue. See, however, the biographical note on Frédéric Baudry. Although Flaubert did not know it when he wrote this letter, Baudry had already been appointed to the post, as of February 17. The article in the *Figaro* was a somewhat garbled gossip item, criticizing the government for not appointing the needy and deserving Flaubert.

live in Paris on a salary of 3,000 francs than I am now at Croisset, and that I should prefer to spend only two or three months in Paris. Moreover, the Princess and Madame Brainne had told me that my friends were trying to get me a position "worthy" of me.

Act Two, Monday. The moment you were gone, Turgenev put on a solemn face and said: "Gambetta asks whether you want Monsieur de Sacy's post: 8,000 francs and living-quarters. You must give me your answer at once." Using eloquence and affection (the latter word is not too strong), and seconded by Laporte, he overcame my distaste for the idea of becoming a functionary. The thought that I should be less of a burden to you was what really made me decide. After a sleepless night, I told him to go ahead. Everything was to be done quietly, and you were not to be told until everything was settled.

Twenty-four hours later I had a letter from Turgenev telling me that he had been mistaken, that the post paid only 6,000, but that he felt he should continue his efforts.

Actually, Gambetta had not promised anything. Goncourt had asked him for a sinecure for me, as had the Charpentiers, who had been quite active about it. They had written to Madame Adam, who was all on my side.

Then came another letter from Turgenev, to say that the post paid not 6,000, but 4,000!

At this point I received a visit from Cordier. He was very helpful and spoke about me to Paul Bert, who said he would do everything for me, and to Père Hugo, who then and there wrote a warm letter recommending me to Ferry.

Then came the article in the *Figaro* and Turgenev's departure for Russia. Shortly before that, I had been warned that Maître Sénard, one of the mainstays of the cabinet, was demanding the post for his son-in-law Baudry, who he insisted had first claim on it.

To his niece CAROLINE [*1879*]

Last Monday came a letter from Baudry, wondering "how in the world" I was and announcing his daughter's marriage. He told me that he was taking steps to get Monsieur de Sacy's post, and made no mention of the steps being taken on my behalf. Taine had spoken to him about it, but (said Baudry) the place would not suit me at all. He also shed some tears over my misfortunes and criticized Bardoux for not giving me the post recently bestowed on Troubat: 3,000 francs and obligatory residence at Compiègne! (Charming thought!) Baudry is an ass. If he had written me frankly and asked me, as a favor to him, to do nothing, my gentlemanly instincts would have obligated me to withdraw from the field. I asked Laporte to answer him that I was too ill to write, and that I would explain the situation to him when I could once again hold a pen. I can be foxy too!

That is how things stand now. But I am sure that Baudry will be appointed and that I will look like a fool. I'll be regarded as a blundering schemer: that will be my sole accomplishment. Furthermore, the article in the *Figaro* will turn Madame Adam against me; and it is already bringing me letters —there was one yesterday from Madame Achille—asking for explanations and requiring answers. Turgenev wrote me from Berlin to apologize. He has no idea of the authorship of this wretched piece, which is partly true, partly false.

I confess it has made me weep with rage. To have my poverty publicized, and to be pitied by those wretches, who talk about my "goodness"! It is cruel, and I did nothing to deserve it. I curse the day when I had the fatal idea of putting my name on a book! Had it not been for my mother and Bouilhet I should never have published. How I regret it now! I only want to be forgotten, left in peace, never mentioned again. I am becoming odious to myself. I long to die, to be left alone! . . .

. . . The *Figaro* had to drag me through the mud to make a political point. Well, it was coming to me. I was a coward, I betrayed my own principles (for I too have principles), and I am punished for it. I must not complain, but I am suffering, and cruelly. This is not a pose. The dignity of my entire life is lost. I consider myself disgraced. Oh, Other People! Always Other People! And all this happened because I did not want to seem stubborn and proud, because I was afraid of seeming to "pose"! . . .

To his niece CAROLINE

Croisset, Friday, 3 o'clock [*March 14, 1879*]

. . . I have every reason to believe that I am going to be *offered* a pension, and I shall accept it, even though to do so *humiliates* me to the marrow of my bones. (That is why I wish the thing to be kept absolutely secret.) Let us hope that the press will keep out of it! I have a bad conscience about this pension, which I have done nothing to deserve, whatever people may say. The mere fact that I mismanaged my affairs is no reason for the government to support me. To save my conscience and live in peace with myself, I have thought of an expedient[47] that I will tell you about and that I am sure you will approve, for you are a decent *man,* something far rarer than a decent woman. Oh, dear child! My poor little girl!

If this thing comes through, as I hope it will, I can await death with serenity.

To FRÉDÉRIC BAUDRY

Croisset, Friday evening, [*May 30, 1879*]

It is decided. I have finally surrendered to a little group of my friends, who want me to be your assistant.

47 His determination to accept any pension only temporarily, and to consider it a loan, to be repaid.

To GEORGES CHARPENTIER *and* MADAME CHARPENTIER [*1879?*]

You yourself expressed this wish to me in February.

My "intractable pride" has resisted up to now. But, my friend, tomorrow or the day after I may very well find myself without means of subsistence. Therefore I accept the position:[48] three thousand francs a year and the *promise* that no duties whatever will be expected of me. For you understand that if I were obliged to live in Paris I should be poorer than before.

Now (between you and me) if you *need* me, it goes without saying that I am and shall be at your orders—hoping, however, that my superior will be merciful?

Your old

Gustave Flaubert

I am *very* worried about my brother's health: the blood-tie is no fiction, I have come to realize.

To GEORGES CHARPENTIER and MADAME CHARPENTIER

Friday evening, [*Paris, September, 1879?*]

Monsieur Gustave Flaubert presents his respects to Monsieur and Madame Charpentier. He will be proud and happy to appear next Friday in response to their honorable invitation.

He finds the fact that no bourgeois will be present a reassuring prospect. For he has now reached such a point of exasperation, when he finds himself in the company of persons of that species, that he is invariably tempted to strangle them, or rather to hurl them into the latrines (if such language be permitted) —an action whose consequences would be embarrassing to the

[48] As of July 1, 1879, Flaubert was appointed special curator, under Baudry, at the Bibliothèque Mazarine, at a salary of 3,000 francs a year. Neither duties nor even residence in Paris were required of him, and some think that the post was a fictitious one, invented by persons friendly to him in the government for the purpose of making a pension slightly more palatable.

publishing house of Charpentier, which, children and dog included,[49] occupies a large place in his heart.

To MAXIME DU CAMP

Thursday, November 13, [Croisset, 1879]

Dear old Max

. . . Now let us speak of your IVth volume.[50] Nothing could be more amusing or more accurate. Your treatment of the subject seems very thorough. You have obviously tried to be impartial, but have not taken sufficient pains to conceal this effort —a defect on the artistic side.

Your book is not an "indictment"—in calling it that you are over-modest—but in many passages it gives the impression of being one. You constantly call the Communards idiots, madmen, criminals. But we know all that! You prove it to us quite clearly. You must allow the reader to think for himself. In my opinion History has a loftier goal than to thunder against crimes. . . .

There is one page that I should like to obliterate from your volume: page 244.

"The dangerous aspects" of Darwin's theory! Are you serious? You yourself admit that the Communards were "rather" unaware of being influenced by this theory.

My own opinion is that they had never even heard of it, and the example of Lebiez, which you mention in a note, does not convince me that the theory is dangerous. And what if it were? Must science accommodate itself to morality? Is the Absolute to be measured in terms of our needs? There are two alternatives: Evolution, or Miracle. We must choose.

49 The reader is reminded of Renoir's portrait of Madame Charpentier and her children (and dog) in the Metropolitan Museum of Art.

50 Of *Les Convulsions de Paris,* a study of the Commune. It has been impossible to identify some of the persons mentioned in this letter and the next.

it is because the Socialists still cling to the old theology that they are so stupid and so harmful. Magic believes in instantaneous transformations by means of formulas, absolutely like Socialism. Neither the one nor the other takes time into account, or the relentless evolution of things. Darwin would not have been understood in the Stone Age, when people believed in gods, or perhaps even in God—in an omnipotent and conscious power.

It is Political Economy (or even the "infamous" Malthus) that inspired Darwin. It is high time for sociology to find inspiration in him. It is doing precisely that in England, incidentally. When these ideas have filtered down into the masses there will be no more revolutions, because everyone will be convinced that *"natura non facit saltus"!*

And it was quite justifiable to criticize that fanatic Robespierre for his Supreme Being, because a man who is in the confidence of the Supreme Being and thinks he has God in his pocket knows no restraint! Science excludes *a priori* "God from the domain of knowledge" (and not from the domain of consciousness). "I do not need that hypothesis," said Laplace. That is why materialism and spiritualism are impertinences. *Quod non pertinet homini.* And it is going too far to accuse Darwin of having contributed to the Commune. . . .

Your

Gustave Flaubert

Severe, but just!

To MAXIME DU CAMP

[*Croisset*] *Wednesday, November 19, 1879*

Thank you for your good letter—this is just a line.

Either I expressed myself badly or you did not understand.

I do not at all defend Darwinism, not being competent to do

so. I merely maintain that it is not responsible for Lebiez, any more than Catholicism is responsible for Mingrat or Lecalonge.

You who are so familiar with the history of the Commune: explain to me why *the bourgeois* who fled from it in terror later defended it. We provincials found this behavior completely incomprehensible and particularly infuriating. There is a psychological riddle here that I cannot solve.

I have come upon something really superb. Do you know why the Naval Ministry and the Sainte Chapelle were not burned? It is because these two buildings had been placed under the protection of St. Benedict's medal! Medals of this saint had been smuggled into the edifices and hidden in different places. (*Origines et effets admirables de la médaille de Saint-Benoît,* pp. 4, 116.)

As a matter of fact I am becoming very learned on the subject of modern Catholicism. For four long months I have been reading nothing but the elucubrations of modern Catholics. They have to be seen to be believed. The freethinkers are ungrateful: they should erect a statue to Pius IX. . . .[51]

To PAUL ALEXIS

Croisset, Monday evening, December 8, 1879

It's very nice, your play![52] But why hasn't it three acts? I am grateful to you for giving it a denouement which is not conventional. It is good because it is outside the vulgar moral code. What surprises me is that the public should have swallowed it.

But between ourselves, my friend, I think that in your preface you attach exaggerated importance to the genital organs. Good Lord—what does it matter whether one copulates or doesn't copulate? The classics went in for cuckoldry, which was

51 Presumably because his proclamation of the dogma of the pope's infallibility won recruits to their ranks.

52 *Celle qu'on n'épouse pas,* in one act.

amusing. The romantics invented adultery—a serious matter. It is high time for the naturalists to regard such doings as of no consequence.

My best to Zola. I long to read his book.

To IVAN TURGENEV

Tuesday evening, [*Croisset, December 30, 1879*]

Thanks! Triple thanks, O Saint Vincent de Paul of the food basket! My word, you treat me like a minion! You spoil me with tidbits. Know then that I eat your caviar almost without bread, like preserves.

As for the novel,[53] its three volumes terrify me. Three volumes just now, not connected with my work, is asking a lot. No matter, I'll read them. I expect to finish my chapter by the end of next week, and they will relax me before I begin the next.

When do you leave, or rather when do you return? It's stupid to love each other as we do and see each other so little.

To IVAN TURGENEV

Wednesday evening, [*Croisset, January 21, 1880*]

Two things only, my friend:

1. When do you leave, or rather when do you return? Are you less worried about the results of your trip?

2. Thank you for making me read Tolstoy's novel. It is first class. What a painter, and what a psychologist! The first two volumes are *sublime;* but the third is a frightful letdown. It repeats and philosophizes. You feel the gentleman, the writer, and the Russian, whereas in the preceding volumes there was only nature and humanity. At times he reminds me of Shake-

[53] *War and Peace.* "I consider [Tolstoy] the foremost living writer," Turgenev had written Flaubert. "You know who, in my opinion, could contest his place."

speare. I cried aloud with admiration as I read—and it's a long haul. Tell me about the author. Is it his first book? He has what's needed. Yes, it's powerful, very powerful.

I have finished my chapter on Religion and am working on the outline of my last chapter: Education. . . .

To GUY DE MAUPASSANT

Croisset, [*February 1, 1880*]

. . . I am impatient to tell you that I consider *Boule de suif* a masterpiece. Yes, young man! Nothing more, nothing less. It is the work of a master. It is original in conception, well constructed from beginning to end, and written in excellent style. One can see the countryside and the characters, and the psychology is penetrating. In short, I am delighted; two or three times I laughed aloud. . . . I have written my schoolmasterish comments on a scrap of paper; consider them, I think they are good. This little story will *live*: you can be sure of it. How beautifully done your bourgeois are! You haven't gone wrong with one of them. Cornudet is wonderful and true. The nun scarred with smallpox, perfect! And the count saying *"Ma chère enfant,"* and the end! The poor prostitute crying while Cornudet sings the *Marseillaise*—sublime. I feel like giving you little kisses for a quarter of an hour! No, really, I am pleased. I enjoyed it and I admire it and you. And now, precisely *because* it is fundamentally strong stuff and will annoy the bourgeois, I would take out two things which are not at all bad but which might bring complaints from fools because they give the impression of saying, "I don't give a damn": 1. *"dans quelle fosse d'aisances avez-vous plongé, ô fusils à tabatière"*—the bourgeois would accuse you of throwing mud at our army, and 2. the word *"tétons."* If you do that, even the most prudish taste could find nothing to reproach you with.

To EMILE BERGERAT [*1880*]

Your prostitute is charming. If you could reduce her stomach a little at the beginning you'd give me pleasure.

Give my excuses to Hennique. I am really overwhelmed by the reading I have to do, and my poor eyes are giving out. I still have a dozen books to read before beginning my last chapter. I am now in phrenology and administrative law, to say nothing of Cicero's *De officiis* and the coitus of peacocks. You who are (or, rather, were) a rustic, have you ever seen these birds celebrate their love-rites?

Certain parts of my book, I think, will be lacking in decency. I have an urchin with improper habits, and one of my protagonists petitions the authorities to establish a brothel in his village.

I embrace you more warmly than ever.

I have ideas on how to make *Boule de suif* known, but I hope to see you soon. I want two copies. Bravo again! *Nom de Dieu!*

To EMILE BERGERAT

Croisset, February 6, 1880

Dear Friend,

Thanks to you I'll be famous in Rouen yet. The *Nouvelliste,* for the first time in its existence, has printed a very favorable article about me, based on your remarks;[54] and last Tuesday the *Journal de Rouen* reprinted, with an introduction, the entire text of your preface. An old domestic of mine, who is deaf, lame, and blind, said something sublime to me yesterday—something inspired by talk she had heard at the grocer's, where the aforesaid issue of the *Journal de Rouen* was being discussed: "It seems that you are a great writer!" You should have seen her expression, and heard her pronunciation! . . .

54 Bergerat's preface to Flaubert's *féerie,* or theatrical fantasy, *Le Château des cœurs,* published in Charpentier's magazine *La Vie Moderne,* January 24. This was the first considerable attention ever paid Flaubert by the press of his native city.

To MAXIME DU CAMP

Croisset, February 27, 1880

First, it was nice of you to tell me at once about your election,[55] and I thank you for doing so.

Next, why should you think that I would be "irritated"? Since it gives you pleasure it also pleases me, but I am surprised, amazed, stupefied, and keep asking myself: "Why? For what purpose?"

Do you remember a skit that you, Bouilhet, and I once acted out at Croisset? We officially welcomed each other into the French Academy . . . a memory that "inspires me with curious reflections," as Joseph[56] used to say.

Will le Mouton please kiss the new academician for me?

To GUY DE MAUPASSANT

Wednesday night, [*Croisset, March 24, 1880*]

Mon cher bonhomme,

I don't yet know what day Goncourt, Zola, Alphonse Daudet, and Charpentier are coming here for lunch or dinner and perhaps for the night. They are to decide tonight and I will know Friday morning. I think it will be Monday. So if the condition of your eye allows, betake yourself to one of the aforesaid characters, find out when they are leaving, and come with them.

Assuming that all of them spend Monday night at Croisset, since I have only four beds available you will occupy the maid's room—she is absent at the moment.

Note: I have been hearing so many silly and implausible things about your illness that I should like very much, purely for my own satisfaction, to have you gone over by *my* doctor, Fortin. He is a simple *officier de santé,* but I consider him excellent.

55 To the French Academy.
56 The dragoman employed by Flaubert and Du Camp in Egypt.

Further observation: if you haven't the cash for the journey, I have a superb double louis at your service. A refusal on grounds of delicacy would be an insult to me.

Last item: Jules Lemaître, whom I told that you would recommend him to Graziani, will call at your office. He has talent and is a real scholar, *rara avis,* worthy of a better post than the one he has at Le Havre.[57]

He too may come to Croisset Monday; and since I intend to get you all drunk I have also invited Fortin, to "heal the sick."

The festival will be lacking in splendor if my disciple stays away.

Yours,

To MADAME ROGER DES GENETTES

[*Croisset,*] *April 18, 1880*

I think you are too harsh about *Nana.* Vulgar, yes, but strong! Why is everyone so severe about this book and so indulgent toward Dumas's *Divorce?* As far as style and temperament are concerned it's the latter that is common and low.

In my opinion *Nana* contains wonderful things: Bordenave, Mignon, etc., and the end, which is epic. It is a colossus with dirty feet, but it is a colossus.

Many things in it shock me, but no matter! One must be able to admire things one doesn't love. My own novel will sin through excess of the opposite kind. There is as much sensuality in it as in a book of mathematics. And no drama, no intrigue, no interesting milieu! My last chapter turns (if a chapter may be said to turn) on pedagogy and moral principles—and this is intended as entertainment! If I heard that anyone I knew was trying to write a book to such specifications I'd urge that

57 Lemaître, then teaching at the Havre lycée, became one of France's most celebrated critics and a member of the French Academy. Graziani is not definitely identifiable.

he be sent to an insane asylum. I can only put my trust in God.

I had hoped to finish the first volume this month; but it won't be done before the end of June, and the second in October. It will probably occupy me all of 1880. I am hurrying, however—driving myself in order not to lose a minute; and my very bones are tired.

From GUY DE MAUPASSANT to IVAN TURGENEV

Paris, May 25, 1880

Cher maître et ami:

I am still prostrated by this calamity, and his dear face follows me everywhere. His voice haunts me, phrases keep coming back, the disappearance of his affection seems to have emptied the world around me. At three-thirty in the afternoon on Saturday, May eighth, I received a telegram from Madame Commanville: "Flaubert apoplexy. No hope. Leave at six." I joined the Commanvilles at six o'clock at the station; but stopping at my apartment on the way I found two other telegrams from Rouen announcing his death. We made the horrible journey in the dark, sunk in black and cruel grief. At Croisset we found him on his bed, looking almost unchanged, except that his neck was black and swollen from the apoplexy. We learned details. He had been well the preceding days, happy to be nearing the end of his novel, and he was to leave for Paris Sunday the ninth. He looked forward to enjoying himself, having, he said, "hidden a nest-egg in a pot." It wasn't a very large nest-egg, and he had earned it by his writing. He had eaten a very good dinner on Friday, spent the evening reciting Corneille with his doctor and neighbor, M. Fortin, slept until eight the next morning, taken a long bath, made his toilet, and read his mail. Then, feeling a little unwell, he called his maid; she was slow in coming, and he called to her out the window to fetch M. Fortin, but he, it turned out, had just left for Rouen by boat. When the maid arrived she found him standing, quite dizzy but not at all alarmed. He said, "I think I am going to have a kind of fainting fit; it's fortunate that it should happen today; it would have been troublesome tomorrow, in the train." He opened a bottle of eau de Cologne and rubbed some on his forehead, and let himself down quietly onto a large divan, murmuring, "Rouen—we aren't far from Rouen—Hellot—I know the Hellots. . . ." And then he fell back, his hands clenched, his face darkened and swollen with blood, stricken by the death which he had not for a second suspected.

His last words, which the newspapers interpreted as a reference to Victor Hugo, who lives in the Avenue d'Eylau, seem to me unquestionably to have meant: "Go to Rouen, we are not far from Rouen, and bring Doctor Hellot, I know the Hellots."

I spent three days near him; with Georges Pouchet and M. Fortin I wrapped him in his shroud; and Tuesday morning we took him to the cemetery, from which one has a perfect view of Croisset, with the great curve of the river and the house he so loved.

The days we consider ourselves happy do not counterbalance days like those.

At the cemetery there were many friends from Paris, especially his younger friends, *all* the young people he knew, and even some whom nobody knew; but not Victor Hugo, or Renan, or Taine, or Maxime Du Camp, or Frédéric Baudry, or Dumas, or Augier, or Vacquerie, etc.

That is all, *mon cher maître et ami,* but I shall have many more things to tell you. We shall attend to the novel when the heirs have settled their affairs. You will be needed for everything.

I wrote the very day of the calamity to Mme. Viardot, asking her to tell you, for I didn't know your address in Russia. I preferred that you should learn this sad news from friends rather than from a newspaper.

I shake your hands sadly, *mon cher maître,* and I hope to see you soon. *Votre tout dévoué.*

INDEX